M000205184

# Driving the
# Pacific Coast

## CALIFORNIA

Sixth Edition

Edited by Kathy Strong

**INSIDERS'** GUIDE®

GUILFORD, CONNECTICUT
AN IMPRINT OF THE GLOBE PEQUOT PRESS

**INSIDERS' GUIDE**®

Text design by Nancy Freeborn
Maps by Trailhead Graphics © Morris Book Publishing, LLC.
Interior photography pp. 2–3: Balboa Beach, Robert Holmes/CalTour; pp. 116–17: Highway 1, Robert Holmes/CalTour.

ISSN 1542-8605
ISBN 0-7627-3869-3

Manufactured in the United States of America
Sixth Edition/Second Printing

The information and rates listed in this guidebook were confirmed at press time. We recommend, however, that you call establishments before traveling to obtain current information.

# Contents

## Northern California

# Introduction

This is as much a tote-along companion as it is a book for reading, reference, and planning a trip to the California coast. Whether you're taking in all 1,100 miles of California's Pacific edge in a single trip or just looking for a place to relax and breathe some salt air for a couple of days, this is your getaway guide. You'll find it conveniently organized and easy to follow, regardless of which way you're traveling—up the coast, down the coast, or to a single destination.

Integral to the book, indeed its essence, is the idea of *getting away,* slipping off physically to a different place, perhaps mentally to a different time, and above all to a different pace. Often as important as getting to where you're going is getting away from where you are, especially if where you are is a throbbing megalopolis with crushing crowds and rushing freeways. Getting away means life in the slow lane.

That's one reason the largest city covered here is San Diego, and most others are considerably smaller. Another reason you won't find chapters on greater Los Angeles and the San Francisco Bay Area is that each would require another volume this size. Indeed, just a cursory coverage of San Francisco's restaurants would take a book as big as this. Besides, there are already plenty of books in print about those cities.

Instead of actual rates for lodging and campgrounds and prices for meals, you will find price ranges in this book expressed as *inexpensive, moderate, expensive,* and so on. Keep in mind that prices change and that these ranges are general. For example, if abalone is the only expensive entree on an otherwise moderately priced menu, prices are considered moderate.

Lodging rates are based on two-person occupancy. Room rates up to $135 are *inexpensive,* up to $195 *moderate,* up to $265 *expensive,* $266 to $500 *very expensive,* and more than $500 *extremely expensive.*

Campground and RV-park rates are based on spaces for one vehicle with water and electrical hookups and either sewer hookup or tank dump available. Up to $20 a day is *inexpensive,* $21 to $30 *moderate,* $31 to $50 *expensive,* and more than $50 *very expensive.*

Prices for meals are given per person. Breakfast up to $4.00, lunch to $8.00, and dinner to $12.00 qualify as *inexpensive.* Breakfasts from $4.01 to $8.00, lunches from $8.01 to $13.00, and dinners from $13.01 to $20.00 are *moderate.* Breakfasts from $8.01 to $13.00, lunches from $13.01 to $18.00, and dinners from $20.01 to $30.00 are *expensive.* Breakfasts more than $13.00, lunches more than $18.00, and dinners more than $30.00 are *very expensive.*

The term *freeway* has become a metaphor to describe the hectic pace of modern life, and nowhere is the freeway more a part of life than in California. Although much of the coast route—Highway 1 and U.S. Highway 101—is simple two-lane highway, those sections in the more populated areas are freeways. So it's impossible to drive the entire California coast without getting onto freeways from time to time.

California freeways are the butt of many jokes, and in some ways deservedly so. But the freeways in Portland, Seattle, Chicago, and New York are just as bad and just as good. They often get clogged, but they also move a lot of traffic. So don't be intimidated by California freeways; they're no different from freeways elsewhere. In fact, you'll find that California drivers have better freeway skills than most, and, believe it or not, they are among the most courteous drivers anywhere.

When traveling through the Los Angeles and San Francisco areas, try to avoid morning and evening rush hours on weekdays. Traffic is usually lightest in these cities early Saturday or Sunday morning, and very early or late on weekdays.

Coastal California is popular with bicyclists, but some narrow and winding portions of the Coast Highway pose hazards for bikers and drivers alike. On the North Coast, from Bodega Bay to Crescent City, beware of log trucks, which often carry timber. Remain alert, and exercise extra caution where the berm is narrow and bike lanes nonexistent.

It's still possible to rent bicycles in some communities, and rental agencies are listed in the following pages. Soaring insurance premiums, however, have forced many California bike shops out of the rental business. Those planning to augment their travels with bike tours should make sure rental equipment will be available or should take their own bicycles along.

Much of the California coast has a pleasant, Mediterranean climate with little variation between summer and winter temperatures. The northern California coast is seldom hot, even in summer. In fact, evenings and foggy or cloudy days can be chilly. Pack appropriate clothing, including a light parka or windbreaker. October to April is the rainy season on the north coast and stretches of the central coast, but that doesn't mean it rains every day. It means there's a chance it will rain or that a storm will come ashore anytime. So don't be put off by the idea of a rainy season. Just carry rainwear if you're traveling then, and take advantage of lower seasonal rates at many establishments and the uncrowded beaches and parks.

Above all, enjoy your visit to California's great Pacific Coast. If you plan to travel up the coast beyond California, be sure to pick up the companion volume—*Driving the Pacific Coast: Oregon and Washington.*

## Help Us Keep This Guide Up to Date

Every effort has been made by the editors to make this guide as accurate and useful as possible. However, many things can change after a guide is published—establishments close, phone numbers change, hiking trails are rerouted, facilities come under new management, and so on.

We would love to hear from you concerning your experiences with this guide and how you feel it could be made better and be kept up to date. Although we may not be able to respond to all comments and suggestions, we'll take them to heart and we'll also make certain to share them with the editors. Please send your comments and suggestions to the following address:

The Globe Pequot Press
Reader Response/Editorial Department
P.O. Box 480
Guilford, CT 06437

Or you may e-mail us at:

editorial@GlobePequot.com

Thanks for your input, and happy travels!

Southern
California

# Southern California

# Coronado

**Location:** Less than 1 mile west of San Diego, via State Route 75 and the San Diego–Coronado Toll Bridge; 16 miles north of the U.S.–Mexico border; 120 miles south of Los Angeles.

**Population:** 23,774

Coronado is sometimes referred to as an island, and it would be were it not for an isthmus called Silver Strand, which connects it to the mainland. Access to the peninsula is by way of the Route 75 loop, west off Interstate 5 in San Diego, or south of San Diego at Palm City, where Palm Avenue (Route 75) leads west to Silver Strand Boulevard.

The most imposing yet graceful landmark on the peninsula is the famed Hotel del Coronado, known locally as The Del. It was for the purpose of building this magnificent structure that two men, Elisha Babcock and H. L. Story, purchased 4,100 acres of peninsula land in 1885. Construction began in March 1887, and the original five-story, 400-room hotel opened for business eleven months later. No doubt today, with our modern equipment and materials and more than a century of technological advances, the job would take at least twice as long.

From the start, a steady stream of celebrities and dignitaries has passed through The Del's portals, beginning with Thomas Edison, who supervised the lighting installation in the original building. Since that time, a dozen U.S. presidents, numerous foreign dignitaries, and countless movie stars and television personalities have stayed at the hotel.

The Del is a star in its own right, having been featured in a number of Hollywood productions, including the zany fifties classic *Some Like It Hot,* which starred Jack Lemmon, Tony Curtis, and Marilyn Monroe. Part of *The Stunt Man,* starring Peter O'Toole, was filmed here, as were episodes of various television series, such as *Lifestyles of the Rich and Famous, Hart to Hart,* and *Simon and Simon.*

To maintain its stature as one of the world's finest waterfront resorts, the hotel has been continually renovated over the years, but without sacrificing any of its original beauty and appeal. Today its 680 rooms stand on thirty-three acres and constitute the largest beachfront hotel on the Pacific Coast of North America. It is also one of the largest wooden structures in the world.

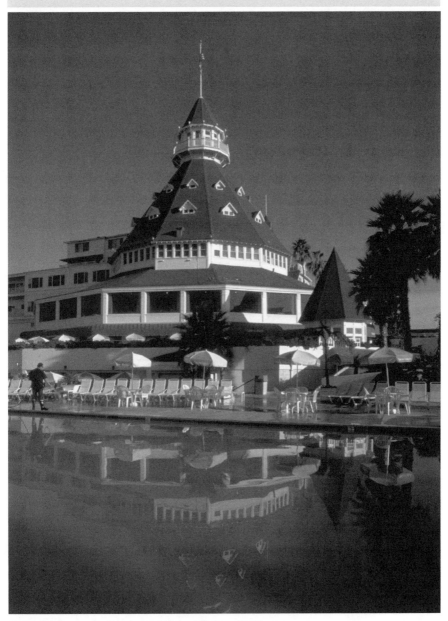

Hotel del Coronado *Courtesy of Robert Holmes/CalTour*

Even those who haven't the inclination or the shekels to shell out for a stay at The Del ought to at least plan to visit the hotel for its historical value and to examine its elegance and its architecture. A self-guided audiocassette tour of the hotel is available to the public during business hours. The tour begins in the lobby and lasts about forty-five minutes.

The town of Coronado grew around this luxurious hotel into what it is today: a lovely year-round resort community flanked by San Diego Bay and the Pacific Ocean.

Coronado's downtown is clustered along Orange Avenue, where visitors stroll and browse in the shops and galleries and enjoy a variety of foods at the area's restaurants and cafes. Ferries provide a pleasant way to travel from the San Diego waterfront, and trolleys serve the Coronado vicinity.

## Lodging

**Best Western Suites Hotel,** 275 Orange Avenue; (619) 437–1666 or (800) 528–1234; www.bestwestern.com. On Orange at Third Avenue, near downtown shops and restaurants. Has 63 units, each with cable TV, refrigerator, microwave, and wet bar. View rooms available. Heated pool, whirlpool, and laundry facilities. Moderate to expensive.

**Hotel del Coronado,** 1500 Orange Avenue; (619) 435–6611; in California, (800) 468–3533; www.hoteldel.com. Southern California's only beachfront resort is on the ocean side of Orange Avenue, between Adella Avenue and Avenida del Sol. A National Historic Landmark with 680 rooms and every desirable accommodation and amenity, including ocean views, in-room bars, room service, health spa, tennis courts, Olympic-size pool, restaurants, lounges, shops, and opulent lobbies. Expensive to extremely expensive.

**Villa Capri,** 1417 Orange Avenue; (619) 435–4137; in California, (800) 231–3954; www.villacapribythesea.com. Overlooks historic Hotel del Coronado. Has 14 rooms and suites with cable TV. Kitchen units available. Heated pool; complimentary continental breakfast. Near eighteen-hole golf course, tennis courts, health spa, restaurants, and shops. Moderate.

## Campgrounds and RV Parks

**Silver Strand State Beach,** 5000 Highway 75; (619) 435–5184; www.parks.ca.gov. On the Strand, southeast of town. En route campsites for overnight use by self-contained RVs only. Fire pits, showers, and facilities for handicapped. Entrance and parking fees. Inexpensive.

## Food

**The Brigantine,** 1333 Orange Avenue; (619) 435–4166; www.brigantine.com. Across from the Hotel del Coronado. Lunch Monday through Friday; dinner daily. Lunch includes seafood fettuccine, batter-fried seafood, steaks, chicken, and an assortment of hearty sandwiches. Lunch-size salads, such as crab Louis, and Cobb. More than a dozen dinner appetizers, including jumbo shrimp and crab cocktails, ahi sashimi, and steamed clams bordelaise. In addition to fresh catch-of-the-day dinners, such regular menu items as pan-roasted king salmon, wok-charred ahi, lamb chops, scallops, steaks, and chicken. Oyster bar. Full bar and wine list. Moderate.

**Coronado Brewing Company,** 170 Orange Avenue; (619) 437–4452; www.coronado brewingcompany.com. This microbrewery serves handcrafted beer, wood-fired pizza, salads, and grill specialties. Live entertainment Thursday, Friday, and Saturday nights from 9:30 to closing. Inexpensive to moderate.

**Miguel's Cocina Restaurant,** 1351 Orange Avenue; (619) 437–4237; www .miguels-cocina.com. In the courtyard of the El Cordova Hotel, across the street from the Hotel del Coronado. Daily lunch and dinner; Saturday and Sunday brunch. Fine Mexican cuisine. Choose from such appetizers as seviche, *taquitos,* and Mexican shrimp cocktail. Soups, salads, tacos, tostadas, burritos, enchiladas, *chile verde,* jumbo Gulf shrimp, calamari jalapeño, steak ranchero, and such house specialties as *carnitas* and fish tacos. Full bar, including Mexican beers. Inexpensive to moderate.

## Shopping and Browsing

**Ferry Landing Marketplace,** 1201 First Street; (619) 435–8895; ferry information, (619) 234–4111. First Street and B Avenue, on the bayfront. Monday through Saturday, 10:00 A.M. to 9:00 P.M.; Sunday, 10:00 A.M. to 6:00 P.M. A shopping center containing specialty shops, galleries, restaurants, boardwalks, fishing piers, and bike rentals. Daily ferry service from the Broadway Pier in San Diego.

**Historic Orange Avenue,** from Eighth Street to the Hotel del Coronado. Galleries, boutiques, and bookstores are housed in finely preserved historical buildings along this street.

## Beaches, Parks, Trails, and Waysides

On the ocean side of Silver Strand Boulevard, south of Coronado, lies the broad, sandy Silver Strand State Beach, popular with swimmers and surfers. This is also an excellent beachcombing area, especially for shells, and a good spot for picnics.

Farther up the Strand, at Coronado, Coronado Shores Beach and Coronado City Beach offer swimming and surfing as their main activities. Avenida Lunar, Avenida de las Arenas, and Avenida del Sol lead west off Silver Strand Boulevard to a concrete promenade overlooking Coronado Shores Beach. City Beach lies north of the Strand and west of Ocean Boulevard. On the bay side of the Strand, across from Coronado Shores Beach, is Glorietta Bay Park, with a picnic area, playground, and municipal swimming pool.

## Water Sports and Activities

Anglers in this part of California enjoy some of the best saltwater fishing in the state, with a great variety of sport and food fishes available in good numbers. In the immediate vicinity of Coronado, surf fishing is popular along the ocean beaches, primarily for bass, croaker, corbina, and perch. Bay waters offer angling for bass, croaker, halibut, mackerel, perch, shark, and smelt, from shore, piers, and boats.

Offshore fishing is good all year for many species, including barracuda, bonito, halibut, kelp bass, rockfish, sheephead, yellowtail, and various bottom dwellers. Summer angling focuses on such game fishes as albacore, yellowfin tuna, shark, and dolphin (fish).

Those who tow boats to the area will find launching facilities at Glorietta Bay Park, off Silver Strand Boulevard, and at Glorietta Bay Marina, on Strand Way, east of Silver Strand Boulevard. Rental boats are also available at the marina.

# Rentals

**Holland's Bicycles,** 977 Orange Avenue; (619) 435–3153; www.hollands bicycles.com. Monday through Friday, 10:00 A.M. to 6:00 P.M.; Saturday, 9:00 A.M. to 6:00 P.M.; Sunday, 11:00 A.M. to 5:00 P.M. Rents, sells, and services Schwinn, Nishiki, and Trek-Klein bikes. Biking clothes available.

**Seaforth Boat Rentals,** 1715 Strand Way; (619) 437–1514; www.seaforthboat rental.com. Rents a variety of watercraft seven days a week, weekdays from 8:00 A.M. to 7:30 P.M. and weekends from 7:00 A.M. to 7:30 P.M. Sailboats include Hobie Cats and Catalinas. Rents powerboats for cruising, fishing, and waterskiing as well as Kawasaki Tandem Sports and WaveRunners. Also rents canoes, rowboats, and pedal boats. Sailing and waterskiing lessons available.

# Tours and Trips

**Coronado Walking Tour,** (619) 435–5892; www.coronadovisitors.com. Guided ninety-minute walking tours of historic Coronado depart from the Glorietta Bay Inn, across the street from the Hotel del Coronado, on Tuesday, Thursday, and Saturday at 11:00 A.M.

**San Diego Harbor Excursion,** 1050 North Harbor Drive, San Diego; (619) 234–4111, ext. 2; www.sdhe.com. Ferry service between Coronado and San Diego. Ferry departs from Old Ferry Landing at Coronado every hour on the hour, Sunday through Thursday, 9:30 A.M. to 9:30 P.M.; Friday and Saturday, 9:30 A.M. to 10:30 P.M. Daily trackless-trolley service to the ferry landing. Also offers one- and two-hour harbor excursions.

**The Gondola Company,** 4000 Coronado Bay Road; (619) 429–6317; www.gondola company.com. Private one-hour gondola cruises through the canals and waterways of the Coronado cays. Tours include complimentary hors d'oeuvres or desserts, blankets, ice bucket, wine glasses, and wine opener. Guests may bring their own beverages. Custom cruises for weddings and groups.

# Golf

**Coronado Municipal Golf Course,** 2000 Visalia Row; (619) 435–3121; www.golf coronado.com. West of the San Diego–Coronado Toll Bridge, via Glorietta Boulevard. A municipal eighteen-hole, 6,466-yard, par-seventy-two course open to the public. Driving range and snack bar.

# Other Attractions

**Coronado Playhouse,** 1335 First Street; (619) 435–4856 (twenty-four hour answering service); www.coronadoplayhouse.com. Thursday, Friday, and Saturday at 8:00 P.M.; Sunday at 2:00 P.M.

# Travel Information

**Coronado Visitors Bureau,** 1100 Orange Avenue; (619) 437–8788 or (800) 622–8300; www.coronadovisitors.com.

# San Diego

**Location:** In the southwest corner of the state, on Interstate 5, Interstate 8, and Interstate 15; 16 miles north of the U.S.–Mexico border and 120 miles south of Los Angeles.

**Population:** 2,600,000

How could San Diego be any better? By most standards, the climate is perfect. Mexico is only minutes away. Warm Pacific and bay waters lapping at the city's edges make surfing and swimming essential elements of the San Diego lifestyle. Scuba diving, snorkeling, and saltwater angling are unsurpassed anywhere in the state. The county is speckled with lakes and reservoirs offering excellent freshwater fishing and some of the biggest largemouth bass in the world. Golf courses galore, plenty of parks, and a myriad of museums, shops, galleries, and superb restaurants—what more could any traveler want?

The current estimate puts the population of greater San Diego at more than two million, making it one of the fastest-growing metropolitan areas and the seventh-largest city in the United States. But San Diego doesn't seem to suffer from those numbers. The city contradicts itself. It has crowds but isn't crowded. Despite all the vehicles, there's no sign of gridlock, and parking seems adequate everywhere. As big as the city is, it's easy to get around in, and it's not intimidating to visitors, who can avoid the freeways altogether if they wish.

So it's the contrasts that make San Diego such a pleasant surprise—the contrasts and the friendly natives. This is a busy, bustling boomtown full of laid-back people. Maybe it's the water—not something in the water that affects the people, but all that water the people spend so much time in, on, and near—that makes them so relaxed and hospitable. After all, there are 70 miles of beach, sprawling bays, and the Pacific Ocean, not to mention countless miles of trails, paths, boardwalks, sidewalks, and grassy parks. It's the joggers and bikers and skaters and hikers, anglers and sailors and surfers and swimmers, shoppers and browsers and theatergoers, picnic lovers and bird-watchers and Margarita sippers—everybody bent on the serious pursuit of fun.

How could San Diego be any better? What more could any traveler want?

# Lodging

**Balboa Park Inn,** 3402 Park Boulevard; (619) 298–0823 or (800) 938–8181; www.balboa parkinn.com. East of I–5, near Balboa Park. Has 26 suites with cable TV, cable movies, wet bars, some fireplaces, and some in-room whirlpools. Complimentary continental breakfast. Walk to the zoo. Moderate to expensive.

**The Beach Cottages,** 4255 Ocean Boulevard; (858) 483–7440; www.beachcottages .com. Located on the beach, west of I–5 and Mission Boulevard, in the Pacific Beach area. Cable TV in 78 units, including motel rooms, one- and two-bedroom apartments, and cottages. All but motel rooms have kitchens. Patios, balconies, barbecues, shuffleboard, and table tennis. Near restaurants and shops. Moderate to expensive.

**Best Western Blue Sea Lodge,** 707 Pacific Beach Drive; (858) 488–4700 or (800) 258–3732; www.bestwestern-bluesea.com. West of I–5 and Mission Boulevard, in the Pacific Beach area. Queen and king beds in 126 rooms with cable TV. Standard and luxury oceanfront rooms with balconies and patios, suites with full kitchens. Skylights and sunken tubs in some rooms. Pool, whirlpool, and beach access. Expensive.

**The Dana Inn and Marina,** 1710 West Mission Bay Drive; (619) 222–6440 or (800) 345–9995; www.thedana.net. West of I–5, in the Mission Bay area. Cable TV and coffeemakers in 196 rooms. Heated pool, whirlpool, tennis courts, and shuffleboard. Two restaurants, a fitness center, and private marina on premises. Paddleboat and bicycle rentals. Walk to Sea World. Expensive.

**Holiday Inn San Diego Bayside,** 4875 North Harbor Drive; (619) 224–3621 or (800) 345–9995; www.holinnbayside.com. West of I–5 and south of I–8, via Rosecrans Street or Nimitz Boulevard, across the street from the marina and sportfishing docks. Cable TV, cable movies, and coffeemakers in 237 rooms. Balconies, bay view, and free newspapers. Pool, putting green, whirlpool, exercise room, volleyball, and shuffleboard. Point Loma Cafe on premises. Moderate to expensive.

**Humphrey's Half Moon Inn,** 2303 Shelter Island Drive; (619) 224–3411 or (800) 542–7400; www.halfmooninn.com. On Shelter Island, west of I–5 and south of I–8, via Rosecrans. Cable TV and cable movies in 182 rooms. Heated pool, whirlpool, bay view, private marina and yacht basin, putting green, gift shop, sightseeing tours, airport and Amtrak limousine service. Humphrey's Restaurant on premises. Expensive to very expensive.

**The Sands of La Jolla,** 5417 La Jolla Boulevard, La Jolla; (858) 459–3336; www.sands oflajolla.com. North of Pacific Beach and west of I–5, in the village of La Jolla. Cable TV in 38 rooms with coffeemakers and minirefrigerators. Kitchen suites available. Near shops, restaurants, tennis courts, golf course, and beaches. Heated pool. Ocean view. Inexpensive to moderate.

## Campgrounds and RV Parks

**Chula Vista RV Park,** 460 Sandpiper Way, Chula Vista; (619) 422–0111; www.chula vistarv.com. West of I–5, south of San Diego. Has 237 full-hookup sites, showers, laundry, and pool. On San Diego Bay, adjacent to 550-slip marina. Tackle shop, cafe, boat ramp, RV supplies, and free shuttle to trolley. Expensive.

**Mission Bay RV Park,** 2727 De Anza Road; (877) 219–6900; www.missionbayrv park.com. West of I–5, on the beach at Mission Bay, near Sea World. Has 259 sites with water and electricity hookups. Showers, tank dump, beach access, and boat ramps. Moderate to expensive.

**San Diego Metro KOA Kampground,** 111 North Second Avenue, Chula Vista; (619) 427–3601; www.koa.com. East of I–5 and west of Interstate 805, between downtown San Diego and the Mexican border. Has 200 full-hookup and 45 tent sites. Pull-through sites and Kamping Kabins available. Tables, fire pits, firewood, showers, pool, whirlpool, recreation room, and horseshoe pits. Propane available. Expensive.

## Food

**Dakota Grill & Spirits,** 901 Fifth Avenue; (619) 234–5554. At the Gaslamp Quarter. Lunch and dinner Monday through Friday; dinner Saturday and Sunday. Award-winning, upscale but casual restaurant with a menu featuring salads, pasta dishes, wood-fired pizzas, mesquite-grilled steaks, the freshest seafood, and house-made desserts. Full bar. Moderate.

**Humphrey's Restaurant and Casablanca Lounge,** 2241 Shelter Island Drive; (619) 224–3577; www.sdro.com/humphrey.com. On Shelter Island, west of I–5 and south of I–8, via Rosecrans. Daily breakfast, lunch, and dinner; Sunday brunch. Sunday brunch features salads, omelets made to order, carved roasts, pasta, pizza, tacos, desserts, and free-flowing champagne. For dinner try such fresh seafood as salmon, halibut, swordfish, Cajun shrimp, or the lobster clambake: live Maine lobster steamed with oysters and crab, served with clarified butter, red potatoes, and an ear of corn. Full bar. Moderate.

**Karl Strauss Brewing Company,** 1157 Columbia Street; (619) 234–2739. Between B and C Streets, downtown. Daily lunch and dinner. A working pub brewery producing and selling beverages brewed on the premises from the private recipes of Karl M. Strauss, a German-born, Bavarian-trained brewmaster. Sample the beers with a variety of snacks and appetizers or with such lunch and dinner entrees as half-pound hamburgers, grilled sausages and chicken, marinated short ribs, beer-batter fish-and-chips, and daily fresh-fish specials. Brewery tours available. Moderate.

**Miguel's Cocina Restaurant,** 2912 Shelter Island Drive; (619) 224–2401. In Point Loma, near Shelter Island and the sportfishing docks. Monday through Friday, lunch and dinner; Saturday, dinner; Sunday, brunch and dinner. Mexican food. Brunch includes a variety of egg dishes—both Mexican and American. Soups, salads, tacos, tostadas, burritos, enchiladas, chimichangas, shrimp fajitas, and Mexican-style steaks. Full bar. Inexpensive to moderate.

## Shopping and Browsing

**Bazaar del Mundo,** 4133 Taylor Street; (619) 296–3161. Daily, 10:00 A.M. to 9:00 P.M. In Historic Old Town. Has ten shops and galleries offering crafts, gifts, collectibles, dinnerware, fabrics, artwork, jewelry, toys, and more. Also two restaurants.

**Horton Plaza,** Fourth and Broadway; (619) 238–1596; www.westfield.com. Between First and Fourth Avenues and Broadway and G Street, 3 blocks east of Harbor Drive, downtown. Enter from Fourth Avenue or G Street. Monday through Friday, 10:00 A.M. to 9:00 P.M.; Saturday, 10:00 A.M. to 9:00 P.M.; Sunday, 10:00 A.M. to 7:00 P.M. Restaurants, theaters, and some shops stay open later. A kaleidoscope of color and design, with several department stores and 140 specialty shops. Shop, browse, and dine inside or out. Fine restaurants and pushcart vendors. Mimes, jugglers, and street musicians. Seven-screen cinema. Live performances at the San Diego Repertory Theatre. Easy walk to and from the Embarcadero, Seaport Village, and other downtown attractions. Adjacent to the historic Gaslamp Quarter.

**Seaport Village,** 849 West Harbor Drive; (619) 235–4014; www.seaportvillage.com. West of I–5, on the waterfront, downtown. June through August, 10:00 A.M. to 10:00 P.M. daily; September through May, 9:00 A.M. to 9:00 P.M. daily. More than seventy-five shops, galleries, and restaurants. Gifts, souvenirs, crystal, posters, nautical items, leather, silver, candles, decorative tiles, music boxes, mugs, clothing, toys and games, antiques, collectibles, candy, fudge, cookies, kites, and more.

## Museums

For those who enjoy visiting museums, San Diego has more to offer than most other cities. Nearly two dozen museums exist here, half of them at Balboa Park. A brochure describing them is available at either of the city's two visitor centers.

**Firehouse Museum,** 1572 Columbia Street; (619) 232–3473; www.globalinfo.com. Wednesday through Friday, 10:00 A.M. to 2:00 P.M.; Saturday and Sunday, 10:00 A.M. to 4:00 P.M. Interesting collection of antique fire-fighting equipment, engines, pictures, and memorabilia.

**San Diego Aerospace Museum,** 2001 Pan American Plaza; (619) 234–8291; www.aerospacemuseum.org. At Balboa Park, east of I–5. Daily, 10:00 A.M. to 4:00 P.M. The San Diego Aerospace Museum displays vintage aircraft, aviation artifacts, and

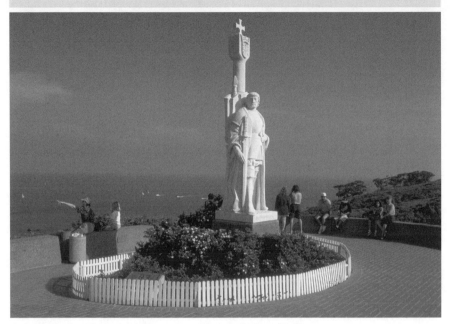

Cabrillo National Monument *Courtesy of Robert Holmes/CalTour*

various aeronautical exhibits. The International Aerospace Hall of Fame pays tribute to pilots, inventors, and industrialists; displays their portraits; and provides biographical information.

**San Diego Maritime Museum,** 1492 North Harbor Drive; (619) 234–9153; www.sdmaritime.org. West of I–5, downtown, at the Embarcadero. Daily, 9:00 A.M. to 8:00 P.M. Three beautifully preserved ships open for public tours: *Star of India,* an iron-hulled bark launched in 1863; *Medea,* a luxurious 1904 steam yacht; and the *Berkeley,* an 1898 San Francisco Bay steam ferry.

**San Diego Natural History Museum,** 1788 El Prado; (619) 232–3821; www .sdnhm.org. At Balboa Park, east of I–5. Daily 10:00 A.M. to 5:00 P.M. Plant and animal displays, gems and minerals, dinosaur skeletons, ecology exhibits, and special hands-on exhibits. Winter whale-watching trips to the Baja lagoons, classes, canyon hikes, and international expeditions.

**Stephen Birch Aquarium-Museum,** 2300 Expedition Way, Scripps Institution of Oceanography, UCSD, La Jolla; recorded message, (858) 534–3474; www.aquarium .ucsd.edu. West of North Torrey Pines Road. From I–5, take La Jolla Village Drive west about 1 mile; then follow the signs. Open 9:00 A.M. to 5:00 P.M. daily, except Christmas Day, Thanksgiving, and New Year's Day. More than 3,000 species of fish and invertebrates from the Pacific Northwest to the tropical waters of Mexico and Indo-Pacific reside in thirty-three tanks and the tidepool plaza. The museum features the largest oceanographic exhibit in the United States. Book-and-gift shop and food concession on premises. Rated *must-see* for anyone interested in sea life.

# Beaches, Parks, Trails, and Waysides

At the entrance to San Diego Bay, west of North Island Naval Air Station, a finger of land known as Point Loma pokes southward into the Pacific. This is the site of the Cabrillo National Monument, which honors the Portuguese navigator Juan Rodriguez Cabrillo, who explored the California coast under the Spanish flag in 1542.

The lofty headland offers spectacular views of the ocean, bay, Coronado, and San Diego. From late December through February, this serves as an excellent place to watch gray whales as they pass the point on their 5,000-mile migration from their summer feeding grounds in Alaska to their winter calving grounds in the lagoons of Baja California, Mexico.

The west side of the point is a good place to explore tidepools. Here you'll find more than a hundred species of plants and animals specially adapted to this harsh environment, among them anemone, crabs, tiny sculpins, and even octopuses. You may watch and photograph them, but don't remove any; they're protected by law. The low tides of autumn, winter, and spring are best for studying the tidepools.

Lighthouse aficionados will delight in finding two here. The old Point Loma Lighthouse was built atop the point, 422 feet above sea level, making its light visible 25 miles out. Its lamp was first lighted on November 15, 1855, but was snuffed only thirty-six years later because fog and low clouds often obscured it. Another light station was erected on the west side of the point, 88 feet above the water, and began operating in March 1891, its light visible 15 miles out.

The monument is open daily from 9:00 A.M. to 5:15 P.M. A visitor center houses a gift shop and offers programs daily in the auditorium. Guided hikes and other activities are also scheduled.

To reach the monument from I-5, take the Rosecrans exit west. Turn right on Canon Street, then left on Catalina Boulevard to Point Loma. From I-8, take Nimitz Boulevard south and turn right on Chatsworth Boulevard, which leads to Catalina Boulevard.

Several beaches and picnic areas are on the bay, at Shelter Island, off North Harbor Drive; Spanish Landing Park, on North Harbor Drive, near Harbor Island; and Embarcadero Marina Park, on Harbor Drive, downtown. South of San Diego, Imperial Beach and Border Field State Park are on the ocean.

Old Town San Diego State Historic Park lies just east of I-5 and south of I-8, near the juncture of the two freeways. Here a number of buildings from San Diego's Mexican and early American periods—1821 through 1872—stand in the shade of cork, eucalyptus, fig, and olive trees. Restaurants and shops are in the vicinity.

At the west end of town, north of Point Loma, is the crown jewel of San Diego's parks: Mission Bay City Park, the largest aquatic park on the West Coast. It encompasses the bay's entire shoreline, as well as Fiesta Island and Vacation Isle, and includes miles of beaches, trails, and sidewalks and plenty of shops and restaurants.

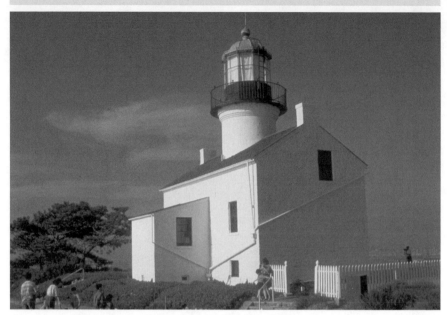

Point Loma Lighthouse *Courtesy of Robert Holmes/CalTour*

South of Mission Bay, on the ocean, are Ocean Beach Park, Ocean Beach City Beach, and Sunset Cliffs Park. North of Mission Bay is the La Jolla area, offering a number of beaches and parks on the ocean, tidepools, the La Jolla Caves, and the Coast Walk—a trail along the La Jolla Bluffs, a good vantage for viewing the caves and the abundant bird life.

# Water Sports and Activities

Life in San Diego is life on the water, with locals and visitors enjoying every form of water recreation imaginable. In addition to swimming and surfing, scuba diving and snorkeling are popular. Waterskiing is good in the protected waters of San Diego Bay and at Mission Bay.

Several yacht clubs and thousands of boat slips attest to the importance of power-boating and sailing. Opportunities exist here for every level of expertise, from the novice who can practice skills in the gentle bays and backwaters to the expert at navigation and offshore cruising who can set out from San Diego for any port in the world.

There are plenty of launch ramps and hoists for travelers who tow boats. For others, rental equipment of every kind and size is available—from kayaks to cruisers. Kayaking, sailboarding, sailing, and waterskiing instructors offer lessons at various levels, for neophytes looking for an introduction or veterans wanting to brush up on certain skills.

No other place in California offers greater opportunities to anglers than San Diego. Experts agree that the next world-record largemouth bass will come from one of San Diego County's reservoirs, which some years ago were stocked with the Florida strain of largemouth. These fish took well to local waters and have grown fast and large, approaching twenty pounds.

For saltwater angling, opportunities are boundless, with something to fit every angler's desires, from shore and pier fishing on the bay to ocean surf fishing. Party boats and charter operators work out of Mission Bay and from the sportfishing docks near Shelter Island.

Those fishing from piers take a wide assortment of species, including surfperch, croaker, sea bass, halibut, mackerel, smelt, and shark. South of San Diego is a fishing pier at Imperial Beach, west of I–5, at the end of Palm Avenue. Downtown, fishing piers are west of Harbor Drive at Embarcadero Marina Park and at the foot of G Street. Shelter Island also has an excellent pier.

Two piers on the west side of town, north of Point Loma, offer ocean fishing. The Ocean Beach Pier is a T-shaped structure, 2,150 feet long, west of Sunset Cliffs Boulevard, at the end of Niagra Avenue. Crystal Pier, in the Pacific Beach area, lies west of Ocean Boulevard at the end of Garnet Street. Although this is a private pier, it's open daily to the public, 7:00 A.M. to 5:00 P.M.

Popular surf-fishing areas south of San Diego are at Border Field State Park and Imperial Beach. Ocean Beach Park, west of Sunset Cliffs Boulevard, is also a good surf-fishing spot. Mission Bay City Park has plenty of shoreline for fishing. In the La Jolla area, Bird Rock, South Bird Rock, Sun Gold Point, and La Jolla Cove are favorite spots for rock and surf fishing.

**Fisherman's Landing,** 2838 Garrison Street; (619) 221–8500. Catch reports, (619) 224–1421; www.fishermanslanding.com. At the sportfishing docks near Shelter Island. Large fleet of fully equipped short- and long-range sportfishing boats. Trips for albacore and yellowtail. Seasonal trips for rockfish. Trips from two and a half hours to nine days. Long-range trips to Mexico from three to twenty-three days. Also whale-watching excursions and private charters. Fisherman's Landing Tackle Shop stocks a full line of saltwater supplies and repairs tackle.

**H & M Landing,** 2803 Emerson Street; (619) 222–1144. Daily catch report, (619) 224–2800; www.hmlanding.com. At the sportfishing docks near Shelter Island. Books half-day, full-day, and long-range deep-sea fishing trips. Party trips and charter cruises. Scuba-diving and whale-watching trips. Skiff and tackle rental. Year-round half-day to four-day trips for marlin, yellowtail, sea bass, barracuda, bonito, and bottom fish, as well as albacore, bluefin, yellowfin, and bigeye tuna. Also four- to eight-day long-range trips.

**Point Loma Sportfishing,** 1403 Scott Street; (619) 223–1627. Daily catch report, (619) 223–1626; www.pointlomasportfishing.com. At the sportfishing docks near Shelter Island. Half-day and longer trips to the Coronado Islands and Baja. Albacore trips, July to October; yellowtail trips, April to December. Two- to four-day long-range trips all year. Large fleet of boats from 48 to 90 feet. Also private charters, twilight trips, night shark-fishing trips, and dive trips.

**Seaforth Sportfishing,** 1717 Quivira Road; (619) 224–3383. Catch report, (619) 224–6695; www.seaforthlanding.com. Half-day, three-quarter-day, full-day, and twilight trips for rockfish, albacore, and other species. Night trips for shark fishing depart at 7:00 P.M. and return at 4:30 A.M. Whale-watching trips in season. Rental tackle available.

# Rentals

**Seaforth Boat Rentals,** 1641 Quivira Road; (619) 223–1681; www.seaforthboat rental.com. On Mission Bay, west of I–5, north of I–8. Kayak, WaveRunner, and boat rentals. Rents beach-cruiser bikes and tandems. Sailing fleet includes Hobie Cats, Capris, Catalinas, and oceangoing sloops. Motor fleet includes cruise boats, speedboats, ski boats, Kawasaki Tandem Sports, WaveRunners, and fishing skiffs. Sailing and waterskiing lessons available.

# Tours and Trips

**Old Town Trolley Tours of San Diego,** 4010 Twiggs Street; (619) 298–8687; www .trolleytours.com. Daily, 9:00 A.M. to 4:00 P.M. (winter) and 5:00 P.M. (summer). Comprehensive, narrated tours of San Diego, including more than one hundred points of interest. Take entire tour in two hours, or get off anywhere to explore and catch the next trolley. Trolleys arrive at stops every twenty to thirty minutes. Included in the route are Old Town, downtown, Harbor Island, the Maritime Museum, San Diego Cruise Ship Terminal, Horton Plaza, Gaslamp Quarter, San Diego Zoo, Balboa Park museums, and the San Diego–Coronado Toll Bridge. Closed Thanksgiving and Christmas.

**San Diego Harbor Excursions,** 1050 North Harbor Drive; (619) 234–4111; www.sdhe.com. At the Embarcadero. Ferry service to Coronado, dinner-and-dance cruises, Sunday brunch cruises, and whale-watching excursions. One- and two-hour narrated harbor tours. Charter cruises and private parties. Bay Ferry departs Broadway Pier for Coronado approximately every hour. Sunday through Thursday, 10:00 A.M. to 10:00 P.M.; Friday and Saturday, 10:00 A.M. to 11:00 P.M.

# Golf

**Balboa Park Municipal Golf Course,** 2600 Golf Course Drive; pro shop, (619) 239–1660; reservations, (619) 235–1184; www.balboapark.org. At Balboa Park, east of I–5, south of I–8. An eighteen-hole, par-seventy-two, 6,267-yard course and a nine-hole, par-thirty-two, 2,175-yard course. Driving range, putting greens, pro shop, clubhouse, showers, lockers, restaurant, and snack bar.

Carmel Mountain Ranch Country Club, 14050 Carmel Ridge Road; (858) 451–8353; www.clubcmr.com. With eighteen holes, this golf course is rated among the top thirty California courses.

Torrey Pines Golf Course, 11480 Torrey Pines Road, La Jolla; (800) 985–4653; www.torreypinesgolfcourse.com. An internationally famous municipal facility with two eighteen-hole courses offering superb ocean views. North course is par seventy-two and 6,847 yards; south course is par seventy-two and 7,605 yards. Driving range, pro shop, resident pro, club rental, restaurant, bar, and snack bar.

## Other Attractions

Reuben H. Fleet Space Theater and Science Center, 1875 El Prado, P.O. Box 33303, 92103; (619) 238–1233; www.rhfleet.org. At Balboa Park, east of I–5, south of I–8. Daily, 9:30 A.M. to 9:30 P.M. An IMAX/OMNIMAX large-screen theater with six-channel sound lets you experience the thrills of mountain climbing, downhill skiing, and more. Shows almost hourly. Some shows may be sold out. Call for current schedule.

San Diego Zoo, 2920 Zoo Drive, P.O. Box 551, 92112; (858) 675–7900 or (800) 628–3066; www.sandiegozoo.org. At Balboa Park, east of I–5, south of I–8. July through Labor Day, 9:00 A.M. to 8:00 P.M. daily; post–Labor Day through June, 9:00 A.M. to 4:00 P.M. daily. World-renowned, hundred-acre botanical garden that's home to more than 4,000 rare and endangered animals and 6,500 varieties of exotic plants. Guided bus tour covers 80 percent of the zoo grounds. Aerial tram allows visitors to view animals from an altitude of 170 feet. Classified *must-see.*

Sea World, 500 Sea World Drive; (619) 226–3901 or (800) 325–3150 for sales promotions; elsewhere, (800) 25–SHAMU; www.seaworld.com. At Mission Bay, west of I–5, north of I–8. Daily, 9:00 A.M. to dusk; extended summer hours with nightly fireworks. Shark exhibit, killer-whale show, undersea theater, sea lions, penguins, and dolphins. A variety of entertainers perform daily. Guided tours. Stroller and wheelchair rentals.

## Travel Information

Cabrillo National Monument, National Park Service, 1800 Cabrillo Memorial Drive; (619) 557–5450; www.nps.gov/cabr

Mission Bay Park Headquarters, Park and Recreation Department, 2581 Quivira Court; (619) 236–6652

Old Town San Diego State Historic Park, San Diego Avenue at Twiggs Street; (619) 220–5422

**San Diego Convention and Visitors Bureau,** 1040 1/3 West Broadway; (619) 236–1212; www.sandiego.org; e-mail: sdinfo@sandiego.org

**Visitor Information Center,** 2688 East Mission Bay Drive; (619) 276–8200; www.infosandiego.com

## events

| March | Mardi Gras in the Gaslamp Quarter, (619) 233–5008 or 233–5227 |
| --- | --- |
| | International Film Festival, (619) 236–1212 |
| April | San Diego Opera, (619) 236–1212 |
| | San Diego Crew Classic, (619) 225–0300 |
| May | Cinco de Mayo (Old Town), (760) 767–5355 |
| June | Mainly Mozart Festival, (619) 236–1212 |
| July | Annual Sandcastle Competition, (619) 424–6663 |
| August | Festival of Sail, (619) 234–9153 |
| September | Street Scene Music Festival, (619) 232–3101 |
| November | San Diego Thanksgiving Dixieland Jazz Festival, (619) 297–5277 |
| December | Parade of Lights Boat Parades, (619) 236–1212 |

# Del Mar / Encinitas

**Location:** Del Mar is 6 miles north of La Jolla and 16 miles south of Carlsbad, west of Interstate 5, on Old Highway 101, now Route S21; Encinitas is 6 miles north of Del Mar and 10 miles south of Carlsbad, also on Route S21, as well as I–5.

**Population:** Del Mar 4,426; Encinitas 58,014

Remnants of the old coast highway, U.S. Highway 101, between La Jolla and Carlsbad connect several small coastal communities, with Del Mar in the south, Encinitas in the north, and Solana Beach, a city of 13,000 people, between the two. Although each is distinctly different from the others, the communities share the main attractions of beautiful ocean beaches and a Mediterranean-type climate that moderates both summer and winter temperatures.

In its various incarnations since 1885, Del Mar has enjoyed booms and suffered busts. It has been rural ranchland, run-down beach community, home of Hollywood stars, and playground of the rich and famous. It seems now to have settled comfortably onto the coastal mesa as a charming seaside village, with sidewalk cafes and trendy little boutiques and galleries.

*Del Mar* is Spanish, meaning "by the sea." The main thoroughfare is the old coast highway, here called the Camino del Mar, or "road by the sea."

Maps and atlases printed before 1986 show the communities of Cardiff-by-the-Sea, Olivenhain, Leucadia, and Encinitas situated between Solana Beach and Carlsbad. But that year Encinitas was incorporated to include all four towns.

Supplying its own orchids and accolades, Encinitas bills itself as the "flower capital of the world." The pleasant climate here—rarely below forty degrees or above eighty-five degrees—is conducive to flower cultivation. Commercial florists of the vicinity produce millions of colorful roses, carnations, poinsettias, and other flowers annually.

In addition to the usual activities associated with beaches and coastal communities, several more exotic pastimes are popular here. Watch the skies for sailplanes, hang gliders, and hot-air balloons. Although sailplaning and hang gliding aren't for everyone, anyone who wishes can take a ride in a balloon, and several local companies offer flights, usually with champagne and hors d'oeuvres afterward.

# Lodging

**Best Western Encinitas Inn at Moonlight Beach,** 85 Encinitas Boulevard, Encinitas; (760) 942–7455; www.bwencinitas.com. West of I–5 via Encinitas Boulevard. Queen and king beds in 94 large rooms and suites, remote-control cable TV, and refrigerators. Kitchenettes, balconies, and in-room whirlpools available. Heated pool, whirlpool, and putting green. Terry robes furnished and daily newspapers delivered. Continental breakfast at poolside cabana. Only 3 blocks to the beach. The Boat House Restaurant on the premises. Moderate to expensive.

**Best Western Stratford Inn of Del Mar,** 710 Camino del Mar, Del Mar; (858) 755–1501; www.stratfordinndelmar.com. South end of town, west of I–5 via Del Mar Heights Road. King beds in 93 rooms and suites with refrigerators, remote-control cable TV, and balcony or terrace. Some ocean views; two outdoor pools and spa; continental breakfast. Bridal suite, executive rooms, and kitchenettes available. Walk to the beach, shops, and bistros. Cribs and roll-aways available. Moderate.

**Comfort Inn Cardiff by the Sea,** 1661 Villa Cardiff Drive, Cardiff; (760) 944–0427; www.choicehotels.com. East of I–5, via Birmingham exit. Queen and king beds and sleeper sofas in 105 rooms with refrigerators and Country French decor. Heated pool and whirlpool. Moderate.

**Del Mar Inn,** 720 Camino del Mar, Del Mar; (858) 755–9765 or (800) 451–4515; www.delmarinn.com. South end of town, west of I–5, via Del Mar Heights Road. Double, queen, and king beds in 81 rooms with satellite TV. Choice of oceanside or poolside rooms. Heated pool, whirlpool. Complimentary English tea and cakes each afternoon. Continental breakfast brought to your room. Walk to beach, shops, and restaurants. Moderate.

**Del Mar Motel,** 1702 Coast Boulevard, Del Mar; (858) 755–1534 or (800) 223–8449; www.delmarmotelonthebeach.com. Refrigerators and cable TV in 44 rooms. Located right on the beach; walk to shopping and restaurants. Moderate to expensive.

**L'Auberge Del Mar,** 1540 Camino del Mar, P.O. Box 2889, Del Mar 92014; (858) 259–1515 or (800) 245–9757; www.laubergedelmar.com. Camino del Mar at Fifteenth Street. An elegant inn opened in the summer of 1989, with 120 rooms and suites with balconies or patios, marble baths, minirefrigerators, wet bars, and canopy beds. Some rooms have cathedral ceilings, fireplaces, and ocean views. European health spa with exercise equipment, steam room, Swiss shower, sauna, and underwater massage tubs. Beauty salon, bar, and Tourla's Restaurant on premises. Walk to shops, restaurants, and beach. Expensive to extremely expensive.

# Campgrounds and RV Parks

**San Elijo State Beach,** (mailing address) 2680 Carlsbad Boulevard, Carlsbad; (760) 753–5091 or (800) 444–7275; www.parks.ca.gov. In Encinitas, west side of Old Highway 101 (Route S21), north of Chesterfield Drive. The southernmost developed state campground in California, with 171 full-hookup sites, each with table, stove, and cupboard. For RVs and trailers up to 35 feet. Showers, laundry, bait shop, convenience store, and beach access. Situated on a high bluff with stairway to the beach. Overflow camping in day-use area for self-contained units only. Moderate.

# Food

**En Fuego Cantina and Grill,** 1342 Camino Del Mar, Del Mar; (858) 792–6551; www.enfuegocantina.com. Open daily for lunch and dinner. Offering authentic Mexican food, Southwestern specials, and a healthy selection of fresh fish in a charming atmosphere with an ocean view. Outdoor seating. Happy hour daily. Moderate.

**Fish Market,** 640 Via Del Valle, Del Mar; (858) 755–2277; www.thefishmarket.com. Lunch and dinner daily. Great fresh seafood in a vibrant, often crowded, and noisy dining room, specializing in family-style meals. Moderate.

**Jake's Del Mar,** 1660 Coast Boulevard, Del Mar; (858) 755–2002; www.jakes delmar.com. West of Route S21, on the beach, near the Amtrak depot. Lunch and dinner daily, Sunday brunch. Serves superb steaks, chicken, and lamb. Specializes in fresh seafood, from Alaskan halibut to Maine lobster. Full bar. Moderate.

**Savory Casual Fare,** 267 North El Camino Real, Encinitas; (760) 634–5556; www .savorycasualfare.com. East of I–5, at the Village Encinitas Plaza. The creative menu is seasonal, using all fresh and local products. Moderate.

# Shopping and Browsing

**The Antique Warehouse,** 212 South Cedros Avenue, Solana Beach; (858) 755–5156. South end of town, just east of Route S21 and the railroad tracks. Wednesday through Monday, 10:00 A.M. to 5:00 P.M. Here are 101 shops selling American and European furniture, jewelry, and other antiques and collectibles.

**Del Mar Plaza,** 1555 Camino del Mar, Del Mar; (858) 792–1555; www.delmarplaza .com. Downtown, Fifteenth Street at Camino del Mar, across from the L'Auberge Del Mar. Seven restaurants with open-air, ocean-view dining. More than thirty shops, galleries, and boutiques.

**The Lumberyard Shopping Center,** 765 First Street, Encinitas; (619) 682–3881. On Route S21 between E and F Streets. Monday through Saturday, 10:00 A.M. to 7:00 P.M.; Sunday, 10:00 A.M. to 6:00 P.M. A small, attractive shopping center with more than two dozen shops and restaurants.

# Beaches, Parks, Trails, and Waysides

The beaches from the Del Mar area north to Encinitas are popular with swimmers and surfers, the former looking for the broad and gently sloping stretches where waves are small and water relatively calm, the latter favoring narrow beaches that slope steeply from the coastal bluffs and create the big waves better for riding. In addition to the predominant sandy beaches are rocky areas where tidepools are exposed as the tide wanes.

Beach access is good, all the way from Torrey Pines State Beach, just south of Del Mar and west of Torrey Pines Road via La Jolla Farms Road, to Leucadia State Beach, west of Old Highway 101, at the north end of Encinitas. Many east-west streets and avenues end at or near the beach. Where there are cliffs and bluffs, stairways and ramps provide beach access.

Torrey Pines State Reserve is south of Del Mar and west of North Torrey Pines Road, 2 miles north of Genesee Avenue, which exits I–5 near the University of California–San Diego campus and connects with Route S21. An extension of the reserve lies to the north, west of I–5, east of Route S21, between Carmel Valley Road and Del Mar Heights Road. Hiking and nature trails provide opportunities to view a variety of wildlife habitat and species, including such rare or endangered birds as the least tern, light-footed clapper rail, snowy plover, and white-tailed kite, as well as the rare Torrey pine.

# Water Sports and Activities

Scuba and skin divers like the area, as do clam diggers. Those fishing the surf take surfperch, flatfish, and other species with some regularity in both sandy and rock areas.

Grunion hunters take the night shift in summer, when the gravid, slender fish ride the surf ashore to spawn in the beach sands. The time to gather grunions is during the extremely high tides that coincide with the full and new moons and occur every two weeks. The runs continue for four or five nights following each of these high tides. Although good tides occur from March through September, current regulations prohibit harvesting the fish before June 1. Check the regulations synopsis, available at sport shops, for additional stipulations.

Beaches from Del Mar City Beach to Solana Beach County Park are good grunion beaches and popular surf-fishing areas. San Elijo and Leucadia State Beaches are other popular angling spots.

# Tours and Trips

**Skysurfer Balloon Company,** 1221 Camino del Mar, Del Mar; (858) 481–6800 or (800) 660–6809; www.skysurferballoon.com. Daily flights over Del Mar with champagne and hors d'oeuvres afterward. Flights last forty-five to sixty minutes. Balloons carry up to eighteen passengers. Call for reservations and information.

## events

| | |
|---|---|
| **April** | Del Mar National Horse Show, Del Mar, (858) 792–4288 |
| | Fiesta del Sol, Solana Beach, (619) 755–4775 |
| **June** | Annual Deep Pit BBQ, Encinitas, (760) 632–9711 |
| | San Diego County Fair (Del Mar), (858) 755–1161 |
| **July** | Hot Air Balloon Classic, Del Mar, (858) 481–6800 |
| **August** | Sunday Summer Concerts by the Sea, Encinitas, (760) 633–2740 |
| **September** | Oktoberfest, Encinitas, (760) 753–6041 |
| **October** | Cardiff Chili by the Sea Cookoff, (760) 436–0431 |
| **December** | Quail Botanical Gardens Garden of Lights, (760) 436–3036 |

## Golf and Tennis

**Encinitas Ranch Golf Course,** 1275 Quail Gardens Drive, Encinitas; (760) 944–1936. East of I–5 via Leucadia Boulevard (north of Encinitas Boulevard exit and south of La Costa Boulevard exit) 1 mile to Quail Gardens Drive. Owned by the City of Encinitas, this is an eighteen-hole, par-seventy-two, 6,821-yard course. Driving range, practice greens, clubhouse, and club and cart rental.

**Lomas Santa Fe Executive Golf Course,** 1580 Sun Valley Road, Solana Beach; (858) 755–0195. East of I–5 via Lomas Santa Fe Drive, then left on Sun Valley Road. An eighteen-hole, par-fifty-six, 2,300-yard executive course open to the public. Driving range, putting green, equipment rentals, restaurant, and cocktail lounge.

## Other Attractions

**Del Mar Thoroughbred Club,** Del Mar; (858) 755–1141; www.dmtc.com. At the north end of town, east of Camino del Mar, west of I–5, south off Via de la Valle. Mid-July through mid-September; daily, except Tuesday; post time, 2:00 P.M. Nine races a day at this famous track founded in 1937 by Bing Crosby and Pat O'Brien. Unreserved and reserved clubhouse seats available. Dining room and lounge in clubhouse.

**Quail Botanical Gardens,** 230 Quail Gardens Drive, P.O. Box 5, Encinitas 92024; (760) 436–3036; www.qbgardens.com. Closed Thanksgiving, Christmas, and New Year's Day. Located ½ mile east of I–5 via Encinitas Boulevard, then north ¼ mile. Daily, 9:00 A.M. to 5:00 P.M.; gift shop, 10:00 A.M. to 4:00 P.M. A lovely twenty-five-acre reserve where exotic tropical and drought-resistant plants grow. Rare flowers, shrubs, and trees flourish in the ravines and on the hillsides, including the largest hibiscus collection on the West Coast and the greatest variety of bamboo plants in the United States.

## Travel Information

**Cardiff by the Sea Chamber of Commerce,** Cardiff Towne Centre, 2501 San Elijo Avenue, Cardiff; (760) 436–0431; www.cardiffbythesea.org

**Del Mar Chamber of Commerce,** 1104 Camino del Mar, Suite #1, Del Mar; (858) 755–4844; www.delmarchamber.org

**Encinitas Chamber of Commerce & Visitor's Center,** 138 Encinitas Boulevard, Encinitas; (760) 753–6041 or (800) 953–6041; www.encinitaschamber.com; e-mail: encchamb@encinitasca.com

**Solana Beach Chamber of Commerce,** 210 West Plaza Street, P.O. Box 623, Solana Beach 92075; (619) 755–4775; www.solanabeach.com

# Carlsbad / Oceanside

**Location:** Carlsbad is 32 miles north of San Diego and 26 miles south of San Clemente, on Interstate 5; Oceanside is immediately north of Carlsbad, 84 miles south of Los Angeles.

**Population:** Carlsbad 87,372; Oceanside 167,082

In the northwest corner of San Diego County, in an area locals call North County, lie the side-by-side cities of Carlsbad and Oceanside. Both are oceanfront communities with broad beaches and ocean-view resorts, but both also rise into the foothills and line the canyons east of the freeway.

Carlsbad has the lion's share of beaches, shops, restaurants, and lodging, but Oceanside has the beautiful harbor, a fine fishing pier, and one of the best stretches of surfing beach in the vicinity.

Locals claim to have the shortest thermometer in the nation, with average high temperatures of about sixty-five degrees in January and seventy-seven degrees in August, coupled with a mere 9 inches of rainfall a year. Naturally, hiking, biking, tennis, and golf are popular here, as are all water sports.

With more than 2,000 hotel and motel rooms available, some right on the ocean, the area is attractive to travelers in its own right but also serves as a good headquarters for visiting attractions north, south, and inland. From here it's an easy drive to Encinitas, Solana Beach, Del Mar, San Diego, and Coronado to the south, or north to San Clemente, Dana Point, Laguna Beach, and Newport Beach. Also within convenient range are Disneyland, Knott's Berry Farm, San Diego Wild Animal Park, and the Palomar Observatory.

Those so inclined can even park their wheels and visit communities north and south by rail. Amtrak makes eight scheduled runs a day between Los Angeles and San Diego, stopping at a number of towns, including Oceanside. Climb aboard the northbound train and be in San Clemente in fifteen minutes, or take a twenty-minute ride to Del Mar on the southbound. From Oceanside to San Diego takes about fifty minutes, and the San Diego station is only 4 blocks from the bay, near the Maritime Museum and Broadway Pier. Take trackless trolleys from there to other points of interest, or use the ferry or water taxi.

# Lodging

**Best Western Beach Terrace Inn,** 2775 Ocean Street, Carlsbad; (760) 729–5951 or (800) 433–5415; www.beachterraceinn.com. West off Carlsbad Boulevard, between Vista Way and Carlsbad Village Drive. From I–5, take Vista Way or Carlsbad Village Drive exit. Cable TV and cable movies in 49 rooms and suites, some with private balconies, fireplaces, and kitchenettes. Oceanfront honeymoon suite with in-room whirlpool. Pool, whirlpool, sauna, and ocean view. Near shops and restaurants. On the beach. Expensive.

**Best Western Marty's Valley Inn,** 3240 East Mission Avenue, Oceanside; (760) 757–7700 or (800) 747–3529; www.bwmartys.com. East of I–5, 1¾ miles on State Route 76. Cable TV and cable movies in 110 rooms and suites. Heated pool, fitness center, continental breakfast. Grove Restaurant and Lounge on premises. Live entertainment and dancing. Moderate.

**Best Western Oceanside Inn,** 1680 Oceanside Boulevard, Oceanside; (760) 722–1821 or (800) 443–9995; www.bestwesternoceansideinn.com. West of I–5, east of Hill Street. Cable TV in 80 rooms, each with a hair dryer, iron, ironing board, and coffeemaker. Heated pool, whirlpool, sauna, laundry, and valet service. Complimentary morning newspaper, continental breakfast, tea, coffee, and evening refreshments. Inexpensive to moderate.

**Carlsbad Inn Beach Resort,** 3075 Carlsbad Boulevard, Carlsbad; (760) 434–7020 or (800) 235–3939; www.carlsbadinn.com. West off I–5 via Carlsbad Village Drive exit. Cable TV in 182 units, some with kitchens. Pool, whirlpools, barbecue area, health club, tennis courts, and laundry facilities. Specialty shops, beauty salon, bakery, and restaurant on premises. Complimentary morning newspaper and continental breakfast. Expensive to very expensive.

**La Costa Resort and Spa,** 2100 Costa Del Mar Road, Carlsbad; (760) 438–9111 or (800) 854–5000; www.lacosta.com. East of I–5 via La Costa Avenue exit. Has 474 rooms and one- and two-bedroom suites. "La Costa" suites are adjacent to golf and tennis facilities. Also 2 three-bedroom presidential suites. Jogging trails, gardens, lakes, and heated pools throughout the 1,000-acre complex. Two PGA golf courses, three restaurants, three lounges, and a theater. Separate spas for men and women, and various spa plans available. Tennis anyone?—2 clay courts and 17 composition courts, some lighted. Resident golf and tennis pros. Expensive to extremely expensive.

**Olympic Resort Hotel and Spa,** 6111 El Camino Real, Carlsbad; (760) 438–8330 or (800) 522–8330. East of I–5 via Palomar Airport Road. Cable TV in 78 rooms and suites with queen and king beds. Fitness center, 5 lighted tennis courts, 2 Olympic-size pools, European spa, sauna, and large golf practice area. Restaurant and cocktail lounge on premises. Moderate to expensive.

**Pelican Cove Inn,** 320 Walnut Avenue, Carlsbad; (760) 434–5995 or (888) 735–2683; www.pelican-cove.com. West of I–5 via Carlsbad Village Drive, then south on Lincoln to Walnut. Twin, queen, and king beds in 10 guest rooms with private baths in this bed-and-breakfast inn. Only 200 yards from the ocean. Near shops and restaurants. Bicycles, beach chairs, in-room massage, and picnic baskets available. Full breakfast. Moderate to expensive.

**Tamarack Beach Resort,** 3200 Carlsbad Boulevard, Carlsbad; (760) 729–3500 or (800) 334–2199; www.tamarackresort.com. West of I–5 via Tamarack Avenue exit, then north on Carlsbad Boulevard. Cable TV in 77 rooms and one- and two-bedroom suites. Heated pool, two whirlpools, balconies, fitness center, outdoor barbecues, complimentary continental breakfast, and ocean views. VCRs in suites. Across the street from the beach. Moderate to expensive.

# Campgrounds and RV Parks

**Oceanside RV Park,** 1510 South Coast Highway, Oceanside; (760) 722–4404. West of I–5 via Oceanside Boulevard, then south on South Coast Highway, ½ block. Has 140 full-hookup sites with cable TV and privacy fences. Heated pool and shuffleboard. Two blocks to the ocean. Expensive.

**South Carlsbad State Beach,** 7201 Carlsbad Boulevard, Carlsbad; (760) 438–3143 or (800) 444–7275; www.parks.ca.gov. West of Carlsbad Boulevard at Ponto Drive. From I–5 take La Costa Avenue west, then Carlsbad Boulevard north. Campground situated on a bluff with stairway to beach. Has 226 campsites with water and electricity, tables, cupboards, and stoves. Showers, laundry, tank dump, convenience store, bait, and beach-equipment rentals. Moderate.

# Food

**Al's In-The-Village Cafe,** 795 Carlsbad Village Drive, Carlsbad; (760) 729–5448; www.alscafecarlsbad.com. At Carlsbad Village. Breakfast and lunch daily, dinner on Friday nights. A large breakfast menu with all the traditional egg dishes, pancakes, waffles, and Hawaiian-style French toast. Also house specialties, including Ben's Wild Man Eggs with bacon, onion, green chilies, and melted Jack cheese; Farm Breakfast, which includes three eggs, ham steak, biscuit and gravy, and home-fried red-skinned potatoes; and Hawaiian Loco Moco, ground sirloin on steamed rice, topped with gravy and a fried egg. Lunches include soups, salads, hot and cold deli-style sandwiches, a half-dozen chicken-breast specialty sandwiches, burgers, and fish-and-chips. Inexpensive.

**Benihana Restaurant,** 755 Raintree Drive, Carlsbad; (760) 929–8311; www.benihana .com. West of I–5 via Poinsettia Lane, then right on Avenida Encinitas, then right on Raintree. Daily lunch and dinner. Specializes in Teppanyaki-style cooking at heated tables where meals are prepared and served by performing chefs. Fresh fish, as well as prime tenderloin, filet mignon, and chicken. Full bar. Moderate to expensive.

**Joe's Crab Shack,** 314 South Harbor Drive, Oceanside; (760) 722–1345. On the harbor with a great view. Lunch and dinner daily. Start with a crab dip, peel-and-eat shrimp, or fried cheese. Then try one of Joe's famous combination fish platters or a meal of crab legs, shrimp, scallops, or surf and turf with top sirloin or chicken. For dessert, try Joe's Chocolate Shack Attack—a six-layer cake with lots of icing. Full bar. Moderate.

**Neimans Fine Dining & Entertainment,** 300 Carlsbad Village Drive, Carlsbad; (760) 729–4131; www.neimans.com. At Carlsbad Village. Daily lunch and dinner, Sunday champagne brunch. Choose from such appetizers as crab cakes, breaded calamari, or garlic spiced shrimp. Check out the soup du jour, or try the vegetarian black bean soup or clam chowder. Specialty salads include Chinese chicken, smoked chicken, and California Cobb salad, as well as Caesar salad, with or without chicken or shrimp. More than a half-dozen gourmet burgers and such specialty sandwiches as oak-fired chicken breast and southern California crab sandwich. Among the many dinner selections are pasta dishes, seafood, rack of lamb, New York pepper steak, and prime rib. Good selection of California wines by the glass or bottle. Nightly entertainment. Moderate to expensive.

**101 Cafe,** 631 South Coast Highway, Oceanside; (760) 722–5220; www.101cafe.net. On Old Highway 101. Breakfast, lunch, and dinner daily; breakfast served all day. Dine indoors or on the patio. The huge breakfast menu includes all the traditional favorites, including corned beef hash and eggs, sirloin steak and eggs, chicken-fried steak and eggs, biscuits and gravy, hot cakes, French toast, and a dozen different omelets. Lunch includes salads, soups, chili, more than a half-dozen different burgers, specialty sandwiches, burritos, and tacos. Among the dinner specialties are fish-and-chips, fried chicken, fried shrimp, meat loaf, beef liver and grilled onions, roast beef, pork chops, and turkey—all served with soup or salad, potato, vegetable, and dinner roll. Children's menu available. Inexpensive.

## Shopping and Browsing

Carlsbad Village, the oldest shopping district in the city, has undergone a major redevelopment. This area, which lies between the beach and the freeway, several blocks each side of Carlsbad Village Drive, contains more than 600 business services, restaurants, specialty shops, antiques shops, and art galleries. Maps of the area are available at the Convention and Visitors Bureau, in the old train depot next to the railroad tracks, just north of Carlsbad Village Drive.

Other shops are scattered about Carlsbad and Oceanside. A major shopping area lies east of the freeway, on and near El Camino Real. The huge Plaza Camino Real mall is flanked by smaller shopping centers. Adjacent North County Plaza has forty stores and restaurants. To the east is Carlsbad Plaza, with sixty-one shops and restaurants.

**Carlsbad Premium Outlets,** 5620 Paseo Del Norte, Suite 100, Carlsbad; (760) 804–9000 or (888) 790–7467; www.premiumoutlets.com. One block east of I–5, between Cannon and Palomar Airport Roads. Opens at 10:00 A.M. daily, closes at 8:00 P.M. Company outlet shopping center with more than 90 nationally renowned designers, manufacturers, specialty retailers, and restaurants represented. Men's and women's apparel, children's fashions, footwear, luggage, leather, home furnishings, jewelry, cosmetics, and more. Bellefleur Winery and Restaurant on premises.

**Westfield Plaza Camino Real,** 2525 El Camino Real, Carlsbad; (760) 729–7927; www.westfield.com. East of I–5 via Carlsbad Village Drive in Carlsbad, or via Vista Way (Route 78) in Oceanside. The second-largest mall in the North County area, with 1.1 million square feet, 5 major department stores, 154 shops, and 2 movie theaters.

# Beaches, Parks, Trails, and Waysides

About 10 miles of beaches border the cities of Carlsbad and Oceanside, beginning with South Carlsbad State Beach, on the west side of Carlsbad Boulevard, near Ponto Drive. Carlsbad State Beach and Carlsbad City Beach are west of Carlsbad Boulevard, in town, between Tamarack and Cypress Avenues.

South Oceanside Beach is just north of Buena Vista Lagoon, west of Pacific Street, at the foot of Cassidy Street. Oceanside City Beach is spread north and south of the Oceanside Pier, along the Strand. Harbor Beach is at the north end of Pacific Street, west of the harbor.

All the beaches in the area are popular with swimmers, sunbathers, and surfers. Access is good and parking ample. At South Carlsbad State Beach, parking is tight in the day-use area, but space is usually available along Carlsbad Boulevard.

Buena Vista Lagoon, at the Carlsbad and Oceanside city limits, is a bird sanctuary where more than 225 species have been recorded. At the north end of Carlsbad Boulevard, turn east on Laguna Drive, then left on Jefferson Street. You can park along Jefferson east of I–5 to watch the reserve's wildlife.

During whale migrations, the bluffs above the beaches are good places for whale watching. Try the Whale Watcher's Walk between Elm and Tamarack in Carlsbad. The Oceanside Pier is another good spot, as is the Blufftop Walkway south of the pier.

# Water Sports and Activities

All the beach areas are popular surf-fishing spots and are enjoyed as well by scuba divers and snorkelers. South Carlsbad State Beach and the Oceanside Pier have bait shops.

South of Tamarack Avenue and Carlsbad State Beach is Agua Hedionda Lagoon. The calm lagoon waters make this a favorite angling spot and a popular waterskiing area.

The Oceanside Pier, once 1,900 feet long, was badly damaged during the 1982–83 winter storms, which reduced its length by about half. Nevertheless, this is a fine fishing pier that also offers a great view of Oceanside. This municipal pier is lighted at night and has fish-cleaning facilities.

The beautiful harbor in Oceanside has more than 900 slips up to 51 feet. This is a popular stopover for sailors traveling between San Diego and Newport Beach, and it's home to the Oceanside charter fleet. There is also access within the harbor for shore fishing. Even if you're not an angler or boater, you should visit the harbor to enjoy its beauty and serenity.

**California Watersports,** 4215 Harrison Street, Carlsbad; (760) 434–3089; www.carlsbad lagoon.com. East of I–5, on Agua Hedionda Lagoon. March through October, 8:00 A.M. to sunset daily; November through February, 8:00 A.M. to sunset Wednesday through Sunday. Concrete launch ramp, fuel dock, snack bar, and picnic area. Also rents waterskiing equipment, jet skis, WaveRunners, motorboats, kayaks, and canoes. Summer day camp for children.

**Helgren's Sportfishing Trips,** 315 South Harbor Drive, Oceanside; (760) 722–2133 or (888) 206–3241; www.helsgrensportfishing.com. At the harbor, near Cape Cod Village. Morning half-day, afternoon half-day, full-day, and twilight fishing trips. Long-range trips to Mexico. Two- and three-day island albacore trips. Charters and group rates available. Rod rental, bait, fishing licenses, and full galley. Two-hour whale-watching trips daily, December 26 through April.

# Rentals

**Boat Rentals of America,** 256 Harbor Drive South, Oceanside; (760) 722–0028; www.boats4rent.com. Rents motorboats, sailboats, pedal boats, WaveRunners, and kayaks.

# Golf

**Emerald Isle Golf Course,** 660 South El Camino Real, Oceanside; (760) 721–4700; www.emeraldisle.net. South off Mission Avenue, then left at the first traffic light (Vista Oceana). An eighteen-hole, par-three executive course with pro shop, equipment and cart rental, driving range, and snack bar.

**Oceanside Center City Golf Course,** 2323 Greenbrier, Box 1088, Oceanside 92051; (760) 433–8590. South on Barnes off Mission Avenue, east on Maxson, south on Grace, then east on Greenbrier. An eighteen-hole, par-sixty-six, 4,426-yard course. Putting green, pro shop, resident pro, equipment rentals, and restaurant.

**Oceanside Golf Course,** 825 Douglas Drive, Oceanside; (760) 433–1360. East of I–5 via Mission Avenue exit, 4½ miles to Douglas, then left. An eighteen-hole, par-seventy-two, 6,400-yard public course. Driving range, putting green, pro shop, equipment rentals, clubhouse, snack bar, restaurant, and cocktail lounge.

**Olympic Resort,** 6111 El Camino Real, Carlsbad; (760) 438–8330. East of I–5 via Palomar Airport Road. A public practice area with nineteen green-size targets, ponds, sand traps, putting green, two fairways, pro shop, and resident pro.

**Rancho Carlsbad Country Club,** 5200 El Camino Real, Carlsbad; (760) 438–1772; www.ranchocarlsbad.com. East of I–5 via Palomar Airport Road, then left on El Camino Real. An eighteen-hole, par-fifty-six, 2,396-yard public executive course. Pro shop, resident pro, driving range, putting green, equipment rentals, and snack bar.

## Other Attractions

**California Surf Museum,** 223 North Coast Highway, Oceanside; (760) 721–6876; www.surfmuseum.org. Open daily, 10:00 A.M. to 4:00 P.M. Internationally recognized world-class surf museum about the sport and lifestyle of surfers.

**Heritage Park Village and Museum,** 220 Peyri Drive, Oceanside; (760) 433–8297, Friends of Heritage Park. Located behind the Mission San Luis Rey, this museum is open Monday through Friday 9:00 A.M. to 4:00 P.M., Sunday 1:00 to 4:00 P.M., and displays a stable and blacksmith shop, city jail, and doctor's office from the 1800s.

**Legoland,** LEGO Drive, Carlsbad; (760) 918–5346; www.lego.com. East of I–5, via Cannon Road; just follow the signs to LEGO Drive. Open 10:00 A.M. to 5:00 P.M. Thursday through Monday, with extended hours during summer and on holidays. America's first Legoland, this 128-acre park is not the usual amusement or theme park, crowded with wild rides. Rather, it features distinct viewing and play areas, many with hands-on play activities: The Beginning, Imagination Zone, Miniland USA, Dino Island, Knight's Kingdom, Explore Village, and Fun Town. The park was designed specifically for kids ages three to twelve, but teens and parents will get a kick out of it too, especially those whose own childhood play included building projects with the ingenious LEGO bricks. Food and beverages are available, and there are more than twenty-five specialty shops, including The Big Shop, with the nation's largest selection of LEGO products. This is a *must see* for every family with children.

**Mission San Luis Rey,** 4050 Mission Avenue, Oceanside; (760) 757–3651; www.sanluis rey.org. Four miles east of I–5 via Mission Avenue. Open daily 10:00 A.M. to 4:00 P.M. Known as the "King of Missions," the largest of California's twenty-one missions. Beautifully restored and open to the public. Self-guided tours. Museum open 10:00 A.M. to 4:30 P.M. daily.

# Travel Information

**Carlsbad Chamber of Commerce,** 5934 Priestly Drive, Carlsbad; (760) 931–8400; www.carlsbade.org; www.carlsbad.com; www.visitcarlsbad.com

**Carlsbad Convention & Visitors Bureau,** 400 Carlsbad Village Drive and State, P.O. Box 1246, Carlsbad 92008; (760) 434–6093 or (800) 227–5722; www.carlsbadca.org

**Oceanside Chamber of Commerce,** 928 North Coast Highway, P.O. Box 1578, Oceanside 92054; (760) 722–1534 or (800) 350–7873; www.oceansidechamber.com; e-mail: info@oceansidechamber.com

## events

| | |
|---|---|
| **January** | Carlsbad Marathon, (760) 434–6093 |
| **March** | Carlsbad 5000 (5K run), (760) 434–6093 |
| **May** | Carlsbad Village Street Faire, (760) 931–8400 |
| | Cinco de Mayo, Oceanside, (760) 722–1534 |
| **June** | Oceanside Triathalon, (760) 722–1534 |
| | NSSA Surf Contest, (714) 378–0899 |
| **July** | Freedom Days Celebration, (760) 754–4512 |
| **August** | Mission Fiesta, (760) 757–3651 |
| **September** | Harbor Days, Oceanside, (760) 722–1534 |
| **October** | Oktoberfest, Carlsbad, (760) 434–6093 |
| **November** | Carlsbad Village Street Faire, (760) 931–8400 |
| **December** | Mission Christmas Craft Sale, Oceanside, (760) 722–1534 |
| | Parade of Lights, Oceanside, (760) 722–5751 |

# San Clemente/Dana Point

**Location:** San Clemente is 23 miles north of Oceanside and 4 miles south of Dana Point, on Interstate 5; Dana Point is 6 miles south of Laguna Beach on California Highway 1 and midway between (60 miles from) San Diego and Los Angeles.

**Population:** San Clemente 57,768; Dana Point 35,745

Relatively unknown outside southern California circles only a few decades ago, San Clemente stepped into the world arena in 1969 when Richard M. Nixon purchased property that once belonged to one of the city's founding fathers. The estate soon became known as the Western White House, and whenever the president and his family occupied it, the network news anchors were sure to mention San Clemente in every broadcast.

With much of that fame, if not notoriety, in its past, San Clemente today is mainly a community of contented retirees and summer vacationers. Rumors, rumblings, and nearby multimillion-dollar property deals, however, indicate that the "Spanish Village" is on its way to resort status and will no doubt begin attracting greater numbers of visitors all year to its pleasant climate and recreational opportunities.

If San Clemente is about to arrive, Dana Point is already there. Named after Richard Henry Dana, who first came to these shores in 1835 aboard the brig *Pilgrim* and later wrote the classic adventure romance *Two Years before the Mast,* Dana Point plays well its role of romantic seaport. Everywhere are reminders of the city's nautical heritage, from its fine little maritime museum to the exquisite sailing replica of the *Pilgrim* moored in the $20-million harbor.

Dana Point is a shipshape town, with sandy beaches and grassy parks shaded by fan palms and eucalyptus trees. Although malls, plazas, shops, and galleries stand here and there, the focal point of interest for most travelers is the beautiful harbor, where there is plenty to see and do, including picnicking, boating, shopping, dining, exploring tidepools, or just relaxing on the beach.

For anyone driving the Pacific Coast, Dana Point is significant as the starting place for California Highway 1, the state's premier coastal route. It hugs the Pacific shores for most of its length, skimming over coastal lowlands and along the edges of mesas, winding switchback by switchback up craggy mountains, descending into the canyons and valleys of rivers and creeks, twisting through forests, hanging precariously on cliff faces, and straightening out on the broad marine terraces and poppy-dotted meadows. This is the Pacific Coast Highway, famous or infamous, depending on your point of view and the hurry you're in. Those of us who enjoy its quirks and kinks say, "Welcome to it." Those who prefer the rush and crush of freeway driving say, "You're welcome to it."

# Lodging

**Best Western Casablanca Inn,** 1601 North El Camino Real, San Clemente; (949) 361–1644; www.bestwestern.com. West of I-5 via Avenida Pico, then left on El Camino Real. Queen and king beds in 80 large rooms and 2 suites with remote-control cable TV, cable movies, and VCRs. Some rooms have balconies and whirlpool tubs. Kitchen suites have wet bars, microwaves, refrigerators, and whirlpool tubs. Moderate to expensive.

**Marriott Laguna Cliffs Resort,** 25135 Park Lantern, Dana Point; (949) 661–5000 or (800) 533–9748; www.lagunacliffs.com. West of Pacific Coast Highway, on a bluff overlooking the harbor. A 376-room, 17-suite resort situated on 42 acres of park and lawn, with 2 lighted tennis courts, 2 pools, Jacuzzis, sauna, exercise equipment, steam room, aerobics, massage. Expensive to extremely expensive.

**San Clemente Beach Travelodge,** 2441 South El Camino Real, San Clemente; (949) 498–5954 or (800) 843–1706; www.travelodge.com. Adjacent to municipal eighteen-hole golf course, east of I-5 via Magdalena. Remote-control cable TV and cable movies in 23 rooms and suites with queen beds and refrigerators. In-room Jacuzzis available. Rooms overlooking golf course or with ocean-view balconies. Walk to beach. Complimentary continental breakfast. Inexpensive to moderate.

# Campgrounds and RV Parks

**Doheny State Beach,** 25300 Dana Point Harbor Drive, Dana Point; (949) 496–6172 or (800) 444–7275; www.dohenystatebeach.org. Pacific Coast Highway at Del Obispo, just south of the harbor. Has 115 sites with drinking water, tables, and fire rings. Tank dump. Trails and beach access. Moderate.

**San Clemente State Beach,** 3030 Avenida del Presidente, San Clemente; (949) 492–3156 or (800) 444–7275; www.parks.ca.gov. West of I-5 via Avenida Calafia exit, south end of town. Campsites on a bluff above the beach, each with table, stove, and cupboard: 85 general sites with water and 72 full-hookup RV sites. Showers and laundry tubs. Trails to beach. Moderate.

**San Onofre State Beach,** Pendleton Coast District, 3030 Avenida del Presidente, San Clemente; (949) 492–4872 or (800) 444–7275; www.parks.ca.gov. South of San Clemente, west off I-5 at Basilone Road exit, then 2½ miles south. Campgrounds are on a bluff above the beach, with 221 trailer spaces and 40 primitive tent sites. No hookups. Water, outside showers, and tank dump. Inexpensive.

# Food

**The Brig Restaurant,** 34461 Golden Lantern, Dana Point; (949) 493–5853. At Mariner's Village, on the harbor. Breakfast, lunch, and dinner daily. Traditional breakfast and Mexican food. Soups, salads, burgers, deli-style sandwiches, mesquite-broiled chicken, shrimp fajitas, fish-and-chips, and pasta dishes. Breakfast served all day. Beer and wine. Inexpensive to moderate.

**New Mandarin Garden,** 111 West Avenida Palizada, San Clemente; (949) 492–7432. West of I–5 and South El Camino Real, in the Old City Plaza. Daily lunch and dinner, Sunday champagne brunch. Chinese restaurant and carryout. Daily lunch specials. Roast duck, barbecued pork and spare ribs, sweet-and-sour pork, Peking fried chicken, beef with broccoli, egg rolls, fried rice, chow mein, and more. Inexpensive.

**Ristorante Ferrantelli,** 25001 Dana Point Harbor Drive, Dana Point; (949) 493–1401; www.ferrantellis.com. West of Pacific Coast Highway, at the Pavilion Shopping Center, adjacent to the harbor. Lunch and dinner daily. Superb antipasti, meal-size salads, calamari, and other fresh seafood. All the usual Italian pasta dishes served with seafood, meat, or vegetable sauces. Full cocktail bar. Inexpensive to moderate.

# Shopping and Browsing

San Clemente and Dana Point have a number of small malls and shopping centers as well as specialty shops, boutiques, and galleries throughout both communities. Serious shoppers and browsers, however, will no doubt want to make the short trek north to Laguna Beach, where there are blocks of shops and galleries.

# Museum

**Orange County Marine Institute,** 24200 Dana Point Harbor Drive, Dana Point; (949) 496–2274; www.ocean-institute.org. At the north end of Dana Point Harbor. Open weekends 10:00 A.M. to 3:00 P.M. Has a number of programs, lectures, and classes, as well as marine-life displays, aquariums, touch tank, and skeleton of a gray whale to examine. The square-rigged brig *Pilgrim* is moored here and is part of many institute programs.

# Beaches, Parks, Trails, and Waysides

Beaches along this stretch of coast—from San Clemente State Beach, in the south, to Doheny State Beach, just south of the Dana Point Harbor—are popular with picnickers, sunbathers, and hikers. Swimmers, however, should not venture into the water without first checking on local conditions. At times, riptides, currents, and undertows can be dangerous.

San Clemente Beach lies west of I–5, off Avenida Calafia, at the south end of town. San Clemente City Beach stretches from the north end of town, south past the Municipal

Pier to San Clemente State Beach. When hiking from bluffs to beaches here, stay on the established trails, as the steep terrain is unstable and dangerous.

Doheny State Beach has bike and horse trails and a popular picnic area with grass, trees, tables, and fire rings. At Dana Point Harbor, a small beach off Ensenada Place offers swimming in warm, protected waters. There's a picnic park adjacent to the beach and others rimming the harbor and on the island, reached via Island Way, off Dana Point Harbor Drive.

## Water Sports and Activities

The same high bluffs, narrow beaches, and underwater contours that sometimes create dangerous conditions for swimmers along this stretch of the coast often form the kinds of waves surfers live for. Surfing is allowed at the north ends of both San Clemente and Doheny state beaches. Salt Creek Beach Park, west of Pacific Coast Highway, north of Dana Point, is also popular with surfers.

The San Clemente Municipal Pier, west of I–5 and South El Camino Real, via Avenida Del Mar, is a favorite of local anglers. Pier concessions sell food, beverages, bait, and tackle.

In Dana Point, anglers usually head for the harbor. This is where the sportfishing fleet operates, where anglers can either launch and moor their own boats or rent skiffs for fishing in harbor waters. Shore-bound anglers will also find opportunities here.

Those fishing offshore will catch bonito, albacore, white sea bass, barracuda, halibut, shark, and a variety of bottom dwellers. Near shore, surf, rock, jetty, and pier, the take will include barred surfperch in good numbers, as well as halibut, bonito, corbina, sargo, croaker, and even the occasional barracuda. Fishing is often good in the harbor and from the jetties, although the west jetty is a dangerous place when the surf's up. Rocky shoreline areas north of Dana Point are also productive.

**Capo Beach Watercraft Rentals,** 3412 Embarcadero Place #B, Dana Point; (949) 661–1690. At Dana Point Harbor, west of Pacific Coast Highway. Open every day. Rents Sea-Doo, WaveRunner, and other personal watercraft models. All rentals include lockers, instruction, life vests, and wet suits in season. Only two minutes from the harbor to the riding area.

**Dana Island Yacht Sales and Charters,** 34551 Casitas Place, Dana Point; (949) 248–7400; www.danaislandyachts.com. At the harbor, west of Pacific Coast Highway. Powerboats and sailboats for hire—bare-boat or with crew. Sportfishing, coastal cruises, cocktail cruises, and brunch cruises to Newport Beach.

**Dana Point Jet Ski,** 34671 Puerto Place, Dana Point; (949) 661–4947 or (800) 865–3875; www.danapointjetski.com. At Dana Point Harbor, west of Pacific Coast Highway. Rents, sells, and services Kawasaki personal watercraft, with the largest fleet of current-year models on the West Coast. Also rents kayaks and surfboards by the hour or day.

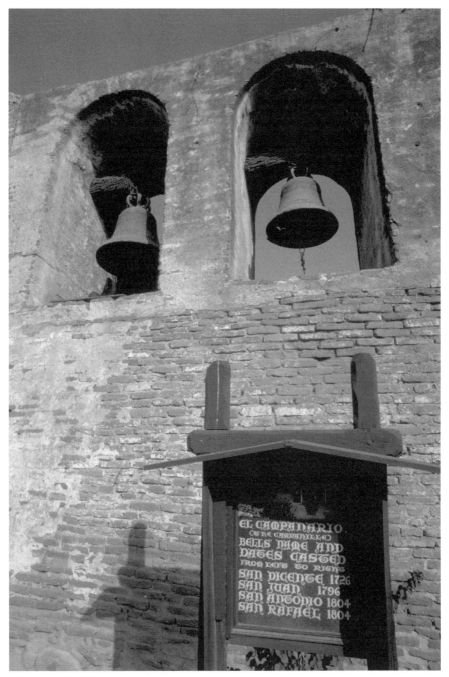

Mission San Juan Capistrano *Courtesy of Robert Holmes/CalTour*

**Dana Wharf Sportfishing Charter and Whale Watching,** 34675 Golden Lantern, Dana Point; (949) 496–5794 or (800) 590–9994; www.danawharf.com. West of Pacific Coast Highway, at the south end of the harbor. Half-day, three-quarter-day, twilight, full-day, and two-day fishing trips aboard a fleet of fine vessels ranging in size from 31 to 65 feet. Licenses and tackle available. Open party and private charters. Galleys serve hot and cold food and beverages. Whale-watching excursions November through April. Parasailing trips. Also twenty-five-passenger half-day trips, private charters, and whale-watching excursions aboard the beautiful 82-foot classic schooner yacht *Kelpie.*

## Other Attractions

**Mission San Juan Capistrano,** Ortega Highway and Camino Capistrano, San Juan Capistrano; (949) 234–1300; www.missionsjc.com. Built in 1776, this historic mission, with gardens and museum, is open daily with guided tours by appointment.

## Golf

**The Links at Monarch Beach,** 22 Monarch Beach Resort Drive North, Dana Point; (949) 240–8247; www.monarchbeachgolf.com. North of Dana Point, east of Pacific Coast Highway, via Niguel Road. An eighteen-hole, par-seventy, 6,600-yard public course with pro shop, restaurant, cart and club rentals, and lessons available.

**San Clemente Municipal Golf Course,** 150 East Magdalena, San Clemente; (949) 361–8384. Great ocean views from this eighteen-hole, par-seventy-two, 6,114-yard course. Driving range, practice greens, club and cart rental, pro shop, resident pro, clubhouse, restaurant, and bar.

## Weather and Tide Information

**Marine weather report;** recorded message, (949) 496–2210

## Travel Information

**Dana Point Chamber of Commerce,** 24681 La Plaza, Suite 120, P.O. Box 12, Dana Point 92629; (949) 496–1555 or (800) 290–DANA; www.danapoint-chamber.com

**San Clemente Chamber of Commerce,** 1100 North El Camino Real, San Clemente; (949) 492–1131; www.scchamber.com; e-mail: scchamber@fia.net

| | |
|---|---|
| **March** | Festival of the Whales Fair, Dana Point, (949) 496–1555 |
| **May** | Cinco de Mayo Festival, San Clemente, (949) 361–8275 |
| | Blues Festival, Dana Point, (949) 496–1555 |
| **July** | Ocean Festival, San Clemente, (949) 492–1131 |
| **August** | Fiesta Street Festival, San Clemente, (949) 492–1131 |
| | Fiesta 5000 (5K run/stride), San Clemente, (949) 492–1131 |
| **September** | Tall Ships Festival, Dana Point, (949) 496–1555 |
| | Doheny Days Music Festival, Dana Point, (949) 496–1555 |
| **October** | Sea Fest, San Clemente, (949) 492–1131 |
| **November** | Thanksgiving Day Turkey Trot 10K Run, Dana Point, (949) 496–1555 |
| **December** | Christmas Festival and Tree Lighting, Dana Point, (949) 496–1555 |
| | Harbor of Lights, Dana Point, (949) 923–2255 |

# Laguna Beach

**Location:** On California Highway 1, 4 miles south of Newport, 10 miles north of San Clemente, and 66 miles north of San Diego.

**Population:** 24,126

In the heart of an area stretching from Corona Del Mar to Dana Point known as the "California Riviera," Laguna Beach is a spotless little town with nothing faintly resembling a slum or anything less than affluence. This is the home base of high culture on the Orange Coast, but without any signs of stuffiness, and with that California sense of humor and laid-back attitude retained.

More than a century ago, the area's natural beauty began attracting visitors who arrived by wagon and stagecoach to camp on the beaches and in the nearby canyons. Ironically, today's traveling camper must head south to Dana Point and San Clemente or north to Newport Beach to pitch a tent or hook up a motor home. Overnighting at Laguna Beach means putting up at one of the many fine motels, resorts, or bed-and-breakfast inns.

The same spectacular seascapes and landscapes that drew vacationers to the area also caught the attention of artists, who began depicting the coastal life and scenery in the 1890s. The tradition continues, and now galleries galore greet visitors to this lovely hamlet.

Those fortunate enough to be in town on the first Thursday of any month enjoy Laguna Gallery Night, during which the Laguna Museum of Art and seventy-five Laguna Beach galleries are open from 6:00 to 10:00 P.M. Galleries plan special showings, often with artists present to meet visitors. The chamber of commerce provides gallery maps and information, and free tram service is available.

The community also stages two art festivals each year, including the one by which all others should be judged—The Festival of Arts and Pageant of the Masters, which lasts seven weeks in July and August. More than 160 area artists display works in all media. The festival grounds are open daily from 10:00 A.M. to 11:30 P.M., and tram service is provided from outlying parking areas on Laguna Canyon Road.

## Lodging

**Aliso Creek Inn,** 31106 Pacific Coast Highway, South Laguna; (949) 499–2271 or (800) 223–3309; www.alisocreekinn.com. On Highway 1, south of Laguna Beach, across the highway from Aliso Beach and fishing pier. Queen beds in 62 studio, one-bedroom, and two-bedroom suites with fully equipped kitchens, cable TV, and cable movies. Restaurant and lounge on premises, with live entertainment and dancing nightly. Beautiful nine-hole golf course on premises, with pro shop. Winter, moderate to expensive; summer, expensive.

**By the Sea Inn,** 475 North Coast Highway; (949) 497–6645 or (800) 297–0007; www.bytheseainn.com. On Highway 1, ½ block from Diver's Cove. Cable TV and cable movies in 36 rooms with skylights and balconies. Kitchenettes and in-room whirlpools available. Heated pool, whirlpool, wet and dry saunas, and steam room. Walk to beach and village. Moderate to expensive.

**Casa Laguna Inn,** 2510 South Coast Highway; (949) 494–2996 or (800) 233–0449; www.casalaguna.com. On Highway 1, between Upland Drive and Solana Way. Cable TV and cable movies in 20 rooms, suites, and cottages—16 with kitchens. Gardens and pathways, patios, decks, and balconies. Most rooms have refrigerators. Antique and contemporary furnishings. Private baths, heated pool, and ocean view. Complimentary tea, wine, and hors d'oeuvres served each afternoon in the library. Continental breakfast also served in the library. Expensive.

**Eiler's Inn,** 741 South Coast Highway; (949) 494–3004 or (866) 617–2696; www .eilersinn.com. On Highway 1, in town. Twin, double, queen, and king beds in 11 rooms and 1 suite—all with private baths. Antique furnishings. Sundeck with ocean view. Courtyard. Fresh flowers, fruit, and candies in rooms. Guests receive bottle of champagne on arrival. Coffee and sun tea available all day. Wine and cheese served in the courtyard each evening. Full breakfast. Steps leading to beach. Expensive; Sunday through Thursday, October through May, moderate to expensive.

**Holiday Inn Laguna Beach,** 696 South Coast Highway; (949) 494–1001 or (800) 228–5691. On Highway 1, in town. Cable TV in 54 rooms and 4 suites. Rooms overlook courtyard. Suites have whirlpool baths. Heated pool. Monte Carlo Restaurant and Lounge on premises, featuring California cuisine. Complimentary continental breakfast, Monday through Friday. Moderate to very expensive.

**Laguna Brisas Spa Hotel,** 1600 South Coast Highway; (949) 497–7272 or (888) 296–6834; www.lagunabrisas.com. On Highway 1, south end of town. Queen and king beds in 66 rooms with remote-control cable TV, refrigerators, hair dryers, and marble baths with whirlpools. Heated pool, whirlpool, and laundry facilities. Complimentary continental breakfast. Walk to beach and village. Moderate to expensive.

**Laguna Riviera,** 825 South Coast Highway; (949) 494–1196 or (800) 999–2089; www.lagunariviera.com. On Highway 1, in town. Cable TV in 41 rooms and suites. Pavilion with pool, whirlpool, and sauna. Decks with ocean view. Beach access. Complimentary continental breakfast. Moderate to expensive.

# Food

**Cedar Creek Inn,** 384 Forest Avenue; (949) 497–8696; www.cedarcreekinn.com. In the Lumberyard Mall, on Highway 1, at the south end of town. Daily lunch and dinner. Large menu featuring contemporary American cuisine. Fresh and delicious salads, big tasty sandwiches, pasta dishes, chicken, beef, and seafood with a flair. Try the turkey and Swiss sandwich on grilled sourdough with bacon, lettuce, tomato, avocado, and mayonnaise. Enjoy salmon poached in spiced apple juice or grilled and topped with apple-pistachio butter. Or cut into a thick New York steak topped with Gorgonzola butter and served with onion rings. Dine indoors, next to a fireplace, or outdoors on one of the garden patios. Full bar. Moderate.

**Las Brisas,** 361 Cliff Drive; (949) 497–5434; www.lasbrisaslagunabeach.com. Breakfast, lunch, and dinner daily; Sunday brunch. Mexican food in an elegant setting. Dine on chicken, beef, and seafood dishes and sip margaritas while you watch the ocean waves crashing below. Full bar. Moderate.

**Rick's Partner's Bistro and Terrace,** 448 South Coast Highway; (949) 497–4441; www.partnersbistro.com. On Highway 1, in town. Daily lunch and dinner, Sunday brunch. Continental cuisine featuring fresh seafood, veal, and vegetarian dishes. Full bar. Moderate.

**The White House,** 340 South Coast Highway; (949) 494–8088. On Highway 1, in town. Monday through Friday, 8:00 A.M. to 10:00 P.M.; weekends, 8:00 to 1:00 A.M. This is a nightclub/restaurant combination, serving health-conscious food, including a full breakfast menu plus a good assortment of salads, sandwiches, fresh seafood, pasta, crepes, and steaks. Food is served in attractive surroundings of warm woods, mirrors, and Tiffany-style light shades. Daily specials. Nightly entertainment. Full bar. Inexpensive to moderate.

# Shopping and Browsing

**Fawn Memories,** 384 Forest Avenue, Suite 7; (949) 494–2071. On Highway 1, south end of town in the Lumberyard Mall, next to Cedar Creek Inn. Sunday through Thursday 10:00 A.M. to 7:00 P.M., 10:00 A.M. to 9:00 P.M. Friday and Saturday. Apparel, jewelry, and hats, as well as porcelain, glass, agate, and ceramic wind chimes.

**Laguna Surf and Sport,** 1088 South Coast Highway; (949) 497–7000; www.laguna surfandsport.net. Highway 1 at Oak Street, 1 block north of the Pottery Shack. Daily, 9:00 A.M. to 9:00 P.M. Bills itself as a "hardcore surf shop." Skateboards, surfboards, boogieboards, wet suits, equipment rentals, T-shirts, and swimsuits.

**Sherwood Gallery,** 460 South Coast Highway; (949) 497–2668; www.sherwood gallery.com. Downtown, between Laguna Avenue and Legion Street. Daily, 11:00 A.M. to 7:00 P.M.; except Sunday, noon to 6:00 P.M. A fascinating gallery featuring ceramics, sculpture, soft sculpture, and neon originals. More than twenty artists represented, with works both serious and whimsical, progressive and eclectic.

# Museum

**Laguna Art Museum,** 307 Cliff Drive; (949) 494–8971; www.lagunaartmuseum.org. Cliff Drive at North Coast Highway, north of Broadway. Daily, 11:00 A.M. to 5:00 P.M. Contemporary California art complements a fine collection of historical works. Also displays private collections. Self-guided and guided group tours; museum store and sales gallery. Stop here before beginning a tour of Laguna Beach galleries.

# Beaches, Parks, Trails, and Waysides

What makes this stretch of the Orange Coast so beautiful is its varied terrain and shoreline. In addition to the long, broad expanse of surf-lined sand at Main Beach are a number of coves beneath cliffs and rocky bluffs, with sandy strands at water's edge known as pocket beaches. Main Beach is in town, on the west side of Highway 1. Pocket beaches and coves are north and south.

Access to Main Beach is via Laguna Avenue, Ocean Avenue, Broadway, and Cliff Drive. Near this fine beach is a grassy picnic area, boardwalk, and playground. This is a good swimming area, except when riptides make swimming dangerous. That's a good time to hike the beach, play volleyball, or just lie back and relax.

A number of trails, walks, and stairways lead to the pocket beaches and coves, most found at the west ends of streets running perpendicular to Highway 1. Off South Coast Highway, beach accesses are at the ends of Moss Street, Diamond Street, Pearl Street, Agate Street, Bluebird Canyon Road, Mountain Road, Cress Street, Brooks Street, Oak Street, Anita Street, Thalia Street, Saint Anne's Street, Cleo Street, and Sleepy Hollow.

Off North Coast Highway, accesses are along Cliff Drive at several places, including the ends of Jasamine Street, Myrtle Street, and Fairview Street. There are rocky coves here with tidepools to explore.

At the north end of Laguna Beach, Crescent Bay Point Park, west of Highway 1, at the end of Crescent Bay Drive, lies a small but lovely park overlooking the coastal bluffs and rocks. This is a good spot to watch sea lions and birds and to photograph the city.

# Water Sports and Activities

Surfers like Aliso Beach County Park, west of Highway 1, at South Laguna. There's good fishing here, as well, from a fine ¼-mile-long pier with a snack bar and tackle shop.

Surf and rock fishing is often good at the pocket beaches and coves at the north end of Laguna Beach. Divers enjoy Heisler Park Marine Life Refuge, which lies offshore from Heisler Park, west of the 400 block of Cliff Drive.

## events

| April | Sawdust "Art Walk," (949) 494–3030 |
|---|---|
| | Laguna Charm House Tour, (949) 760–7062 |
| June | Sawdust Festival, (949) 494–3030 |
| | Art–a-Fair, (949) 494–4514 |
| July | Sawdust Festival continues |
| | Art-a-Fair continues |
| | Festival of Arts and Pageant of the Masters, (800) 487–3378 |
| August | Festival of Arts and Pageant of the Masters continue |
| | Sawdust Festival continues |
| | Art-a-Fair continues |
| September | Festival of Arts and Pageant of the Masters continue |
| October | Festival of Arts continues |
| November | Sawdust Winter Fantasy, (949) 494–3030 |
| December | Sawdust Winter Fantasy continues |

# Golf

**Aliso Creek Golf Club,** 31106 South Coast Highway, South Laguna; (949) 499–1919. On Highway 1, south of Laguna Beach, across the highway from Aliso Beach and the fishing pier. A nine-hole, par-thirty-two, 2,500-yard course. Clubhouse, locker room, pro shop, club and cart rentals, restaurant, and cocktail lounge.

# Weather and Tide Information

**Weather, tide, surf, and diving report;** recorded message, (949) 494–6573

# Travel Information

**Laguna Beach Visitors Bureau,** 252 Broadway; (949) 497–9229 or (800) 877–1115; www.lagunabeachinfo.org; e-mail: lbvb@lagunabeachinfo.org

**Laguna Beach Chamber of Commerce,** 357 Glenneyre; (949) 494–1018; www .lagunabeachchamber.org

# Newport Beach

**Location:** On California Highway 1, 4 miles north of Laguna Beach, 70 miles north of San Diego, and 49 miles south of Santa Monica.

**Population:** 78,043

Newport Beach is startling to the southbound traveler who has just left the concrete, asphalt, and smog of Los Angeles. The first impression is of how green the city is. That's the color of money.

It's soon obvious to the newcomer why Newport Beach was nicknamed "the Gold Coast." Everywhere are signs of affluence, from the chic shops of Fashion Island to the gleaming yachts moored on Newport Bay.

The city's boundaries encompass a number of distinct communities and small villages that have retained much of their character and individuality. On the seaward side of Highway 1, for example, lie the Balboa Peninsula, Balboa Island, and Lido Island—each unique in some way. The islands are on Lower Newport Bay, and the peninsula lies northwest to southeast, reaching to the harbor entrance, across the channel from Corona del Mar.

Brothers James and Robert McFadden, who started the shipping and lumber business in 1873 that eventually grew into the city of Newport, began trading at a landing on the Santa Ana River. When the shoal-filled waters of the river mouth and lower bay proved too hazardous for seagoing vessels, the McFaddens moved their business to the beach and built the Newport Pier in 1888. Originally a commercial wharf, now a fishing pier, this is the longest-standing pier on the entire southern California coast.

The famous Newport Dory Fishing Fleet has been fishing here since 1891. Each morning, the dorymen launch their flat-bottomed boats in the surf at dawn and return to the pier to sell their catch about 9:30 A.M.

Newport Boulevard exits south off Highway 1 and leads past the Lido Peninsula and Lido Island toward Newport Pier. As the thoroughfare curves east, it becomes Balboa Boulevard and leads to Balboa and beyond, ending at the west jetty and harbor entrance.

The cupola surmounting the roof of the Balboa Pavilion rises above other nearby buildings, making this landmark easy to spot. Local promoters built the pavilion and Balboa Pier in the early 1900s to attract tourists and help establish Balboa as a beach resort. Balboa became part of Newport Beach in 1906. In the past the pavilion served as a casino and a dance hall where all the big bands played—the Dorsey brothers, Glenn Miller, Benny Goodman—and such stars as Gene Krupa and Bing Crosby appeared. Restored in 1962, the building is now headquarters for sightseeing and sportfishing trips and contains a tackle shop and restaurant.

The Balboa Ferry operates nearby, transporting vehicles and their passengers, as well as bikers and foot traffic, between Balboa and the south side of Balboa Island. A small bridge connects the mainland to the north side of the island.

The biggest festival of the year is the Sea Fest. It takes place in September and includes such activities and events as a bike tour, boat races, harbor sailing, fishing tournament, kite contest, marine-art festival, sand-castle contest, surfing championships, tall-ships festival, sailboarding, volleyball tournament, and wooden-boat festival. And, of course, there's plenty of grub and grog to go around.

# Lodging

**Balboa Inn,** 105 Main Street, Balboa; (949) 675–3412 or (877) 225–2629; www.balboa inn.com. On the Balboa Peninsula, south of Highway 1 via Newport and Balboa Boulevards, 1 block past Washington Street. Has 34 rooms and suites in a recently renovated historical landmark. Ocean and bay views. Fireplaces and in-room whirlpool spas available. Pool and whirlpool. Room service and complimentary continental breakfast. Walk to Balboa Pier, harbor, beach, restaurants, and shops. Expensive; reduced winter rates.

**Best Western Bay Shores Inn,** 1800 West Balboa Boulevard; (949) 675–3463 or (800) 222–6675; www.thebestinn.com. On the Balboa Peninsula, south of Highway 1 via Newport Boulevard. Queen and king beds in 21 rooms, suites, and 2-bedroom apartments that accommodate up to 8 persons. Cable TV and cable movies. Some rooms with bay or ocean views. Walk to beach, Newport Pier, harbor, public tennis courts, and biking/jogging trails. Moderate to expensive.

**Doryman's Inn Bed & Breakfast,** 2102 West Ocean Front; (949) 675–7300. South of Highway 1 via Newport Boulevard, then east on Balboa Boulevard to McFadden Place. Inn is on Ocean Front at McFadden, near the Newport Pier. Queen and king beds in 11 spacious, elegantly appointed rooms with private baths and sunken marble tubs. Fireplaces, ocean views, and in-room whirlpools available. Full breakfast. Restaurant 21 Oceanfront on premises. Near many restaurants, shops, and other attractions. Walk to the pier, harbor, and beach. Moderate to very expensive.

**Newport Channel Inn,** 6030 West Coast Highway; (949) 642–3030 or (800) 255–8614; www.newportchannelinn.com. On Highway 1, west of Newport Boulevard, opposite the beach. Queen beds and waterbeds in 30 rooms with local TV. Sundeck, ocean view. Continental breakfast and beach towels provided. Short walk to beach—just across the highway. Near shops, restaurants, and charter services. Adjacent shopping center with coin-operated laundry and minimarket. Moderate.

## Campgrounds and RV Parks

**Newport Dunes,** 1131 Back Bay Drive; (949) 729–3863; www.newportdunes.com. Located ¼ mile northeast of Highway 1 via Jamboree Road. More than 350 RV sites plus 24 cottages. Everything for the RV traveler, and built to order for boaters and anglers. Pool, whirlpool, cable TV, clubhouse, grocery store, snack bar, restaurant, coin-operated laundry, and video arcade. Complete marina services, launch ramp, marine sales and repairs, boat rentals, slips, and dry boat storage. Expensive to very expensive.

## Food

**Newport Landing,** 503 East Edgewater; (949) 675–2373; www.newport-landing.com. South of Highway 1 via Newport and Balboa Boulevards, on the Balboa Peninsula, 1 block from the Balboa Ferry. Daily lunch and dinner; Sunday brunch. A Newport Beach fixture—enjoy it from the main dining room or the casual oyster bar and lounge, which overlooks the busy harbor. Specialties include prime rib, rack of lamb, deep-water shrimp, and abalone. Full bar and live entertainment nightly; dancing on weekends. Moderate to expensive.

**Ruby's Diner,** #1 Balboa Pier, Balboa; (949) 675–7829; www.rubysdiner.com. On the Balboa Peninsula, south of Highway 1 via Newport and Balboa Boulevards. Sunday through Thursday, 7:00 A.M. to 10:00 P.M.; Friday and Saturday, 7:00 A.M. to 11:00 P.M. A 1940s-style diner at the end of the pier. Breakfast choices include an assortment of omelets and other egg dishes, French toast, hotcakes, biscuits and gravy, and Rubymuffins. Salads of all sizes and varieties, chowder, chili, hot dogs, chili dogs, and an assortment of burgers and other sandwiches. From the fountain—malts, shakes, ice-cream sodas, floats, sundaes, and banana splits. Various beverages, including beer and wine. Inexpensive.

## Shopping and Browsing

**Fashion Island,** Newport Beach; (949) 721–2000; www.shopfashionisland.com. North of Highway 1, between MacArthur Boulevard and Jamboree Road—follow the signs. Monday through Friday, 10:00 A.M. to 9:00 P.M.; Saturday, 10:00 A.M. to 6:00 P.M.; Sunday, noon to 5:00 P.M. Orange County's premier open-air shopping center, with more than 200 shops, boutiques, and department stores. Here you'll find the famous Farmers Market at the Atrium Court, forty restaurants, two cinema complexes, and many food kiosks offering pastries, hot dogs, candies, ice cream, frozen yogurt, sushi, coffee, fruits, salads, and deli delights. Browse and shop at more than sixty men's,

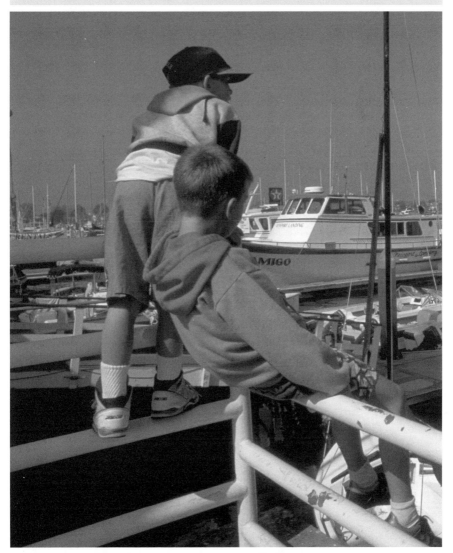

Newport Beach Marina *Courtesy of Robert Holmes/CalTour*

women's, and children's apparel and shoe stores, as well as jewelry, leather, luggage, and gift shops.

**Lido Marina Village,** 3400 Via Oporto, Suite 104; (949) 675–8662; www.shoporange county.com. South of Highway 1 on Newport Boulevard, then left on Via Lido, and left to the parking structure at the village. A beautiful waterfront area with tree-lined cobblestone streets, restaurants, sidewalk cafes, more than thirty-five shops and boutiques, and galleries. Enjoy the sun and salt air while strolling the harbor boardwalk. Yacht brokers, charter services, and sailing clubs are headquartered here. Browse amid the beautiful watercraft.

# Beaches, Parks, Trails, and Waysides

Near the entrance to Newport Bay, just east of the east jetty, lies the broad, sandy Corona del Mar State Beach. For swimmers there are changing rooms and outdoor showers.

Newport Beach stretches more than 5 miles from its narrow northwest end past the Newport Pier, where it is much wider. Access is via Newport Boulevard, south off Highway 1.

Six-mile-long Balboa Beach is a broad strand that extends from Newport Beach to the west jetty at the end of the Balboa Peninsula. Most of the streets running perpendicular to Balboa Boulevard provide beach access.

Balboa Island, reached by bridge south of Highway 1 or by ferry from Balboa, is rimmed by a boardwalk that makes a scenic hiking route and leads to several small beaches.

The upper end of the Newport Bay estuary is a wildlife reserve reached by way of Back Bay Drive off Jamboree Road. This 752-acre wetland habitat, consisting mainly of intertidal mudflats and salt marsh, harbors numerous species of waterfowl, shorebirds, and songbirds. During the winter, when the reserve is crowded with migratory species, an organization known as Newport Bay Naturalists and Friends offers guided tours on Saturday mornings.

**Newport Bay Naturalists and Friends,** 600 Shellmaker Road; (949) 640–6746.

# Water Sports and Activities

Southeast of the city of Newport Beach, between Arch Rock and Irvine Cove, is Crystal Cove State Park, one of the newer parks in the system. The adjacent offshore area is an underwater park popular with divers. Divers, snorkelers, and surfers also like Corona del Mar State Beach, east of the east jetty.

West of the west jetty and reached by way of Balboa Boulevard are Jetty View Park and a beach area famous for bodysurfing. The water here, where the jetty joins the peninsula, is known as "the Wedge" and is renowned for its enormous waves. Big waves can be dangerous, so it's no place for beginners.

Several natural features, an abundance of man-made ones, and a good variety of inshore and offshore species make this an extraordinarily good and diverse angling area. Those who tow boats will want to get familiar with Newport Dunes Aquatic Park, just north of Highway 1 on Back Bay Drive off Jamboree Road. There's a full-service marina here and launching facilities open twenty-four hours a day. From here, anglers can set out for offshore fishing grounds or can find plenty of action in Newport Bay, where there are probably a dozen species in abundance, with halibut, bass, croaker, and sargo topping the list.

A submarine canyon lies offshore and comes closest to shore near the Newport Pier. This deepwater structure has a dampening effect on incoming waves, keeping them small along this stretch of the beach. It also brings species near shore that are usually found many more miles out to sea. A number of charter operators are specialists in finding and catching these gamesters, including marlin and tuna.

There are ample shore-fishing opportunities as well, and good fishing from Newport Pier and Balboa Pier.

**Adventures at Sea,** 3101 West Coast Highway; (866) 872–7313; www.boatcharter .com. Romantic sunset cruises of the Newport harbor aboard quiet, graceful, electric-powered gondolas. Some of the canopied craft are painted gleaming white and have cushioned seats covered with tapestry or velvet. Others are black-hulled, mahogany-decked beauties with glove-leather upholstery. All have CD players on board. Three harbor tours available: after-dinner cruise for two, champagne cruise for two, and gourmet dinner cruise for two. Gondolas accommodate an extra person or couple for an additional charge.

**Bongos Sportfishing Charters,** 2130 Newport Boulevard; (949) 673–2810; www.bongosportfishing.com. South off Highway 1. Fishing charters aboard a fleet of fast, powerful, tournament-rigged boats for fishing trips to local hot spots, deepwater banks, and Catalina Island for marlin, tuna, bonito, halibut, yellowtail, barracuda, and shark. All the latest electronics, as well as stereo and color TV.

**Davey's Locker,** 400 Main Street, Balboa; (949) 673–1434; www.daveyslocker.com. Fishing reports, (949) 972–9818. South of Highway 1 via Newport and Balboa Boulevards, at Balboa Pavilion. Davey's 50- to 80-foot boats fish local waters and Catalina Island. Half-day, all-day, and three-quarter day trips. Whale-watching excursions. Private charters. Tackle store with a complete line of tackle, rental gear, licenses, bait, and local fishing information. Boat rentals for fishing and harbor cruising.

**Newport Landing, Sportfishing, and Fuel Service,** 309 Palm Street, Balboa; (949) 675–0550. On the Balboa Peninsula, near the Balboa Ferry terminal. Weekdays, 6:00 A.M. to 6:00 P.M.; weekends, 5:00 A.M. to 7:00 P.M. Sportfishing, whale-watching, and harbor cruises. Complete marine service. Gas and diesel fuel, live and frozen bait, fishing tackle, licenses, beer, soft drinks, and ice.

# Rentals

**Balboa Boat Rentals,** 510 East Edgewater, Balboa; (949) 673–7200. At Edgewater Avenue and Palm Street, between Adams and Washington Streets, north of Balboa Boulevard. Rents powerboats, sailboats, and kayaks.

There are also boat rentals at Davey's Locker. See above.

# Tours and Trips

**Catalina Passenger Service,** 400 Main Street, Balboa; (949) 673–5245. At the Balboa

Pavilion, south of Highway 1 via Newport and Balboa Boulevards or via ferry from Balboa Island. One round-trip daily departs Newport Beach at 9:00 A.M. and Catalina at 4:30 P.M.; December 26 to Easter, weekend service only. Travel to Catalina Island aboard the largest catamaran in the United States—only seventy-five minutes from Newport Beach to Avalon, Catalina Island. Only hand-carried luggage and backpacks permitted. No diving equipment.

## Golf

**Newport Beach Golf Course,** 3100 Irvine Avenue; (949) 852–8681. Southwest of Corona del Mar Freeway, between Jamboree Road and Newport Boulevard, northeast of Pacific Coast Highway. An eighteen-hole, 3,200-yard public course. Pro shop with lessons available. Pull-cart and club rental. Lighted for night play. Driving range, restaurant, and cocktail lounge.

**Pelican Hill Golf Club,** 22651 Pelican Hill Road South, Newport Coast; (949) 760–0707; www.pelicanhill.com. East on Newport Coast Drive off Highway 1, between Corona del Mar and Laguna Beach. Two challenging eighteen-hole courses in spectacular coastal hills, canyons, and pine forests. Practice range with putting, pitching, and chipping greens. Pros, lessons, club and cart rentals, pro shop, and food-and-beverage service at The Grill at Pelican Hill Restaurant.

## Travel Information

**Newport Beach Conference and Visitors Bureau,** 110 Newport Center Drive, Suite 120; (949) 719–6100 or (800) 942–6278; www.newportbeach-cvb.com

**Newport Beach Chamber of Commerce,** 1470 Jamboree Road; (949) 729–4400; www.newportbeach.com; e-mail: info@newportbeach.com

## events

| | |
|---|---|
| **February** | Newport Beach Jazz Party, (949) 759–5003 |
| **March** | International Film Festival, Newport Beach, (949) 851–6555 |
| **April** | Newport Harbor Boat Show, Newport Dunes Resort, (949) 729–3863 |

| | |
|---|---|
| **May** | "Back" Bay Classic, Back Bay, Newport Beach, (949) 776–7490 |
| | Newport Beach Jazz Festival, Hyatt Newporter, (949) 650–5483 or (949) 729–1234 |
| | Wine & Food Festival, Balboa Bay Club, (949) 630–4146 |
| **June** | Ocean Discovery Day, Upper Newport Bay, (949) 640–6746 |
| | Baroque Music Festival, Corona del Mar, (949) 760–7887 |
| **July** | Fireworks Extravaganza, Newport Dunes Resort, (949) 729–3863 |
| | Independence Day Celebration, Mariners Park, (949) 644–3151 |
| | Flight of the Lasers, Newport Harbor, (949) 729–4400 |
| | Old Glory Boat Parade, Newport Harbor, (949) 673–5070 |
| | Summer Concert Series, Fashion Island, (949) 721–2000 |
| | Summer Jazz Series, Hyatt Newporter, (949) 729–1234 |
| **August** | Summer Concert Series continues |
| **September** | Sand Castle Contest, Corona del Mar, (949) 729–4400 |
| | Balboa Arts and Music Festival, Balboa Pier, (949) 644–3151 |
| | Wooden Boat Festival, Newport Harbor, (949) 642–5031 |
| **December** | Christmas Boat Parade, Newport Harbor, (949) 729–4400 |

# Oxnard / Ventura

**Location:** Side by side along Highway 1 and U.S. Highway 101, 60 miles northwest of Los Angeles and 30 miles south of Santa Barbara.

**Population:** Oxnard 162,216; Ventura 105,000

One of the most dazzling scenic drives in California extends along the coastline between tony Santa Barbara and the northern Ventura County cities of Ventura and Oxnard. The two adjacent cities lie less than an hour from celebrity-laden Santa Barbara, but their slightly less known charms are equally inviting—their diversity downright intriguing. Rich Mission-era history, revitalized old town offerings, and marinas that connect you to the wealthy ecological treasures of the Channel Islands are among the area's gifts to those who come to explore for a weekend or a week.

Once called the "Land of Everlasting Summers" by Spanish explorer Juan Rodriguez Cabrillo, the city got its name from the Oxnard brothers who built a sugar beet factory there in 1898. This once quiet little town known for its plentiful fields of produce, mainly strawberries (Oxnard still produces 20 percent of the state's crop), is emerging as a real competitor in tourism on the coast. The city still gives claim to its strawberry production, hosting the California Strawberry Festival each spring, but its harbor area and its recent old town revitalization are bringing more and more tourists to sample its many other delicacies.

Oxnard's beaches are not as popularized as its southern counterparts in Zuma and Malibu, but the absence of towel-touching-towel bronzing bodies and wide expanse of sandy beaches and occasional dunes make them highly desirable. Rudolph Valentino filmed *The Sheik* on Oxnard's beach and later bought a vacation home there. Clark Gable became his neighbor, throwing show business-style parties that granted the sandy expanse the nickname "Hollywood Beach."

Next is the reincarnated city of Ventura. It is not that Ventura needed reinvention. It is and always has been a charming Mission town endowed with an enviable combination of history and panoramic vistas of the sparkling Pacific. However, in recent years the area has been uplifted significantly, granting its sagging downtown area a more cosmopolitan feel with a delightful infusion of culture, entertainment, and bistro allure. All the while, Ventura has stayed loyal to its heritage; the glowing cross, established by Father Serra, sitting high on a hill overlooking town, reminding all of the city's historical beginnings.

You can pretty much park the car in downtown Ventura and walk a few blocks in any direction around the 1782-established San Buenaventura Mission to experience the charming, restored old town area. Instead of the secondhand stores that once occupied the area, dozens of antiques dealers line East Main Street, offering quality antique furnishings, china, silver, and jewelry. Walking tours are scheduled throughout the year and range from a look at Ventura's historic saloon district to a "Lost Treasures Tour" that covers both the folklore and the architectural treasures of the city. To get a copy of the tour schedules, drop in the Ventura Visitors & Convention Bureau at 89 South California Street or call them at (800) 333–2989.

Don't want to walk all over town? The Buenaventura Trolley takes passengers from Ventura Harbor to downtown and back. The trolley conveniently stops at the Ventura City Hall (an impressive Neo-Classical Revival structure with fluted columns capped with Doric headings and a magnificent stained-glass dome), the Mission, the Albinger Archaeological Museum (boasting "3,500 years of history in 1 block"), and the Ventura County Museum of History and Art.

If you're standing on Ventura's shoreline, on a clear day the Channel Islands look close enough to touch. Five of the eight islands and their surrounding 1-nautical mile of ocean, brimming over in kelp forests, make up the Channel Islands National Park. The park is now the protected habitat for marine life ranging from microscopic plankton to the earth's largest creature, the blue whale. The history of the islands is as rich as its natural resources, ranging from the Chumash Indians who established villages on the islands to explorers like Cabrillo, Gaspar de Portola, and Sebastian Vizcaino.

Check with Island Packers for schedules, costs, camping reservation requirements, and special tour packages. To learn more about the Channel Islands you can visit the Channel Islands National Park Headquarters at the Ventura Harbor. The modern, three-story building with observation tower offers several attractive displays dedicated to the islands and sanctuary. The interior lobby of the building hosts topographical maps of each island, and an interior tide pool display contains live starfish, crabs, anemones, sea urchins, and more. The visitor center is open 8:30 A.M. to 5:00 P.M. daily.

# Lodging

**Bella Maggiore Inn,** 67 South California Street, Ventura; (805) 652–0277or (800) 523–8479. A half block south of Main Street is this intimate, European-style inn, easily identifiable by its exterior ornate carvings; the interior is Mediterranean in feel with two dozen cozy guest rooms and a lobby with fireplace and piano. Moderate.

**Casa Serena Hotel & Marina Resort,** 3605 Peninsula Road, Channel Islands Harbor, Oxnard; (805) 985–6311 or (800) 447–3529. The resort is located at the tip of the Peninsula overlooking Channel Islands Harbor and just ¼ mile from the beach. The 271 rooms include 30 suites. A tennis court, putting green, several pools, fitness center, and spa keep guests occupied; dine in the resort's Lobster Trap restaurant. Expensive.

**The Clocktower Inn,** 181 East Santa Clara Street, Ventura; (805) 652–0141 or (800) 727–1027; www.clocktowerinn.com. Located on Mission Park in the heart of down-town Ventura. The stay includes breakfast and wine-and-cheese reception every evening. Moderate.

**Mandalay Beach Resort,** 2101 Mandalay Beach Road, Oxnard; (805) 984–2500 or (800) 362–2779; www.embassymandalay.com. Now an Embassy Suites property, the Mandalay stands as the only all-suite beachfront resort in California. Spread over eight acres of lush tropical vegetation, the resort offers two- and three-room suites with two marble baths, and comfortable living room and dining areas, as well as a complimen-tary cooked-to-order breakfast each morning. On-site is award-winning Capistrano's Restaurant, serving breakfast, lunch, and dinner, a spa, an attractive outdoor heated pool, tennis courts, and, most importantly, a great beach for swimming, sunning, and spectacular sunset watching. Expensive.

**Pierpont Inn,** 550 Sanjon Road, Ventura; (805) 643–6144. The Pierpont Inn made its mark on Ventura in 1891 when a former doctor, Ernest Pierpont, and his family built The Overlook as a popular winter resort. The completely renovated inn has been hon-ored as one of only 192 Historic National Hotels in the United States by the National Trust. Check into reasonable packages for touring the Channel Islands. Moderate to expensive.

**Victorian Rose Bed & Breakfast,** 896 East Main Street, Ventura; (805) 641–1888; www.victorian-rose.ca. This former Methodist church now serves as a unique bed-and-breakfast inn. Innkeepers offer five attractive rooms with a unique ecclesiastical flair. Moderate.

## Campgrounds and RV Parks

**Faria Beach,** 4350 West Pacific Coast Highway, Ventura; (805) 654–3951. Oceanside campground with 42 sites, hot showers, flush toilets, concession stand, surf fishing, playground, and horseshoe pits. Four sites have full hookups.

**Hobson Beach,** 5210 West Pacific Coast Highway, Ventura; (805) 654–3951. Oceanside campground with 31 sites, showers, flush toilets, concession stand, surf fishing, sandy shoreline, surfing, and one of the best reefs for exploration at low tide. Ten sites have full hookups.

**McGrath State Beach Campground,** (805) 968–1033. Located 5 miles south of Ventura off US 101. One hundred seventy-four campsites, 2 miles of beach, nature trails. One of the best bird-watching areas in the state.

**Ventura Beach RV Resort,** 800 West Main Street, Ventura; (805) 643–9137. Private RV park offering full hookups, showers, supplies, and recreational facilities. The resort offers 168 sites and is a short walk from the beach.

# Food

**Kampai Japanese Restaurant,** 2367 North Oxnard Boulevard, Oxnard; (805) 988–0252. Multiple dining rooms with personal chefs provide a dining experience.

**Jonathan's at Peirano's,** 204 East Main Street, Ventura; (805) 648–4853; www.jonathansatpeiranos.com. Dinner and lunch in historic downtown prepared by chef/owner Jason Collis. Live jazz Thursday through Saturday.

**Progressive Dining/Channel Islands Water Taxi Service,** 3600 South Harbor Boulevard, Suite 1240, Oxnard; (805) 985–5828; www.channelislandsharbor.org. Visitors may now combine two of the best area pastimes, touring the harbor (known as the cleanest in the state) and dining, by booking a Progressive Dining Package, also referred to as the "dine around." Provided by the Channel Islands Water Taxi Service that transports customers to shopping, dining, and recreational points in the harbor, the evening is composed of a relaxing cruise in the harbor with stops at various harbor restaurants for each course of your meal. You actually customize your own itinerary and menu given several choices. A typical dining adventure would involve an appetizer at one restaurant, followed by a water taxi cruise to a second bistro for your entrée. The water taxi then embarks to a third locale for coffee and dessert. Dinner cruises run seven days a week; advanced reservations advised.

**71 Palm Restaurant,** 71 North Palm Street, Ventura; (805) 653–7222. Chef Didier Poirier and his interior designer wife, Nanci, moved and transformed the former Norton House into an intimate bistro with homelike warmth and upstairs veranda. The converted historic bungalow serves French classics; try the warm duck salad or the chicken ravioli with sage sauce. The wine list offers good variety and value. Reservations are recommended.

# Attractions

**Heritage Square,** 200 West Seventh Street, Oxnard; (805) 483–7960. Between 1986 and 1991, the city's redevelopment agency and some of the area's most notable, historically significant families joined together to preserve and bring new life to a handful of turn-of-the-century homes and historical structures that would have otherwise been demolished for progress' sake, as well as a few finely replicated buildings, to form a city block known as Heritage Square. Finely restored, the more than two dozen vintage structures include a former church (now the Town Hall for meetings, weddings, and special events), the former home of a Union Oil Company president, and the Justin Petit Ranch House, which is now the home of the Elite Theatre Company

| | |
|---|---|
| **January–March** | Whale watching, (805) 642–1393 |
| **February** | Whalefest Celebration, Ventura Harbor Village, (805) 642–8538 or (877) 89–HARBOR |
| **April–May** | Ventura Music Festival, (805) 648–3146; www.venturamusicfestival.org |
| **May** | California Strawberry Festival, (805) 385–4739 or (888) 288–9242; www.strawberry-fest.org |
| **June** | Seafest Celebration, Ventura Harbor, (805) 642–8538 or (877) 89–HARBOR |
| **July** | Oxnard Salsa Festival; www.oxnardsalsafestival.com. Fourth of July Street Fair, Ventura, (805) 648–2075 |
| **July–August** | Dallas Cowboys Training Camp, Oxnard |
| **August** | Tall Ships Festival; www.tallshipschannelislands.com Ventura County Fair, Seaside Park, (805) 648–3376 |
| **October** | Annual Pier Under the Stars Food & Wine Tasting, Ventura, (805) 658–4726 |
| **December** | Annual Parade of Lights Festival, Ventura Harbor Village, (805) 642–8538 or (877) 89–HARBOR Annual Parade of Lights, Channel Islands Harbor, Oxnard, (805) 642–8618 |

(805–483–5118), an intimate theater group. The Victorian-designed grounds of the Square hold courtyards with fountains, colorful blooms, and a central gathering area that is the locale of Friday night summer concerts, weddings, and other cultural events. Self-guided and docent-led tours are offered year-round on Saturday from 10:00 A.M. to 2:00 P.M.; call (805) 483–7960 for information.

**Rubicon Theatre,** 1006 East Main Street, Ventura; (805) 667–2900; www.rubicon theatre.com. Proclaimed the "anchor" of the cultural district of downtown Ventura, this theater is located in a renovated church originally constructed in the 1920s and offers just 200 seats and an ambitious season of productions. Founded in 1998, the Rubicon's mission is to present a diverse selection of classic and contemporary comedies, dramas, and musicals for the enjoyment of the community and visitors. Call the box office at (805) 667–2900 for a schedule or check the Web site.

# Travel Information

**Island Packers,** 1691 Spinnaker Drive, Ventura Harbor; (805) 642–1393 (Ventura), (805) 382–1779 (Oxnard), (805) 642–7688 (recorded information); www.islandpackers .com. Visitors to the Channel Islands may depart from either Ventura's or Oxnard's harbors. Island Packers offers year-round excursions from both harbors with nature tours, whale watching, hiking, snorkeling, kayaking, and camping. Anacapa is the most popular day-trip destination in the islands, located just 11 miles from Oxnard and 14 miles from Ventura. A hefty flight of stairs leads from the boat landing to the eastern end of the island that may be explored by a self-guided 1½-mile nature walk. The vegetation stays fairly brown year-round on the island except during spring and summer, when the low-lying ice plant blooms in spectacular bright hues. The beaches, down long cliffs, aren't accessible, but you are apt to see some sunbathing seals. Due to the rich sealife surrounding Anacapa, scuba and skin diving are popular and minimal camping is allowed for those wanting to stay longer.

**Ventura Visitors & Convention Bureau,** 89 South California Street, Ventura; (805) 648–2075 or (800) 333–2989; www.ventura-usa.com

**Oxnard Convention & Visitors Bureau,** 200 West Seventh Street (in Heritage Square), Oxnard, (805) 385–7545 or (800) 269-6273; www.oxnardtourism.com

# Santa Barbara

**Location:** On U.S. Highway 101, 89 miles south of Grover Beach, 90 miles northwest of Los Angeles.

**Population:** 88,251

---

Coastal California serves up several superb entree cities, but sweet Santa Barbara is the gourmet dessert—as beautiful to look at as it is to savor. It's one of the few cities in the nation that's as stunning in reality as it is in the travel magazines and books.

The mild climate keeps flowers blooming and lush greenery thriving all year, with palms lining the boulevards and eucalyptus trees shading and scenting parks and neighborhoods. Houses, shops, government buildings, and historic landmarks—as white as the frosting on a wedding cake and capped with red tile roofs—stand amidst all this splendor, from the ocean's edge to the rolling foothills.

It's ironic that the tragedy and devastation of an earthquake should have led to the preservation of and adherence to the Spanish-style architecture employed here. Although most of the city's early structures were of Spanish-Moorish design, in the early 1900s other styles began to encroach. But following the widely destructive earthquake of 1925, the city established an Architectural Board of Review to ensure conformity to certain building standards. The result is an eye-pleasing landscape of Mediterranean grace and grandeur.

Santa Barbara's downtown area is compact and just right for walking. So park your vehicle and stroll along the shady sidewalks, through the courtyards, to the cafes, galleries, antiques shops, and boutiques. The self-guided "Red Tile Tour," with map and guide available at the visitor center, is a good way to see the area and visit many of the historical structures along the way.

No matter what activities you enjoy, you're never far from the beach in Santa Barbara. In fact, State Street, the city's main thoroughfare, leads directly to the beach and historic Stearns Wharf, the oldest operating wharf on the West Coast.

In addition to a good many annual events that take place throughout the year, an ongoing exhibit of arts and crafts draws locals and visitors to the shoreline east of Stearns Wharf every Sunday and holiday. More than 200 local artists and artisans offer their works for sale from 10:00 A.M. to dusk.

Along most of the California coast, the ocean lies west of Highway 1 or US 101, with the foothills and mountains to the east. In the vicinity of Santa Barbara, however, US 101 runs east to west, with the ocean to the south and foothills in the north. Keep that in mind as you travel to the various attractions.

# Lodging

**Best Western Pepper Tree Inn,** 3850 State Street; (805) 687–5511 or (800) 338–0030. North of US 101 via Las Positas Road, in Northside. Queen and king beds in 150 rooms with cable TV, cable movies, and coffeemakers. Private balconies, room service, limo service, pool, whirlpool, massage facilities, gym, hair salons, and gift shop. Near eighteen-hole golf course and shopping center. Fichera's Treehouse Restaurant on premises, featuring American cuisine, fresh seafood, and local wines. Cocktail lounge with nightly entertainment. Moderate to expensive.

**Mason Beach Inn,** 324 West Mason Street; (805) 962–3203 or (800) 446–0444; www.masonbeachinn.com. South of US 101, 1 block north of Cabrillo Boulevard, between Castillo and Bath Streets. Queen and king beds in 45 rooms with cable TV. Pool, whirlpool, and continental breakfast. Walk to shops, restaurants, beach, Stearns Wharf, charter docks, and marina. Moderate to expensive.

**Secret Garden Inn & Cottages,** 1908 Bath Street; (805) 687–2300 or (800) 765–6255; www.secretgarden.com. About 2 blocks north of US 101 via Mission Street. Queen and king beds in 11 rooms and suites decorated with antiques. Private and shared baths. Walk or bike to downtown shops, galleries, and restaurants. Full breakfast. Wine and hors d'oeuvres. Moderate to expensive.

**Simpson House Inn,** 121 East Arrellaga Street; (805) 963–7067 or (800) 676–1280; www.simpsonhouseinn.com. About 2½ blocks north of US 101. Double, queen, and king beds in 15 rooms decorated with antiques, original artwork, English lace, Oriental rugs, and fresh flowers. Complimentary vegetarian breakfast and evening wine and hors d'oeuvres. Some private baths. Expensive to very expensive.

**The Upham Victorian Hotel & Garden Cottages,** 1404 De La Vina Street; (805) 962–0058 or (800) 727–0876; www.uphamhotel.com. North of US 101 via Mission Street or Arrellaga Street, downtown. Beautiful, cupola-topped Victorian hotel with great verandas and exquisite interiors, located on an acre of gardens. Private baths and cable TV in 50 rooms and suites in the hotel, carriage house, and 5 garden cottages. Some porches, patios, and gas fireplaces. Master suite with fireplace, whirlpool tub, wet bar, and private yard with hammock. Double, queen, and king beds. Valet laundry and dry cleaning. Continental breakfast served in the lobby and on the garden veranda. Complimentary wine and cheese each afternoon. Louie's Restaurant, off the main lobby, serves daily lunch and dinner, featuring seafood, pasta, and California cuisine. Walk to shops, galleries, restaurants, and theaters. Expensive to very expensive.

**West Beach Inn,** 306 West Cabrillo Boulevard; (805) 963–4277 or (800) 423–5991. South of US 101, across from the marina, via Castillo Street or State Street. Cable TV and cable movies in 44 rooms and suites with ocean or garden views. Complimentary continental breakfast and afternoon wine and cheese. In-room refrigerators. Walk to beach, Stearns Wharf, charter docks, shops, and restaurants. Expensive.

## Campgrounds and RV Parks

**Carpinteria State Beach,** 5361 Sixth Street, Carpinteria; (805) 968–1033 or (800) 444–7275; www.parks.ca.gov. South of US 101, 12 miles east of Santa Barbara. Has 101 tent and RV sites in Anacapa and Santa Cruz campgrounds that accommodate RVs to 33 feet; some hookups. Santa Rosa and San Miguel campgrounds have 37 sites for RVs from 22 to 30 feet. Full hookups available at Santa Rosa campground. Sites have tables and fire rings. Showers and tank dump. Easy beach access. Moderate.

## Food

**The Harbor Restaurant,** 210 Stearns Wharf; (805) 963–3311; www.stearnswharf.org. South of US 101, at Stearns Wharf. Daily lunch and dinner, Sunday brunch. Oak-grilled steaks, fish, and shellfish. Prime rib and chicken dinners. Full bar. Moderate.

**Moby Dick Restaurant,** 220 Stearns Wharf; (805) 965–0549. On Stearns Wharf, south of US 101. Breakfast, lunch, and dinner daily. Breakfast includes hot and cold cereals and egg dishes. Specialty is open-face crab Benedict. Lunch is burgers and traditional sandwiches, salads, fish-and-chips. Dinners are steaks, chicken, and fresh seafoods. Choose from such specialties as scallone (scallop and abalone patty), Maryland crab cakes, Cajun catfish, and Idaho trout. Full bar and cocktail patio. Moderate.

**Woody's BBQ,** 5112 Hollister Avenue; (805) 967–3775; www.woodysbbq.com. Lunch and dinner daily. From the sawdust on the floor to the oak-smoked country cooking, this is a local favorite, featuring chili, beans, charbroiled burgers, charbroiled chicken sandwiches, barbecued ribs, slowly smoked chicken and combination dishes. Beer and wine. Inexpensive to moderate.

## Shopping and Browsing

Santa Barbara's compact downtown area is a shopper's and browser's delight. In addition to all the shops and galleries are more than forty antiques dealers, most within 1 or 2 blocks on each side of State Street.

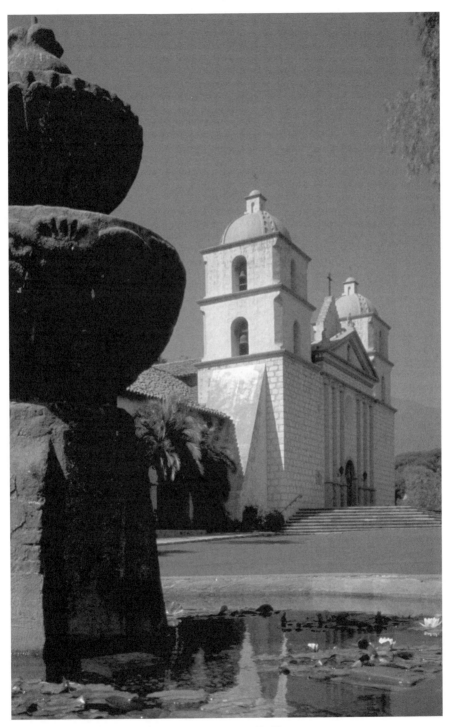
Mission Santa Barbara *Courtesy of Robert Holmes/CalTour*

Scattered around Santa Barbara County are nearly two dozen wineries, most of which offer tasting and sales, many of which offer tours. Pick up a copy of the "Vintners' Association Wine Touring Map" at the visitor center.

**Antique Market Place,** 26 East Ortega Street; (805) 966–5655. Three blocks north of US 101, between State and Anacapa Streets. Monday through Friday, 11:00 A.M. to 5:00 P.M.; Saturday, 11:00 A.M. to 4:00 P.M.; closed Sunday. Oriental, European, and American antiques. Oriental rugs, paintings, porcelain, clocks, artwork, furniture, silver, bronze, cut glass, and American Indian artifacts.

# Museums

**Old Spanish Days Carriage Museum,** 129 Castillo Street; (805) 962–2353; www.carriage museum.org. South of US 101, next to Pershing Park. Open daily 9:00 A.M. to 3:00 P.M.; Sunday 1:00 to 4:00 P.M. More than sixty restored antique horse-drawn vehicles, including fine carriages, stagecoaches, a hearse, and a pumper fire engine. Also on display are saddles and horse tack once owned by such notables as the Cisco Kid, Clark Gable, and Will Rogers.

**Santa Barbara Museum of Art,** 1130 State Street; (805) 963–4364; www.sbmuseart .org. Northeast of US 101. Open Tuesday through Sunday 11:00 A.M. to 5:00 P.M. An exquisite collection that spans more than 4,000 years, from early Greek and Roman sculpture to modern acrylics and photographs. Paintings by O'Keeffe, Hopper, Monet, Matisse, and Chagall; bronzes, drawings, and antiquities. Special exhibits and guided tours.

**Santa Barbara Museum of Natural History,** 2559 Puesta del Sol Road; (805) 682–4711; www.sbnature.org. North of US 101, 2 blocks north of the Old Mission, via Mission Street and Mission Canyon Road. Open daily 10:00 A.M. to 5:00 P.M.; the third Sunday of each month is free to the public. Closed Thanksgiving, Christmas, and New Year's Day. Exhibits of the flora, fauna, geology, and prehistoric Indians of the Pacific Coast and Channel Islands. Planetarium and museum store.

**South Coast Railroad Museum,** 300 North Los Carnero Road, Goleta; (805) 964–3540; www.goletadepot.org. South of US 101, west of Santa Barbara. Wednesday through Sunday, 1:00 to 4:00 P.M. Located in a restored Victorian-style depot built in 1901, the museum exhibits railroad memorabilia and photographs. Outside displays include a bay-window caboose. Miniature train rides around the grounds; Trackside Shop museum store.

# Beaches, Parks, Trails, and Waysides

Most of the beaches in the Santa Barbara area are easy to reach. Carpinteria State Beach, located on the south side of the city of Carpinteria, lies about 12 miles east of

Santa Barbara. This is a broad, sandy beach popular with sunbathers and swimmers. A shallow offshore shelf that prevents riptides makes this one of the safest swimming beaches on the coast.

In the Montecito area, there's good beach access south of US 101 via the Olive Mill exit. In Santa Barbara the beach parallels Cabrillo Boulevard, reached by a number of streets, including State Street, south off US 101.

Cabrillo Boulevard becomes Shoreline Drive near the harbor. This street leads to Leadbetter Beach and Shoreline Park, west of the Harbor, both of which have picnic areas.

At the east end of Cabrillo Boulevard, between Cabrillo and US 101, is forty-two-acre Andree Clark Bird Refuge. A bike path and grassy area along the south and east shores of the marsh provide areas for viewing the abundant bird life, including ducks, geese, herons, and egrets.

# Water Sports and Activities

The east-west orientation of the coastline makes some of the beaches near Santa Barbara among the best in the world for surfing. Particularly popular are those from Santa Barbara west to Gaviota. El Capitan Point at El Capitan State Beach, south of US 101, about 12 miles west of Goleta, is famous among surfers.

Offshore fishing is good for rockfish, calico bass, lingcod, halibut, and other species. Charter operators at the Santa Barbara Harbor offer trips to local hot spots as well as to the Channel Islands.

The harbor has launching facilities, rental boats, bait, and tackle. Goleta Beach County Park, west of Santa Barbara, also has a boat hoist, boat and motor rentals, fishing tackle, bait, and licenses. There's also good pier fishing here and at Stearns Wharf.

**Captain Don's Sportfishing,** 219–G Stearns Wharf, Box 6; (805) 969–5217. Charter fishing trips and whale-watching cruises to the productive waters off the Santa Barbara coast.

**Hook, Line & Sinker,** 4010 Calle Real; (805) 687–5689. Just north of US 101. Bait-and-tackle shop with a full line of freshwater and saltwater gear, custom rods, tackle repair, and fishing licenses. Good source of local fishing information.

**Santa Barbara Sailing Center,** 133 Harbor Way; (805) 962–2826 or (800) 350–9090; www.sbsail.com. A fleet of forty power and sail craft from 14 to 50 feet for rent, skippered charters, harbor tours, island cruises, champagne cruises, and dinner cruises. Sailing instruction and certification offered.

**Stardust Sportfishing at Sea Landing,** 301 West Cabrillo Boulevard; (805) 963–3564; www.stardustsportfishing.com. Cabrillo Boulevard at Bath Street, on the waterfront, south of US 101. Half-day, three-quarter-day, and all-day coastal and island fishing

## events

| | |
|---|---|
| **May** | Cinco de Mayo, (805) 965–8581 |
| **June** | Summer Solstice Parade, (805) 965–3396 |
| **July** | Semana Nautica Swim Competition, (805) 897–2680 |
| | Santa Barbara National Horse Show, (805) 687–8711 |
| | Greek Festival, (805) 683–4492 |
| **August** | Old Spanish Days, (805) 688–4815 |
| | Sand Castle Contest, (805) 963–1391 |
| **September** | Danish Days, (800) 468–6765 |
| **October** | Harbor and Seafood Festival, (805) 967–8778 |
| | Avocado Festival, Carpinteria, (805) 684–0038 |
| **December** | Fifty-third Annual Downtown Santa Barbara Holiday Parade, (805) 962–2098 |

trips. Twilight trips in season. Live bait available. Tackle rental. Also private charters and scuba-diving trips. Full-service galley serving breakfast, lunch, snacks, beer, and drinks.

**Sunset Kidd's Sailing,** 125 Harbor Way #13; (805) 962–8222. On the waterfront, south of US 101. Hour-long harbor cruises, sunset and evening cruises, and overnight island trips—all under sail. Private charters also available.

# Golf

**Glen Annie Golf Club,** 405 Glen Annie Road, Goleta; (805) 968–6400; www.glen anniegolf.com. A half-mile east of US 101, via Glen Annie Road. Spectacular coastal views with the Santa Ynez Mountains as a backdrop on this eighteen-hole, par-seventy-one, 6,420-yard course. Pro shop, resident pro, clubhouse, club and cart rental, driving range, practice greens, restaurant, and bar.

**Sandpiper Golf Course,** 7925 Hollister Avenue, Goleta; (805) 968–1541; www.sand pipergolf.com. South of US 101 in Goleta, west of Santa Barbara. An eighteen-hole, par-seventy-two, 7,068-yard golf course on a bluff overlooking the ocean. Snack bar, pro shop, and equipment rentals.

**Santa Barbara Golf Club,** Las Positas Road and McCaw Avenue; (805) 687–7087. Just north of US 101 via Las Positas Road. An eighteen-hole public course, pro shop, resident pro, equipment and cart rentals, and snack bar.

## Other Attractions

**Botanic Garden,** 1212 Mission Canyon Road; (805) 682–4726; www.sbbg.org. North of US 101, 1½ miles past the mission, off Foothill Road. Tours: daily at 2:00 P.M.; also at 11:00 A.M. Saturday, and Sunday. A sixty-five-acre garden along upper Mission Creek with native trees and shrubs, cacti, and wildflowers. Three miles of nature trails.

**Mission Santa Barbara,** 2201 Laguna Street; (805) 682–4713. North of US 101 at the upper end of Laguna Street via Los Olivos Street off State Street. Daily, 9:00 A.M. to 5:00 P.M. Founded in 1786 and known as the "Queen of the Missions," this certainly ranks among the most beautiful of the twenty-one California missions. Museum, chapel, cemetery, garden, and gift shop. Tours by appointment.

## Travel Information

**Santa Barbara Chamber and Visitor Information Center,** One Santa Barbara Street, P.O. Box 299, 93102; (805) 965–3021 or (800) 927–4688; www.sbchamber.org

# Grover Beach / Pismo Beach

**Location:** Side by side along Highway 1 and U.S. Highway 101, 89 miles north of Santa Barbara and 12 miles south of San Luis Obispo, about midway between Los Angeles and San Francisco.

**Population:** Grover Beach 13,030; Pismo Beach 8,560

In the vicinity of Grover Beach and Pismo Beach, the foothills push westward and slope quickly to the ocean, forcing the highway seaward, within view of the resorts atop the bluffs overlooking the beach and surf. Miles of wide beach extend southward from the city of Pismo Beach to the Pismo Dunes and beyond. To the north, at the base of the cliffs are tiny pocket beaches and tidepools.

*Pismo* is a Chumash Indian word roughly translating to "tar" and referring to the natural asphalt that bubbles up through fissures in the ocean bottom and washes ashore along the beaches of central California. The Indians used it to caulk their plank canoes and waterproof their baskets. The same material has combined with the extremely fine sands here to create beaches hard enough to drive on.

Pismo Beach has been a resort town for the better part of a century, and Grover Beach has been attracting fun seekers and outdoor enthusiasts for nearly as long. Most of the resort motels and hotels are in Pismo Beach and Shell Beach along the bluffs, while the campgrounds and RV parks are at Grover Beach and Oceano.

## Lodging

**Best Western Shore Cliff Lodge,** 2555 Price Street, Pismo Beach; (805) 773–4671 or (800) 441–8885; www.shorecliff.com. West of US 101 and Highway 1 on a bluff overlooking the ocean. Remote-control cable TV in 99 rooms and kitchen suites. Pool, whirlpool, sauna, and lighted tennis courts. Ocean view and stairs to beach. Restaurant and bar on premises. Moderate to very expensive.

**The Cliffs at Shell Beach,** 2757 Shell Beach Road, Shell Beach; (805) 773–5000 or (800) 826–7827; www.cliffsresort.com. West of US 101, north of Pismo Beach, via Spyglass Road. Remote-control cable TV in 165 large rooms and 27 deluxe suites loaded with such amenities as marble bathrooms, whirlpool tubs, and private balconies. Heated pool with waterfalls, whirlpool, fitness center, and beach access. Restaurant on premises. Room service available. Moderate to very expensive.

**Edgewater Inn and Suites,** 280 Wadsworth Avenue, Pismo Beach; (805) 773–4811 or (888) 248–1354; www.edgewater-inn.com. West of US 101. Queen and king beds in 93 rooms and kitchen suites with refrigerators and remote-control cable TV. Pool, whirlpool, ocean view, and beach access. Continental breakfast. Moderate to expensive.

**Holiday Inn Express,** 775 North Oak Park Boulevard, Grover Beach; (805) 473–3609 or (866) 270–5110; www.hi.hotelsvalued.com. West of US 101, south of Pismo Beach. Double and king beds in 78 rooms with cable TV and cable movies. Some fireplaces and in-room whirlpools. Continental breakfast. Restaurant and cocktail lounge on premises. Moderate.

**Pismo Lighthouse Suites,** 2411 Price Street, Pismo Beach; (805) 773–2411 or (800) 245–2411; www.pismolighthousesuites.com. West of US 101. Cable TV and cable movies in 70 suites, some with wet bars, microwave ovens, and fireplaces. Heated pool, whirlpool, ocean view, and beach access. Moderate to expensive.

**Sea Crest Resort Motel,** 2241 Price Street, Pismo Beach; (805) 773–4608 or (800) 728–8400; www.sea-crest.com. West of US 101 on a bluff overlooking the ocean. Queen and king beds in 160 large rooms and executive, family, and Jacuzzi suites. Heated pool, whirlpools, glass-enclosed sundeck, barbecue area, and shuffleboard court. Ocean view. Moderate to expensive.

**SeaVenture Resort,** 100 Ocean View Avenue, Pismo Beach; (805) 773–4994 or (800) 760–0664; www.seaventure.com. West of US 101, off Dolliver. Cable TV in 50 units, 43 with spas—all with fireplaces, wet bars, and refrigerators. Heated pool and barbecue area. Continental breakfast. Rooftop restaurant open for dinner as well as weekend brunch. Cocktail lounge. Moderate to very expensive.

# Campgrounds and RV Parks

Oceano Memorial Campground, Oceano; (805) 781–5930; www.slocountyparks.com. South of Grover Beach, west of US 101, off Highway 1, south of Pier Avenue. Has 22 campsites with hookups available, fire pits, and showers. Picnic areas. Moderate.

**Pismo Coast Village,** 165 South Dolliver, Pismo Beach; (805) 773–1811; in California, (888) 782–3224; www.pismocoastvillage.com. Has 400 full-hookup, grassy sites with trees, tables, and fire rings. Showers, laundry, heated pool, ocean-view sites, beach access. Bicycle, barbecue-grill, umbrella, boogieboard, and beach-chair rentals. Restaurant, general store, arcade, basketball and volleyball courts, and horseshoe pits. Propane, firewood, and ice available. Expensive.

**Pismo State Beach North Beach Campground,** South Dolliver Street, Oceano; (805) 489–2684 or (800) 444–7275. West of US 101 and Highway 1, south of Pismo Beach. Has 103 campsites with tables and stoves, some hookups. Tank dump. Ocean view, beach access, dunes access. Inexpensive.

**Pismo State Beach Oceano Campground,** Pier Avenue, Oceano; (805) 489–2684 or (800) 444–7275; www.parks.ca.gov. West of US 101, off Highway 1, south of Grover Beach. Has 124 campsites, 42 with full hookups. Each site has table and stove. Showers, ocean view, trail to the beach. Moderate.

# Food

**F. McLintock's Saloon & Dining House,** 750 Mattie Road, Pismo Beach; (805) 773–1892; www.mclintocks.com. Lunch and dinner daily. Historic old saloon and restaurant serving great oak-barbecued ribs, ten-ounce filet mignon, and T-bone steaks. Seafood includes rainbow trout, stuffed sole, and scampi. Live country-western music nightly. Full bar. Moderate.

**Old West Cinnamon Rolls,** 861 Dolliver Street, Pismo Beach; (805) 773–1428. West of US 101, downtown. Monday through Saturday, 6:30 A.M. to 5:30 P.M.; Sunday, 6:30 A.M. to 2:00 P.M. An assortment of huge, fresh, sticky cinnamon rolls—the best you've ever had. Moderate.

**Steamer's,** 1601 Price Street, Pismo Beach; (805) 773–4711. Daily lunch and dinner. Specializes in California cuisine. Fresh seafood, steaks, and prime rib. Homemade cheesecake and other desserts. Beer, wine, and cocktails. Dancing and live entertainment nightly. Moderate.

# Shopping and Browsing

**Art Mesquit,** 1353 Shell Beach Road, Shell Beach; (805) 773–1776. West of US 101, north of Pismo Beach. Monday through Saturday, 10:30 A.M. to 5:30 P.M.; Sunday, noon to 4:30 P.M. Oriental antiques, Art Deco items, antique radios, lamps, chairs, small tables, and fine furniture.

# Beaches, Parks, Trails, and Waysides

South of Oceano and west of Highway 1 are the Pismo Dunes, the highest dunes in the state. In the past, when Hollywood needed footage of the Sahara Desert, camera crews headed for Pismo Dunes. In fact, the desert scenes in the silent classic *The Sheik,* starring Rudolph Valentino, were filmed here. Even today, the area is used in commercials and feature films.

All kinds of four-wheel-drive and off-road vehicles regularly descend on the dunes, and ordinary highway vehicles are allowed on the beach in designated areas. Those so inclined can rent four-wheelers locally and enjoy cruising the surfline or the exhilarating experience of a full-throttle climb up the slipface of a dune. Parts of the dunes are off-limits to vehicular traffic of any kind, so be sure to pick up maps and regulations before roaring off.

Hiking provides a pleasant way to enjoy the resplendent beauty of the dunes and adjacent beach. Among the wildlife hikers might encounter are more than fifty species of

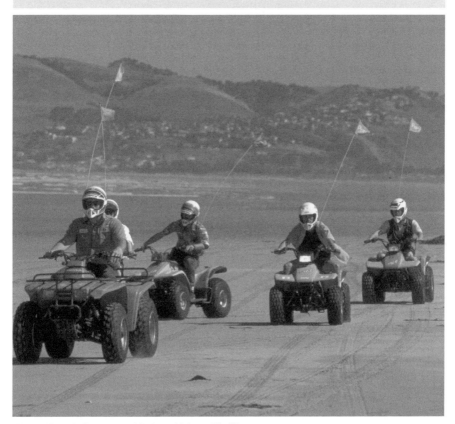

Pismo Beach *Courtesy of Robert Holmes/CalTour*

songbirds, shorebirds, and migratory waterfowl, as well as dune mice, cottontail rabbits, jack rabbits, and black-tailed deer. A lucky few will catch a glimpse of a fox, coyote, or bobcat.

Beach access is good from the city of Pismo Beach southward. You can reach the beach from the end of Wilmar Avenue, west off Price Street, and from Cypress Street at the west end of several intersecting streets, such as Wadsworth Avenue, Main Avenue, Stimson Avenue, Ocean Avenue, Park Avenue, and Addie Street.

In Grover Beach, beach access is at the west end of Grand Avenue, near LeSage Riviera Golf Course, and off Strand Way at the west end of most intersecting streets. Auto ramps leading to the beach are at the west end of Grand and Pier Avenues and at the Oceano Beach entrance.

In the Shell Beach area, off Shell Beach Road, several overlooks and small parks along Ocean Boulevard and Seacliff Drive offer excellent views of the ocean and offshore rocks and islets that harbor sea lions as well as nesting and roosting populations of several bird species, including pigeon guillemot and brown pelicans. Access to pocket beaches and tidepools is via paths or stairways along Ocean Boulevard at the end of

Palomar Avenue, Morro Avenue, and Vista del Mar and at Spyglass City Park on Seacliff Drive.

To reach Avila State Beach and Port San Luis Beach, take the Avila Beach exit off US 101, 3 miles north of Pismo Beach.

# Water Sports and Activities

The Pismo Beach area is another popular spot with surfers. The best surfing is south of the Pismo Beach Pier.

Three piers in the area serve anglers. Pismo Beach Pier is 950 feet long and lighted for night fishing. Concessions sell snacks, beverages, bait, and tackle. There's another pier at Avila Beach, with fish-cleaning facilities at the end of the pier. The 1,320-foot pier at Port San Luis is also lighted at night. It's equipped with boat hoists, and fuel docks and a boat-trailer parking area are nearby.

Although the pismo clam is still the most sought-after clam on the central coast, populations of this great bivalve are a fraction of what they once were. The large clams, with shells 7 inches or more across, fed the Chumash Indians for centuries. Early white settlers literally plowed the beaches to harvest the clams by the thousands to use as fertilizer and livestock feed. By 1911 the clams' numbers had sufficiently dwindled to require regulation of the harvest, yet an incredibly liberal limit of 200 clams per day was imposed. Commercial harvest continued until 1947, when it was finally prohibited.

The limit is now ten clams, 4½ inches or larger, per person per day, which is enough for anyone. The problem is that most legal-size clams are found beyond the low-tide line and are available only to those willing to wade into the surf for them. The fear now among some biologists is that the growing numbers of sea otters along the central coast will ultimately wipe out the remaining clam colonies.

# Rentals

**Arnie's ATV Rentals,** 171 North Second Street, Grover Beach; (805) 473–1610 or (800) 213–1590. Also, located at 311 Pier Avenue, Oceano; (805) 474–6060. All ATV rentals serving the Pismo Dunes.

**Sun Buggie Fun Rentals,** Oceano Dunes Park, 368 Pier Avenue, Oceano; (866) 728–4443. Rents six different styles of dune buggies with one, two, three, or four seats.

# Golf

**Avila Beach Golf Resort,** 6464 Avila Beach Road, P.O. Box 2140, Avila Beach 93424; (805) 595–4000; www.avilabeachresort.com/golf. Located 2½ miles west of US 101, via Avila Beach exit, 3 miles north of Pismo Beach. An eighteen-hole, par-seventy-one, 6,500-yard course open to the public. Clubhouse, pro shop, resident pro, cart and club rentals, driving range, coffee shop, snack bar, and restaurant.

**Pismo State Beach Golf Course,** 9 LeSage Drive, Grover Beach; (805) 481–5215; www.pismogolf.com. West of US 101, 1 block north of Grand Avenue, 1 mile south of Pismo Beach. A nine-hole public course on the beach. Clubhouse, pro shop, hand-cart rentals, club rental, driving range, and restaurant.

## Travel Information

**Grover Beach Chamber of Commerce,** 180 Highway One, Grover Beach; (805) 489–9091; www.groverchamber.com

**Pismo Beach Chamber of Commerce,** 581 Dolliver Street, Pismo Beach; (805) 773–4382 or (800) 443–7778; www.pismochamber.com

## events

| | |
|---|---|
| **June** | Pismo Beach Car Show, Pismo Beach, (805) 773–4382 |
| **July** | Old Fashioned Fourth of July and Fireworks on the Beach, Pismo Beach, (805) 773–4382 |
| **August** | Saint Anthony's Celebration, Pismo Beach, (805) 481–8012 |
| **October** | Clam Festival, Pismo Beach, (805) 773–4382 |
| | Jubilee by the Sea Jazz Festival, Pismo Beach, (805) 773–2241 |
| | Pumpkins on the Pier, Pismo Beach, (805) 773–4382 |
| **November** | Marching Band Review, Pismo Beach, (805) 773–4382 |
| | Christmas Tree Lighting, Pismo Beach, (805) 773–4382 |

# Morro Bay

**Location:** Morro Bay is on California Highway 1, 18 miles south of Cambria, 16 miles northwest of San Luis Obispo; neighboring Los Osos (population 8,000) is 5 miles to the south, and Cayucos (population 3,000) is 4 miles to the north.

**Population:** 10,372

Resting on the east shore of a small estuary of the same name, Morro Bay is a compact and charming resort community with a busy and interesting port minutes from the open ocean. The city, bay, sand spit, and state park are all named after the area's most prominent landmark—the huge rock early Spanish explorers dubbed El Morro, meaning "The Knob" or "The Knoll."

Morro Rock stands 576 feet high and is the core of an ancient volcanic plug, one of several in a chain stretching from here to San Luis Obispo. When early settlers first came to these shores, Morro Rock was an islet standing 1,000 feet offshore and was larger than it is today. In the 1930s construction of a revetment and causeway connected the rock to the mainland. From the late 1800s until 1969, when the state designated Morro Rock an ecological reserve, more than a million tons of rock were quarried from the face of the dome to build breakwaters and the causeway.

The reserve was established to protect the endangered peregrine falcons that nest on the rock and feed on the abundant local and migratory birds and waterfowl. Although climbing the rock is prohibited, it's possible to drive or hike to the base and to view it from anywhere on the Morro Bay waterfront or the hills above town. Alert and lucky observers spot the raptors on hunting forays, diving on their prey at speeds in excess of 200 miles per hour, making them the fastest birds in the world.

Visitors flock to Morro Bay to dine on fresh local seafood and to enjoy outdoor activities on the bay, on the beaches, and at nearby state parks. There are a beautiful golf course and superb museum here, as well as numerous natural areas to explore. The many shops and galleries of Cambria are a short drive north; downtown San Luis Obispo is an equal distance to the southeast.

# Lodging

**Bay View Inn,** 225 Harbor Street; (805) 772–2771 or (800) 742–8439; www.bay viewinn.net. Southwest of Highway 1, 1 block from the waterfront. Queen and king beds in 22 rooms with cable TV, cable movies, and coffeemakers. Some rooms with fireplaces, refrigerators, and views of the waterfront and ocean. Whirlpool. Laundry facilities. Walk to shops and restaurants. Moderate to expensive.

**Best Western San Marcos Motor Inn,** 250 Pacific Street; (805) 772–2248 or (800) 772–7969; www.bestlodging.worldres.com. Southwest of Highway 1 via Morro Bay exit to Morro Avenue at Pacific Street. King beds in 32 rooms with cable TV, cable movies, and refrigerators. Whirlpool, balconies, and ocean view. One block to the waterfront. Moderate to expensive.

**Blue Sail Inn,** 851 Market Avenue; (805) 772–7132 or (888) 337–0707; www.blue sailinn.com. Southwest of Highway 1, 1 block from the waterfront. Cable TV and cable movies in 47 rooms with refrigerators, wet bars, coffeemakers, and private balconies; some fireplaces. Whirlpool. Bay view. Moderate.

**The Breakers Motel,** P.O. Box 110, 93442; (805) 772–7317 or (800) 932–8899; www.breakersmorrobay.com. Southwest of Highway 1, Morro Bay Boulevard at Market Avenue. Double, queen, and king beds in 25 rooms with remote-control cable TV, cable movies, and refrigerators. In-room coffee and tea. Heated pool, spa, ocean view, some fireplaces. Continental breakfast. Walk to shops, restaurants, and waterfront. Moderate.

**El Morro Masterpiece Motel,** 1206 Main Street; (805) 772–5633 or (800) 527–6782; www.masterpiecemotel.com. Southwest of Highway 1. Queen and king beds in 27 rooms and suites with cable TV, cable movies, coffeemakers, and hair dryers. Some rooms with refrigerators, ceiling fans, and fireplaces. Complimentary continental breakfast and evening wine and cheese. Penthouse suite with Roman spa, fireplace, wet bar, VCR, sundeck, and great panoramic view. Whirlpool and ocean view. Moderate to expensive.

**Embarcadero Inn,** 456 Embarcadero; (805) 772–2700 or (800) 292–7625; www .embarcaderoinn.com. Southwest of highway 1, on the waterfront. Queen and king beds in 32 bay-view rooms and suites with refrigerators, remote-control TV, and VCRs; 30 of the rooms with balconies. Suites also have fireplaces and wet bars. Walk to shops and restaurants. Moderate to expensive.

# Campgrounds and RV Parks

Bay Pines Travel Trailer Park, 1501 Quintana Road; (805) 772–3223; www.baypines rv.com. South of Morro Bay on Highway 1 at Los Osos exit. Has 112 full-hookup sites with satellite TV. Heated pool, showers, and laundry. Moderate.

**Montana de Oro State Park,** Pecho Road, Los Osos; (805) 528–0513 or (800) 444–7275; www.parks.ca.gov. Near park headquarters along Islay Creek. Has 50 sites with tables and stoves for tents, trailers, and motor homes to 27 feet. Also a horse camp east off Pecho Valley Road, at northern park boundary: three individual horse camps and two group camps with tables, wood stoves, pit toilets, and corrals. Inexpensive to moderate.

**Morro Bay State Park,** State Park Road, (805) 772–2560 or (800) 444–7275; www.parks.ca.gov. Has 135 campsites, 30 with electricity and water hookups. Table, stove, and food locker at each site. Showers, laundry tubs, and tank dump. Campground set amid a pine and eucalyptus forest. Exercise trail and eighteen-hole golf course with driving range, pro shop, and cafe. Moderate.

**Morro Dunes Travel Trailer Park and Resort Campground,** 1790 Embarcadero; (805) 772–2722; www.morrodunes.com. Has 178 campsites, 137 with full hookups. Table and stove at each site. Showers, laundry, tank dump, ocean view, and beach access. Store, RV supplies, firewood, and ice. Moderate to expensive.

**Morro Strand State Beach,** (805) 772–2560 or (800) 444–7275; in winter, (805) 772–7434; www.parks.ca.gov. West of Highway 1, between Ascadero Road and Yerba Buena Avenue. Has 104 sites with tables and stoves for tents, trailers, and RVs to 24 feet. Showers. Campground is protected from wind by small dunes. Moderate.

**Tratel Morro Bay,** 1680 Main Street, 93442; (805) 772–8581. East of Highway 1, south of Route 41. Has 53 full-hookup sites with cable TV and concrete patios. Showers and laundry. Minimarket 1 block away. Moderate.

# Food

**The Coffee Pot Restaurant,** 1001 Front Street; (805) 772–3176. On the waterfront, downtown. Breakfast and lunch daily. More than a dozen omelets, quiche, and egg dishes, served with O'Brien hash browns and choice of biscuit, muffin, or toast. Pancakes and French toast. Soups, salads, sandwiches, and fish-and-chips. House specialties include huge homemade cinnamon rolls, blueberry muffins, and French toast stuffed with cream cheese, walnuts, and marmalade. Inexpensive to moderate.

**Dorn's Original Breakers Cafe,** 801 Market Street; (805) 772–4415; www.dorns cafe.com. Southwest of Highway 1, 1 block east of Embarcadero. Breakfast, lunch, and dinner daily; breakfast served till 2:00 P.M. daily. Almost a dozen omelets to choose from, including Dorn's special seafood omelet. Choice of seven kinds of pancakes. Waffles, French toast, and eggs. Large assortment of lunch appetizers, salads, soups, chowder, sandwiches, and seafood entrees. Large dinner menu includes steaks, fish, and shellfish, and such house specialties as seafood brochette, linguine and clam sauce, and sole Florentine. Full bar. Moderate.

**The Great American Fish Company,** 1185 Embarcadero; (805) 772–4407. Southwest of Highway 1, on the waterfront. Lunch and dinner daily. A variety of seafood and meat sandwiches, seafood crepes, and fish-and-chips. More than a dozen appetizers, including smoked albacore, squid strips, artichokes, oysters, and stuffed potato skins. In addition to steaks, chicken, and ribs, mesquite-broiled shark, salmon, shrimp, halibut, swordfish, albacore, giant squid, and mahimahi. Full bar. Moderate.

**Harbor Hut,** 1205 Embarcadero; (805) 772–2255. On the waterfront, in town. Daily lunch and dinner, Sunday brunch. Lunch menu features award-winning clam chowder, salads, omelets, crepes, stuffed potato skins, deli-style sandwiches, and such seafood entrees as calamari, clam strips, oysters, prawns, and fresh fish. Half-dozen seafood appetizers. Dinners include five different steaks, teriyaki chicken, and seafood favorites such as king-crab legs, bouillabaisse, lobster, and seafood platter, as well as fresh salmon, halibut, and abalone when available. Full bar. Moderate to expensive.

**Margie's Diner,** 1698 Main Street; (805) 772–2510. North of downtown, east of Highway 1, just south of Route 41 intersection. Breakfast, lunch, and dinner daily. Good selection of omelets and other egg dishes, pancakes, French toast, and biscuits and gravy. Lunch includes soup, chili, salads, juicy burgers, deli-style sandwiches, and open-face turkey and roast-beef sandwiches with mashed potatoes and gravy. All lunch items available through dinner, plus such entrees as barbecued chicken, fried chicken, ham steak, and roast beef. Milk shakes, malts, and root-beer floats. Homemade pies. Inexpensive to moderate.

# Museum

**Museum of Natural History,** Morro Bay State Park; (805) 772–2694; www.morrobay museum.org. At White Point, in the park, southeast of town. Daily, 10:00 A.M. to 5:00 P.M.; closed Thanksgiving, Christmas, and New Year's Day. Interpretive displays of the wildlife and history of the Morro Bay area. Slide shows, movies, lectures, and field trips. Superb view of bay and ocean. Good place for watching whales in season.

# Beaches, Parks, Trails, and Waysides

Montana de Oro State Park in Los Osos is a large, relatively undeveloped natural area lying south of Morro Bay. Within its 8,000 acres are creeks, woodlands, grassy coastal plains rising to 1,500-foot hills, and 7 miles of ocean shoreline varying from sandy beaches to rocky bluffs and cliffs.

Trails wind among the pine, eucalyptus, and live oak trees on the hillsides and along creek bottoms where willow, myrtle, maple, box elder, and cottonwood trees grow. A variety of small mammals reside here, as do fox, bobcat, deer, and even cougar.

From Morro Bay, take South Bay Boulevard to Los Osos Valley Road, and turn west. From US 101, Los Osos Valley Road leads west to Pecho Road.

## events

| | |
|---|---|
| **January** | Polar Bear Dip, Cayucos, (805) 995–1200 |
| **July** | Fireworks and Fourth of July Celebration, Cayucos, (805) 995–1200 |
| | Fourth of July Parade, Cayucos, (805) 995–1200 |
| | Fourth of July Fireworks, Morro Bay, (805) 772–4467 |
| **September** | Peddler's Faire, Cayucos, (805) 995–1200 |
| **October** | Harbor Festival, Morro Bay, (805) 772–1155 |
| **November** | Christmas Street Faire, Morro Bay, (805) 772–4288 |
| **December** | Lighted Boat Parade, Morro Bay, (805) 772–6278 |

Morro Bay State Park borders the southeast end of the city and lies adjacent to the bay. It contains the Natural History Museum and an eighteen-hole golf course, as well as hiking trails and picnic areas.

The Morro Bay State Park Sand Spit is a long finger of land separating the ocean from the bay. This undeveloped stretch of beach and dunes, popular with bird-watchers and clam diggers, is reached on foot by trail off Pecho Road or by boat, which is the easier and more popular way to go. Those who don't have boats can rent them or take the water taxi from the Embarcadero.

Morro Strand State Beach and Cayucos State Beach lie north of town, west of Highway 1, with access at the end of Twenty-fourth Street and in the town of Cayucos near the pier.

The Morro Bay area is a popular spot for watching and photographing a wide variety of birds. The large salt marsh attracts puddle ducks, diver ducks, seabirds, shorebirds, and songbirds by the thousands. Eucalyptus trees near the bay also serve as roosts and rookeries for great blue herons and egrets.

The eucalyptus trees also attract beautiful monarch butterflies, which arrive by the tens of thousands in October and remain through the winter months. Each evening, the butterflies gather in the trees in great clusters to keep warm.

## Water Sports and Activities

Surfers like the beaches near Morro Rock and north of town. The bay is popular with sailboarders, canoeists, and kayakers. And on minus tides, mudflats are exposed, providing access to clam beds. Both Dungeness and rock crabs are found in the bay, and local bait shops rent crabbing gear.

Anglers take surfperch, mackerel, rockfish, and various bottom fish from several small piers on the bay. The Cayucos Pier is on the ocean and serves as a popular fishing spot north of town. It's lighted for fishing at night, and there's no need for a fishing license.

Offshore anglers take chinook salmon from spring well into fall. Fall months are good for albacore, and the halibut fishery runs from midsummer through autumn. Lingcod, rockfish, cabezon, and a host of reef and bottom species are available all year, weather permitting.

## Rentals and Supplies

**Liquid Soul,** 701 Embarcadero; (805) 772–3244. On the waterfront, downtown. Monday through Friday, 10:00 A.M. to 6:00 P.M., Saturday and Sunday, 10:00 A.M. to 8:00 P.M. Sells surfboards, boogieboards, and other water gear.

**Morro Bay Marina,** 699 Embarcadero #9; (805) 772–8085. On the waterfront, downtown Pacific at Embarcadero. Rents boats by the hour. Open 10:00 A.M. to 5:00 P.M.

**Morro Bay State Park Marina,** 10 State Park Road; (805) 772–8796. South of town. Daily, 9:00 A.M. to 5:00 P.M. Rents canoes and rowboats by the hour.

**Wavelengths Surf Shop,** 998 Embarcadero; (805) 772–3904. West of Highway 1, downtown. Monday through Saturday, 9:30 A.M. to 8:00 P.M.; Sunday, 9:30 A.M. to 6:00 P.M. Rents surfboards, boogieboards, and wet suits by the day.

## Tours and Trips

**Bay Taxi,** Virg's Landing, 1215 Embarcadero; (805) 772–1222; www.virgs.com. Transportation to the sand spit for hikers, bird-watchers, clam diggers, and picnickers. Also, thirty-minute bay tours and whale watching tours.

***Tiger's Folly II,*** 1205 Embarcadero; weekdays, (805) 772–2257; weekends, (805) 772–2255. Docked at the Harbor Hut Restaurant. One-hour harbor cruises, weekends only. Full bar on board. Reservations not required. Also Sunday champagne brunch cruises, for which reservations are required.

# Golf

**Sea Pines Golf Club,** 1945 Solano Street, Los Osos; (805) 528–1788. A mile west of Los Osos via Los Osos Valley and Pecho roads. A nine-hole, par-twenty-eight, 1,465-yard public course. Clubhouse, pro shop, resident pro, club and cart rentals, driving range, and restaurant.

# Travel Information

**Cayucos Chamber of Commerce,** 158 North Ocean Avenue, Cayucos; (805) 995–1200 or (800) 563–1878; www.cayucoschamber.com or www.cayucosbythe sea.com

**Los Osos Chamber of Commerce,** 781 Palisades Avenue, P.O. Box 6282, Los Osos 93402; (805) 528–4884; www.losososbaywoodpark.org

**Morro Bay Chamber of Commerce,** 880 Main Street, P.O. Box 876, 93442; (805) 772–4467; in California, (800) 231–0592; www.morrobay.net; e-mail: baywatch@the grid.net

# Cambria / San Simeon

**Location:** Cambria is on California Highway 1, 16 miles north of Morro Bay and 34 miles northwest of San Luis Obispo; San Simeon, on California Highway 1, is 6 miles north of Cambria and 67 miles south of Big Sur.

**Population:** Cambria 6,232; San Simeon 600

Cambria is on the coast in the pine-forested foothills. San Simeon, also on the coast, is situated on the coastal benchlands that rise into rolling ranch country on the west slope of the Santa Lucia Mountains. Although the two communities evolved in the mid-nineteenth century nearly simultaneously, to some extent for similar reasons, they could scarcely be more different from each other today.

When copper and cinnabar, from which mercury is extracted, were discovered in the nearby mountains in the early 1860s, the Cambria area expanded rapidly. Dairy farming and cattle ranching grew with it, and soon dairy products, tallow, and hides were being shipped from here.

The cove just south of San Simeon Point developed as a whaling station in the early 1850s. During the annual migration of gray whales past the point, whale spotters watched for the spouting mammals and signaled the whalers, who set out after them in small boats. The blubber was rendered and oil shipped from here until the industry declined in the 1870s.

George Hearst, father of William Randolph Hearst, was an illiterate Missourian who made millions mining California silver and gold and later became a U.S. senator. He bought Rancho San Simeon in 1865 and in 1878 built a new wharf at the cove near San Simeon Point, where schooners could load cattle hides, quicksilver, and other locally produced goods.

The coastal shipping trade flourished until 1894, when the railroad came to Cambria. Completion of the Coast Highway between Carmel and Cambria began a new era. But even before then, changes were taking place that would have far-reaching effects on the local landscape and economy.

In 1919 construction began on what would eventually become the greatest tourist attraction on this stretch of coast: William Randolph Hearst's extravagant monument to himself at San Simeon, known as the Hearst Castle. More than a million people visit this complex every year to see the hundred-room Casa Grande, three guest houses, works of art collected from around the globe, and grounds landscaped with shrubs, flowers, and more than 100,000 trees.

Construction, modification, and alteration continued for more than thirty years, leaving the complex still unfinished at Hearst's death in 1951. His heirs deeded the property to the state in 1958, and it's now operated as the Hearst San Simeon Historical Monument.

Cambria burgeoned in the 1950s and ultimately flowered into a busy artists' hamlet where dozens of galleries and shops, restaurants, and pubs stand amid the mixed architecture of California contemporary and English Tudor styles.

Between trips to the beach, visitors to the area can combine tours of Hearst Castle with shopping, browsing, and dining.

## Lodging

**Beach House Bed & Breakfast,** 6360 Moonstone Beach Drive, Cambria; (805) 927–3136; www.moonstonebeach.com. West side of Highway 1, on the beach. Has 7 rooms, some with fireplaces and oceanviews, all with private baths and cable TV. Decks, patios, and living room with fireplace. Bicycles available. Continental breakfast. Expensive to very expensive.

**Best Western Cavalier Beachfront Resort,** 9415 Hearst Drive, San Simeon; (805) 927–4688 or (800) 826–8168; www.cavalierresort.com. West side of Highway 1, on the ocean, 3 miles south of Hearst Castle. Remote-control cable TV, cable movies, and VCRs in 90 rooms, some with fireplaces, wet bars, and refrigerators. Two heated pools, whirlpool, ocean view. Two restaurants, cocktail lounge, room service, and adjacent shopping plaza. Expensive to very expensive.

**Castle Inn by the Sea,** 6620 Moonstone Beach Drive, Cambria; (805) 927–8605; www.cambriacastleinn.com. West of Highway 1, on the beach. Queen and king beds in 31 rooms with ocean views, cable TV, VCRs, and refrigerators. Large picnic area, heated pool, and whirlpool. Continental breakfast. Moderate.

**Olallieberry Inn,** 2476 Main Street, Cambria; (805) 927–3222 or (888) 927–3222; www.olallieberry.com. One mile east of Highway 1. Has 9 individually decorated rooms with private baths, 6 with fireplaces. On weekends, wine and appetizers served in the parlor. Continental breakfast. Moderate to expensive.

**Quality Garden Inn,** 9260 Castillo Drive, P.O. Box 200, San Simeon 93452; (805) 927–3998 or (800) 821–7914; www.choicehotels.com. East side of Highway 1. Queen and king beds in 56 rooms and suites with cable TV, some with fireplaces, in-room whirlpool, wet bars, and refrigerators. Garden courtyard with waterfalls. Heated pool and whirlpools. Restaurant on premises. Moderate to expensive.

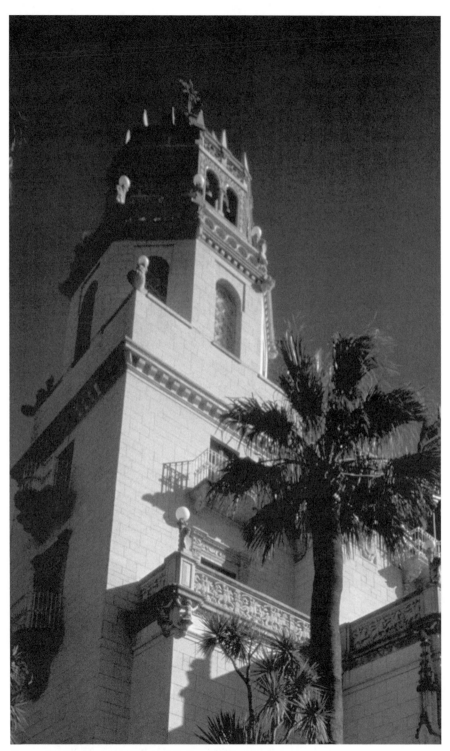
Hearst Castle *Courtesy of Robert Holmes/CalTour*

## Campgrounds and RV Parks

**San Simeon State Park,** P.O. Box 8, San Simeon; (805) 927–2020 or (800) 444–7275; www.parks.ca.gov. Beach is west of Highway 1, campground east of the highway. Has 115 developed campsites and 70 primitive sites with tables and fire pits. Showers, tank dump, ocean view, fishing, hiking, and nature trails, and a ⅙-mile walk to the beach. Moderate.

## Food

**The Brambles Dinner House,** 4005 Burton Drive, P.O. Box 746, Cambria 93428; (805) 927–4716; www.bramblesdinnerhouse.com. East of Highway 1, 2 blocks southwest of Main Street. Dinner daily as well as Sunday brunch. Clam chowder, oyster soup, and pea soup. Top sirloin, filet mignon, and New York steaks, as well as lamb chops broiled over oak. Barbecued chicken, baby pork ribs, and beef ribs. Prawns, scallops, scallone, fish, and bouillabaisse. Full bar. Moderate to expensive.

**The Hamlet Restaurant,** Highway 1, Cambria; (805) 927–3535. At Moonstone Gardens, Highway 1 at Moonstone Beach Drive. Daily lunch and dinner, Sunday brunch with jazz. Such lunch offerings as quiche Lorraine, brisket of beef sandwich, fish-and-chips, calamari and chips, clam chowder and salad, and mariner's salad. Dinners include breast of chicken, filet mignon, king-crab legs, brisket of beef, and rack of lamb. Full bar; great ocean view from inside restaurant; lunch outdoors on garden patio. Moderate to expensive.

**Linn's Main Bin,** 2277 Main Street, Cambria; (805) 927–0371; www.linnsfruitbin.com. East of Highway 1. Breakfast, lunch, and dinner daily. Extraordinary three-egg omelets, such as the Moonstone Beach, stuffed with seafood, Jack cheese, and sour cream; the Mexi-cali, stuffed with Jack cheese, chili peppers, onions, and bell peppers and topped with salsa and guacamole; and the Granatino Special, filled with Italian sausage, mozzarella cheese, onions, and bell peppers, then topped with marinara sauce. Other breakfast offerings are Belgian waffles, fresh fruit plate, and freshly baked muffins and granola. Quiches and hearty soups are lunch favorites, as are specialty sandwiches. For lunch and dinner, chicken and beef pot pies in two sizes are local favorites. Wonderful homemade cakes, pies, and cheesecakes. Inexpensive to moderate.

**Mustache Pete's Italian Eatery,** 4090 Burton Drive #1, Cambria; (805) 927–8589; www.mustachepetes.com. East of Highway 1, 1 block southwest of Main Street, Burton at Center Street. Lunch and dinner daily. Among the appetizers are shrimp cocktail, steamer clams, and buffalo wings. Soups, salads, shrimp Louis, and such sandwiches as sausage parmigiana hero, turkey and Swiss, and Italian submarine. Fettuccine, linguine, tortellini, rigatoni, ravioli, lasagna, manicotti, cannelloni, and spaghetti served for lunch and dinner. Also a large selection of veal, beef, poultry, and seafood entrees served with soup or salad and pasta. Carryout service available. Full bar. Moderate.

**The Sow's Ear Cafe,** 2248 Main Street, Cambria; (805) 927–4865; www.thesows ear.com. East of Highway 1. Dinner daily. Appetizers include fried Brie, stuffed mushrooms, and calamari strips. Among dinner entrees are salmon in parchment, beer-spiced shrimp, chicken and dumplings, baby pork ribs, sautéed calamari, and chicken-fried steak with country gravy. Fresh seafood specials nightly. Freshly baked breads and homemade desserts. Local wines. Moderate to expensive.

## Shopping and Browsing

**Linn's Fruit Bin Farmstore,** Rural Route #1, Box 600, Cambria 93428; (805) 927–1499; www.linnsfruitbin.com. On Santa Rosa Creek Road, 5 miles east of Cambria. Daily, 8:00 a.m. to 5:00 p.m. Fruit and berry preserves, fruit and nut pies, chicken and beef frozen pot pies, and country craft items.

**Moonstones American Craft Gallery,** 4070 Burton Drive, Cambria; (805) 927–3447 or (800) 424–3827; www.moonstones.com. Daily, 10:00 A.M. to 10:00 P.M. Boxes and carvings of exotic woods, kaleidoscopes, sculptured glass, crystals, ceramics, kinetic sculpture, jewelry, and candles.

**Seekers Glass Gallery,** 4090 Burton Drive, P.O. Box 521, Cambria 93428; (805) 927–4352 or (800) 841–5250; www.seekersglass.com. Southwest of Main Street, Burton Drive at Center Street, East Village. Daily, 10:00 A.M. to 10:00 P.M. An exquisite collection of contemporary American glass artwork, beautifully displayed. More than 250 artists represented.

## Museum

**Hearst San Simeon State Historical Monument,** 750 Hearst Castle Road, P.O. Box 8, San Simeon 94352; (805) 927–2020 or (800) 444–4445; www.hearstcastle.com. Daily, except Thanksgiving, Christmas, and New Year's Day, 8:00 A.M. to 4:00 P.M. in winter; extended summer hours. Evening tours, spring and autumn, with costumed actors representing the guests who frequented the castle. Commonly known as Hearst Castle, this was once the opulent home of newspaper publisher William Randolph Hearst. Since the Hearst family donated it to the state, it has become one of the most popular attractions on the West Coast. Architect Julia Morgan designed and implemented all the plans, seeing to every detail of the vast undertaking. Four different guided tours take place concurrently—each lasting about an hour and three-quarters and each with limited capacity. Tour 1 (fifty-three persons): guest house, esplanade and gardens, the castle, assembly room, refectory, morning room, billiard room, and theater. Tour 2 (twelve persons): Doge's Suite, The Cloisters, the library, Gothic Suite,

Celestial Suite, Della Robbia Room, and the pantry and kitchen. Tour 3 (fourteen persons): "B" House (or Casa del Monte), new wing, the old versus the new, and special feature—a film of celebrity guests of the 1920s and 1930s. Tour 4 (fourteen persons): "A" House (or Casa del Mar), wine cellar, hidden terrace, and Neptune Pool dressing rooms. Tickets cost $14 to $25 and you can order by calling (800) 444–4445. In summer reservations are essential.

## Beaches, Parks, Trails, and Waysides

Leffingwell Landing, west of Highway 1, off Moonstone Beach Drive, provides vantages for watching whales and sea otters. Trails along the bluffs overlook a rocky beach and tidepools.

Moonstone Beach, west of Moonstone Beach Drive, is a good spot for hiking and exploring tidepools. It's also a popular beachcombing area for driftwood and gemstones. In fact, it's named after the moonstone agates—along with jasper and jade—found here.

The William R. Hearst Memorial State Beach, west of Highway 1 on San Simeon Road, is a favorite swimming area because San Simeon Point protects it from wind and moderates the surf. A grassy picnic area can be found in a nearby eucalyptus grove.

Most of the year, sea otters and sea lions are visible off the beaches. Binoculars help in finding these sea mammals. In the vicinity of the San Simeon Ranch near Hearst Castle, turn your binoculars on the hillsides east of the highway, and you might spot zebra grazing. They're remnants of the herds of exotic animals the Hearsts imported years ago.

## Water Sports and Activities

Rock and surf fishing are productive along Moonstone Beach. The 1,000-foot pier at William R. Hearst Memorial State Beach is another favorite angling spot, with tackle and bait available nearby.

## Other Attractions

**Pewter Plough Playhouse,** 824 Main Street (at Sheffield), West Village, Cambria; (805) 927–3877; www.pewterploughplayhouse.com. Live local theater; call for dates, times, and a list of shows.

## Travel Information

**Cambria Chamber of Commerce & Visitor Information,** 767 Main Street, Cambria; (805) 927–3624; www.cambriachamber.org

**San Simeon Chamber of Commerce,** 9511 Hearst Drive, P.O. Box 1, San Simeon 93452; (805) 927–3500; www.sansimeonchamber.org

| | |
|---|---|
| **January** | Art & Wine Festival, (805) 927–3624 |
| **March** | Chili Cookoff and Classic Car Show, Cambria, (805) 927–3624 |
| **May** | A Day in Old San Simeon Barbecue, (805) 927–2014 |
| **June** | Cambria Heritage Celebration, (805) 927–3130 |
| | Arts & Craft Faire, Cambria, (559) 887–3474 |
| **July** | Picnic in the Park and Fireworks, Cambria, (805) 927–8020 |
| **August** | Greenspace Art Auction, Cambria, (805) 927–2866 |
| **September** | Central Coast Woodcarvers Show, Cambria, (805) 534–1292 |
| | Allied Arts Art Show, Cambria, (805) 927–0528 |
| | Arts & Craft Faire, Cambria, (559) 877–3474 |
| **November** | Cambria Crafters Guild Christmas Boutique, (805) 929–3391 |
| | Rosemary Festival, Cambria, (805) 927–5224 or (800) 266–4372 |
| **December** | Cambria Farmers Market Christmas at the Market, (805) 927–4715 |

# Big Sur

**Location:** On California Highway 1, about 65 miles north of San Simeon and about 25 miles south of Carmel.

**Population:** 520

Draped along the western slope of the Santa Lucia Mountain Range between San Simeon and Carmel, California Highway 1 achieves its reputation for being one of the nation's scenic wonders. For 90 miles this narrow, winding, two-lane road climbs the chaparral-covered shoulders of the mountains, descends into the wooded canyons, clings to oceanside bluffs, and courses through switchback after switchback, sending travelers east and west to get north or south.

Construction began on this highway in 1919 and took until 1937 to complete, at a cost of $10 million. But those were Depression-era dollars. To put that figure in better perspective, in 1983 a major slide closed the highway and took one year to repair. That cost $7.4 million.

Certainly, the cost of labor was cheaper when the highway was built. Most of the work was done by convicts who lived at several labor camps along the course of the highway. The prisoners, from San Quentin, earned from 35 to 75 cents a day in cash and were credited with three days' shortening of their sentences for every two days they worked.

This is no hurry-up highway; nor should it be. It's a scenic route through spectacular mountain and ocean vistas that must be savored. Those in a rush to reach destinations north or south should use U.S. Highway 101 instead.

Although there is a spot on the map named Big Sur, don't expect to find a city, or a village for that matter. Even *community* is an inappropriate term to describe the loose gathering of people and property called Big Sur. It's better to think of Big Sur as a region, an overwhelming presence, even an attitude or notion or experience. Many of us think of this whole 90-mile expanse of rugged coastline and highway with its unmarked trails to hard-to-find beaches as Big Sur, and we're probably as close to the right idea as anyone.

The river after which the area and several specific locations are named the Spaniards called *El Rio Grande del Sur,* meaning, quite unromantically, "The Big River of the South." They dubbed another smaller stream *El Rio Chiquito del Sur,* which means "The Little River of the South." We have shortened and Americanized them to Big Sur River and Little Sur River.

Big Sur has few amenities to distract the traveler or detract from the area's scenic splendor—no nightclubs, golf courses, theaters, trendy boutiques, or fast-food joints. Mostly, what you see is what you get. Big Sur is an outdoor experience. It's having a scenic drive, hiking up a canyon or along a coastal bluff, fishing the surf or one of several mountain streams, hunting jade in a rocky cove, photographing seascapes, watching birds on a coastal lagoon, or camping among the redwoods.

Campgrounds are fairly plentiful, but they fill up fast. Those that take reservations are often booked weeks or months ahead for the summers and weekends, especially weekends. Those available on a first-come, first-served basis fill up early in the day. So plan ahead, and make reservations for the busy times.

Although lodging is relatively scarce, a few resorts and cabins provide overnight accommodations. They can be booked solid much of the year, so make reservations, no matter when you plan to travel.

Big Sur climate is considered moderate, with January temperatures usually from the low forties to the low sixties and July temperatures from the low fifties to the high sixties. Summer days can get hot, though, especially inland. Rain, which averages about 40 inches a year, falls mainly from October to April. May through September is dry.

Rock hounds enjoy searching creek beds and rocky beaches along the surf line. In addition to agates and jasper, jade and garnets are among the treasures found.

Big Sur wildlife is abundant and varied. The entire shoreline is a sea-otter refuge that is also frequented by California and Steller sea lions. Gray whales migrate up and down the coast from summer feeding grounds in Alaska to winter calving grounds in Mexico, and stragglers linger and feed near shore much of the year.

Cormorants and tufted puffins use the cliffs and rocks as rookeries. Shorebirds, such as sanderlings and willets, feed along the shoreline, while red-tailed hawks and golden eagles soar on the updrafts, hunting rodents and reptiles.

Among the numerous small mammals are ground squirrels, gray squirrels, possums, rabbits, raccoons, and ring-tailed cats. Gray fox and bobcat compete with the raptors for food. Large mammals include deer, wild pig, and the occasional black bear and cougar.

For years Big Sur has also attracted an odd admixture of humankind from ranchers to mystics but has been particularly attractive to writers, artists, photographers, and self-styled intellectuals and eccentrics. Artist and novelist Henry Miller lived here, part of the time in an abandoned labor camp. Poet Lawrence Ferlinghetti called *Big Sur* home, and author Jack Kerouac based his novel Big Sur on his many visits with the beat-generation poet. Photographer Ansel Adams lived here and photographed Big Sur extensively.

In its December 1988 issue, the slick monthly *M* magazine (for "The Civilized Man") listed offshore sailing, Swiss railroads, the Tibetan side of the Himalayas, *The Oxford English Dictionary*, "The William Tell Overture" (with fireworks), gold, real Bermuda onions, and Big Sur among the one hundred things on earth that haven't been ruined yet.

# Lodging

**Big Sur Campground and Cabins,** Highway 1; (831) 667–2322. Just over 67 miles north of San Simeon, just under 24 miles south of Carmel. Three A-frames and nine cabins with fireplaces, fully equipped kitchens, queen beds, and sleeping lofts. River units with redwood decks. Moderate.

**Big Sur Lodge,** 47225 Highway 1, Big Sur State Park, P.O. Box 190, 93920; (831) 667–3100 or (800) 424–4787; www.bigsurlodge.com. At Pfeiffer Big Sur State Park, 64 miles north of San Simeon, 26 miles south of Carmel. Has 61 lodge rooms and cabins, some with kitchens, some with fireplaces. Heated pool, restaurant, gift shop, two grocery stores, and coin-operated laundry on premises. Moderate.

**Big Sur River Inn,** 47225 Highway 1, Pheneger Creek; (831) 667–2700 or (800) 548–3610; www.bigsurriverinn.com. About 65 miles north of San Simeon, 25 miles south of Carmel. Twenty rooms and family suites—all with private baths. Suites have balconies overlooking the river. Heated pool, restaurant, bar, general store, and gift shop on premises. Live entertainment in the bar on weekends. Moderate to expensive.

**Ventana Inn;** (831) 667–2331, (831) 624–4812, or (800) 628–6500; www .ventanainn.com. About 63 miles north of San Simeon, 27 miles south of Carmel. Queen and king beds in 62 rooms, suites, town-house suites, and cottages, most with fireplaces, some with hot tubs as well. Suites with dining alcoves and wet bars available. TVs and VCRs. Refrigerators in some suites, including the town houses. Private terraces with mountain or ocean views. One-day reservations Sunday through Thursday only; nonholiday weekends, two-day reservations only; holiday weekends, three-day reservations only. Continental breakfast served in lobby, library, or guests' rooms. Complimentary wine and cheese buffet every afternoon. Restaurant, two pools, and spa. Children not encouraged. Expensive to extremely expensive.

# Campgrounds and RV Parks

Camping outside designated areas in the Los Padres National Forest requires permits, available at two ranger stations on Highway 1. The Big Sur Station is less than 1 mile south of Pfeiffer Big Sur State Park; Pacific Valley Station is 32 miles north of San Simeon. Information, permits, and maps are also available from the U.S. Forest Service, District Headquarters, 406 South Mildred Street, King City; (408) 385–5434.

**Andrew Molera State Park,** P.O. Box A, 93920; (831) 667–2315; www.parks.ca.gov. About 21 miles south of Carmel, 3 miles south of Point Sur. Has 24 campsites with fire pits at a walk-in campground about ¼ mile from the parking area. Trail to beach. Miles of hiking trails. Inexpensive.

**Big Sur Campground & Cabins,** Highway 1; (831) 667–2322; www.campingfriend .com. Just over 67 miles north of San Simeon, just under 24 miles south of Carmel. Has 81 full-hookup campsites in the redwoods and along the river, 36 pull-through sites, plus 4 tent cabins. Tables, fire pits, showers, laundry, and tank dump. Store. Tent rentals. Swimming, fishing, playground, volleyball, basketball. Tent cabins and 8 A-frame cabins. Moderate to expensive.

**Fernwood Resort Campground;** (831) 667–2422; www.fernwoodbigsur.com. About 65 miles north of San Simeon, about 25 miles south of Carmel. Has 60 campsites with electricity hookups and fire pits. Tent cabins available. Showers, restaurant, bar, and grocery store on premises. Firewood available. Moderate.

**Kirk Creek Campground,** Los Padres National Forest; (805) 434–1996; www.parks man.com. West of Highway 1, 35 miles north of San Simeon, 55 miles south of Carmel. Has 34 campsites with fire pits and a bike-camp area. Trails to the beach. Moderate.

**Limekiln Creek Redwoods Campground State Park,** Highway 1; (831) 667–2403 or (800) 444–7275; www.parks.ca.gov. About 26 miles south of Big Sur, 2 miles south of Lucia. Has 33 campsites with water hookups and fire pits for tents, trailers, and RVs to 24 feet. Showers, tank dump, trail to beach, hiking trails, trout stream, and nearby surf fishing. General store with groceries, beer, wine, bait, tackle, firewood, and ice. Moderate.

**Pfeiffer Big Sur State Park Campground,** Highway 1; (831) 667–2315 or (800) 444–7275; www.parks.ca.gov. East of Highway 1, 26 miles south of Carmel, 64 miles north of San Simeon. Has 214 campsites with tables, stoves, and food lockers along the river, in redwood groves, in oak forests, and in meadows. Accommodates RVs to 32 feet, but no hookups. Showers, laundry, tank dump, and store. Hiking trails with swimming spots, summer guided nature walks, campfire programs, and Junior Ranger programs. Moderate.

**Plaskett Creek Campground,** Los Padres National Forest; (805) 434–1996 or (877) 444–6777; www.parksman.com. East of Highway 1, 35 miles north of San Simeon, about 40 miles south of Big Sur. Has 44 campsites with tables, fire pits, and grills. Water available, but no hookups. Also has hike and bike sites. Moderate.

**Riverside Campground and Cabins,** P.O. Box 3, 93920; (831) 667–2414; www.river sidecampground.com. About 66 miles north of San Simeon, 24 miles south of Carmel. Has cabins and 45 campsites with electricity hookups, tables, and fire pits. Tent rentals, firewood, showers, laundry, playground, and hiking trails. Moderate.

# Beaches, Parks, Trails, and Waysides

The Big Sur area is a vast system of canyons and streams, beaches and coves, cliffs and bluffs, and many miles of trails. Although there are plenty of sandy beaches, swimming is not a major pastime at most, because of cold ocean water and dangerous currents.

The steep, unstable terrain can be hazardous, so stay on established trails when possible, especially when descending hills and bluffs to beach areas. Poison oak grows throughout the Big Sur region and is abundant in some places. Learn to recognize it so that you can avoid it. Be aware, too, that this is rattlesnake country. Don't let unnecessary fear of these interesting reptiles prevent your enjoying Big Sur; just exercise caution, and watch where you walk.

More of a nuisance than a hazard is the fact that so many trails, gravel roads, and beach areas are unmarked; it's sometimes difficult to tell where trails and roads lead and whether you're on public land or private property. Seems some of the locals have an aversion for signs of any sort and take them down about as fast as they're put up. Rely on maps to guide you.

At the south end of the Big Sur area, about 25 miles north of San Simeon, just north of Gorda, lies Willow Creek Picnic Area, on the west side of Highway 1. On the east side of the highway, at the south end of the bridge, a road leads to the rocky beach where rock hounds sometimes find jade. Upstream, gold and silver mines operated in the late 1800s and early 1900s but have been closed since 1915.

North of Willow Creek, about 12½ miles south of Lucia, is Jade Cove, so named for the deposits of nephrite jade here. Rock hounds are allowed to take this jade only below the mean high-tide line. This cove is where divers worked in 1971 to remove a chunk of jade weighing 9,000 pounds.

Limekiln Beach, 26 miles south of Big Sur, is privately operated, and a nominal day-use fee is charged. The beach at the creek mouth was once the site of Rockland Landing. A trail leads about ½ mile to four old lime kilns once used to smelt lime that was shipped in kegs from Rockland Landing in the 1870s.

About 11 miles south of Pfeiffer Big Sur State Park and 37 miles south of Carmel is Julia Pfeiffer Burns State Park, encompassing 2,405 acres of mountainous and forested terrain. A paved trail leads to a viewpoint overlooking McWay Waterfall. Another trail leads to a picnic area.

Pfeiffer Beach is south of Pfeiffer Big Sur State Park, west of Highway 1, 1 mile south of the park entrance via Sycamore Canyon Road. This picturesque beach, popular with hikers and photographers, provides views of spectacular surf crashing amid sea stacks and rocky rubble. Parts of the Richard Burton–Elizabeth Taylor movie *The Sandpiper* were filmed here. This beach is also a good place for watching and photographing shorebirds.

Pfeiffer Big Sur State Park offers a wide variety of activities, including picnicking, hiking, photography, and wildlife watching. The park is east of Highway 1, 26 miles south of Carmel. During summer months, docent-led nature walks are among the activities.

The Big Sur River flows through Andrew Molera State Park, then empties into the ocean. A lagoon near the river mouth is a sanctuary that attracts a variety of shorebirds. There are 10 miles of hiking trails and 2½ miles of sandy beach in this 4,749-acre park. Coast redwoods and big-leaf maples grow in the park. The eucalyptus grove along the river attracts monarch butterflies, which overwinter here. The park lies 21 miles south of Carmel.

Two miles south of Malpaso Creek is Garrapata State Park. Here a 1%0-mile trail leads along coastal bluffs to Soberanes Point, a good spot for watching whales and sea otters.

## Water Sports and Activities

Many pocket beaches and coves along this great stretch of Pacific coastline are popular with divers. A major attraction is 35 miles south of Carmel at Julia Pfeiffer Burns State Park, where a trail leads through Partington Canyon to Partington Cove. Offshore is the 1,680-acre Julia Pfeiffer Burns Underwater Area.

Surf and rock anglers catch fish from about any stretch of beach or rocky shore where there's access. Among the most plentiful species are surfperch, flounder, sanddabs, croaker, rockfish, cabezon, and lingcod.

Freshwater fishing is restricted to those coastal streams with sufficient year-round flow to support a native population of trout and to attract the anadromous steelhead. Both the Big Sur and Little Sur rivers are such streams, as are Big Creek, Garrapata Creek, Limekiln Creek, and Salmon Creek.

## Other Attractions

**Point Sur State Historic Park and Lighthouse;** recorded message, (831) 625–4419; www.pointsur.org. Additional information available from Andrew Molera State Park Headquarters. West of Highway 1, 3 miles north of Andrew Molera State Park. Docent-guided tours of the park and lighthouse start at 10:00 a.m. and 2:00 p.m. on Saturday, 10:00 a.m. on Sunday; visitors advised to arrive half an hour before the tour starts. Moonlight tours are given in the evening. Drive past the gate to the small parking area (no motor homes or trailers). Tours, which last two hours or so, require hiking along a trail that rises 300 feet and is ½ mile each way. This is not a good tour for young children.

## Travel Information

**Big Sur Chamber of Commerce,** P.O. Box 87, 93920; (831) 667–2100; www.big surcalifornia.org; e-mail: info@bigsurcalifornia.org

**Big Sur Natural History Association,** P.O. Box 189, Big Sur 93920

## events

| | |
|---|---|
| **April** | Big Sur International Marathon, Pfeiffer Big Sur State Park, (831) 625–6226 |
| **June** | Big Sur Garden Tour, (831) 667–1530 |
| **October** | Big Sur 10K River Run, Big Sur State Park, (831) 624–4112 |
| | Big Sur Jade Festival, (831) 659–3857 |
| **November** | Big Sur Harvest & Craft Fair, (831) 667–2557 |

# Carmel / Pebble Beach

**Location:** Carmel is on California Highway 1, 26 miles north of Big Sur, 90 miles north of San Simeon, 350 miles north of Los Angeles, and 130 miles south of San Francisco; Pebble Beach lies west of Carmel, via 17-Mile Drive.

**Population:** Carmel 4,700; Pebble Beach 4,700

Imagine a village so quaint it has no parking meters along its narrow, shaded streets and no neon signs advertising its many chic shops and charming cafes. Imagine a coastal hamlet with more than a hundred galleries but no streetlights, where houses have names instead of addresses, and where all the trees are registered.

If you're planning to visit the village of Carmel at the north end of the Monterey Peninsula, you can stop imagining—you've found the place described. For years, Carmel has been just such a village, as well as a home to artists, poets, novelists, musicians, and freethinkers. It also attracts the affluent and the famous, as does the neighboring Pebble Beach.

There are four ways to get into the exclusive community of Pebble Beach, all of them guarded gateways where starched-and-pressed security personnel will charge you five bucks a car for the privilege—money well spent if you're interested in the scenic drive. In the vicinity of Carmel, the Highway 1 Gate is just north of town and west of the highway. To reach the Carmel Gate, take Ocean Avenue west from Highway 1; then go right on San Antonio. In Pacific Grove the Pacific Grove Gate and the Country Club Gate are off Sunset Drive.

If you're a guest at The Inn at Spanish Bay, or if you plan to dine, the gate fee is refunded. If you're planning to visit a Pebble Beach resident, have that person leave word at the gate so that you can enter free of charge.

Without the toll, no doubt the narrow and winding roadways of Pebble Beach would be congested, noisy, and littered, instead of as wonderfully enjoyable, quiet, and scenic as they are.

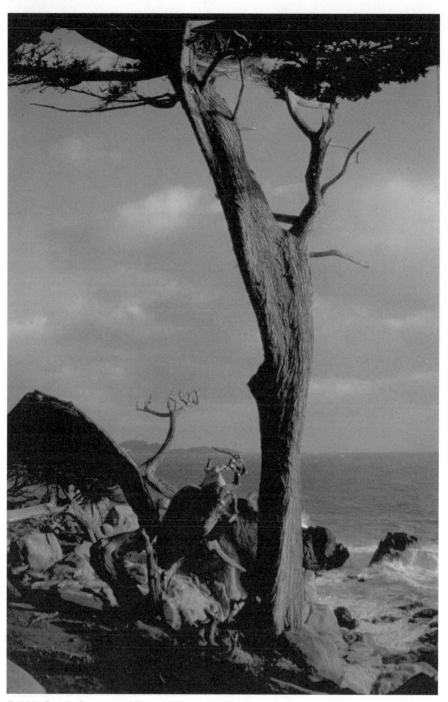

Pebble Beach *Courtesy of Robert Holmes/CalTour*

# Lodging

**Carmel River Inn,** P.O. Box 221609, Carmel 93922; (831) 624–1575 or (800) 882–8142; www.carmelriverinn.com. At the south end of Carmel on Highway 1 at the bridge. Twin, double, and king beds in 43 rooms, suites, and cottages with cable TV, some with fireplaces, some with kitchens. Perhaps the best lodging bargain in the Carmel area. Moderate to expensive.

**The Cobblestone Inn,** P.O. Box 3185, Carmel 93921; (831) 625–5222 or (800) 833–8836; www.cobblestoneinncarmel.com. At Eighth and Junipero Avenues, west of Highway 1 on Ocean Avenue, then north on Junipero. Cable TV in 24 rooms with private baths. Quilts, pillows, fireplaces, and antiques enhance the country comfort of the inn. Complimentary tea, sherry, wine, and hors d'oeuvres in the afternoon. Buffet breakfast served in the dining room each morning. Picnic lunches provided on request. Easy walk to village shops and restaurants. Moderate to expensive.

**Highlands Inn,** P.O. Box 1700, 120 Highlands Drive, Carmel 93923; (831) 620–1234 or (800) 233–1234; www.highlandsinn.hyatt.com. Just south of Carmel on Highway 1. "Understated elegance" perhaps best describes this California-style inn, with its ocean-view rooms, one-bedroom suites, town-house suites, and two-bedroom town-house suites. Fireplaces, decks, kitchens, and spa baths available. Heated pool and hot tubs. Wine tasting and afternoon tea. Cocktail lounge, superb restaurant, gift shop, and deli-cafe on premises. Valet parking, concierge service, and room service. Very expensive to extremely expensive.

**Hofsas House,** P.O. Box 1195, Carmel 93921; (831) 624–2745 or (800) 221–2548; www.hofsashouse.com. On San Carlos Street, near Fourth, west of Highway 1, via Ocean Avenue, only 2 blocks from village center. Queen and king beds in 38 individually decorated rooms and suites with cable TV, some with fireplaces, some with kitchens, some with balconies. Also available are two-bedroom, two-bath suites with wet bars. Walk to shops, galleries, and restaurants, and avoid Carmel's parking hassles. Heated pool and sauna. Moderate to expensive.

**Inn at Spanish Bay,** 2700 17-Mile Drive, Pebble Beach; (831) 647–7500 or (800) 654–9300; www.pebblebeach.com. West of Highway 1, between Carmel and Pacific Grove. A beautiful, full-service resort with 269 rooms and suites, offering fireplaces, sofas, chairs, four-posters, and marble baths. Most rooms with balconies or patios. Ocean-view rooms and suites. Three restaurants, twenty-four-hour room service, two cocktail lounges, eight tennis courts, eighteen-hole golf course and privileges at three others. Pool, spa, and beach access. Extremely expensive.

**Lamplighters Inn,** P.O. Box 604, Carmel 93921; (831) 624–7372; www.carmel lamplighter.com. West of Highway 1 on Ocean Avenue to Camino Real. Twin, queen, and king beds in 4 rooms, 2 cottages to accommodate 2 to 6 guests. Cable TV and fireplaces. Three blocks to the beach, easy walk to village shops. This is the most photographed inn in California. Moderate to expensive.

**Pine Inn,** P.O. Box 250, Carmel 93921; (831) 624–3851 or (800) 228–3851; www.pine-inn.com. West of Highway 1 on Ocean Avenue at Lincoln Street. Twin, double, queen, and king beds in 49 rooms in this beautiful, full-service, 1889 hotel decorated with period furnishings, artwork, and fabrics. Shops, boutiques, cocktail lounges, and restaurant on premises, fireplace in the library. Walk to other village attractions. Moderate to expensive.

## Campgrounds and RV Parks

**Carmel by the River RV Park,** 27680 Schulte Road, Carmel; (831) 624–9329; www .carmelrv.com. East of Highway 1, 4½ miles on Carmel Valley Road, then south 1 mile on Schulte Road. Has 35 sites on the Carmel River with full hookups and cable TV. Showers, barbecue area, and horseshoe pits. Pets allowed. Expensive.

## Food

**Anton & Michel Restaurant,** P.O. Box 4425, Carmel 93921; (831) 624–2406; www.carmelsbest.com. West of Highway 1, on Mission Street between Ocean and Seventh Avenues. Daily lunch and dinner, Sunday brunch. Appetizers include escargots in puffed pastry and homemade ravioli. Such dinner specialties as classic rack of lamb and shellfish paella. Extensive wine list and full bar. Expensive to very expensive.

**Flaherty's Seafood Grill and Oyster Bar,** P.O. Box 2265, Carmel 93921; (831) 625–1500 or 624–0311. West of Highway 1, on Sixth Avenue between San Carlos and Delores Streets. Lunch and dinner daily. Fresh seafood is the specialty here: oysters, scallops, clams, Maine lobster, Dungeness crab, and abalone. Superb soups and chowders. Shellfish kept alive in large saltwater tanks. Cocktails and imported and domestic beers and wines. Moderate.

**Rio Grill,** 101 Crossroads Boulevard, Carmel; (831) 625–5436; www.riogrill.com. Just east of Highway 1, via Crossroads Boulevard. Lunch and dinner daily. A local favorite with a creative menu. Start with a marinated and fire-roasted artichoke with sun-dried tomatoes, crisp-fried calamari with orange-sesame dipping sauce, smoked-salmon tostada, crisp rock-shrimp taco, or any of several other tempting appetizers. House-made soups and big, meal-size salads. Oak-grilled burgers and inventive deli-style sandwiches. Entrees include barbecued baby back ribs, herb-crusted chicken breast, smoked duck, grilled prawns on penne pasta, pumpkin seed–crusted salmon, and lamb shank with wild mushrooms braised in ale. Among the great desserts are caramel apple bread pudding, pecan brownies with chocolate sauce and vanilla cream, and the house-famous ice cream sandwich. Full bar. Moderate to expensive.

# Shopping and Browsing

**The Barnyard,** 3618 The Barnyard, Carmel; (831) 624–8886; www.thebarnyard.com. About ½ mile east of Highway 1, via Carmel Valley Road or Rio Road to Carmel Rancho Boulevard. Nothing here even faintly resembles the typically homogenized suburban mall. Instead, fifty-five shops and boutiques and ten restaurants are housed in pleasing buildings in the California-country style of architecture. Cobblestone walks meander amid colorful gardens. Among the shops are those specializing in men's and women's apparel, gifts, toys, jewelry, antiques, collectibles, and kitchenware.

**Carmel Plaza,** P.O. Box 4814, Carmel 93921; (831) 624–0137; www.carmelplaza.com. West of Highway 1, on Ocean Avenue between Junipero and Mission Streets. Monday through Sunday, 10:00 A.M. to 6:00 P.M. Restaurants and some stores open later. In the village of Carmel with courtyard, fountain, flowers, and more than fifty stores, shops, galleries, and restaurants. Shops include Banana Republic, Ann Taylor, Tiffany's, Chico's, and J.Jill.

**The Crossroads,** 159 Crossroads Boulevard, Carmel; (831) 625–4106; www.cross roadsshoppingvillage.com. East side of Highway 1 at Rio Road. Monday through Saturday, 10:00 A.M. to 6:00 P.M.; Sunday, noon to 5:00 P.M. Among the more than one hundred establishments in this English-style shopping village are eighteen restaurants and cafes and more than eighty boutiques and shops.

**Masterpiece Gallery,** P.O. Box 6477, Carmel 93921; (831) 624–2163; www.master piecegallerycarmel.com. West of Highway 1, on Delores Street at Sixth Avenue. Daily, 11:00 A.M. to 5:00 P.M. Closed on Saturday. A gallery featuring the works of a number of contemporary masters, as well as Californian and French Impressionists of the late nineteenth and early twentieth centuries. Paris street scenes, California and East Coast landscapes, and waterscapes.

# Beaches, Parks, Trails, and Waysides

The Point Lobos State Reserve is a 1,300-acre natural area west of Highway 1, 3 miles south of Carmel at Riley Ranch Road. *Lobo* is Spanish for "wolf"; however, it's not the wild canine that the point was named for but, rather, the abundant "sea wolves" or sea lions that haul out on nearby rocks. The name has been shortened from the original Spanish *Punta de los Lobos Marinos,* or "Point of the Sea Wolves."

Many consider the reserve to be the best of California's state parks. The rocky shoreline is intriguing and beautiful, and stands of Monterey pine and Monterey cypress add to its natural splendor. Hikers enjoy more than a dozen trails, and park rangers carefully limit the number of visitors to prevent crowding.

Off Point Lobos, 750 submerged acres have been designated the Point Lobos Ecological Reserve, where all marine life is protected. In fact, everything natural in the park is protected. So don't remove anything but litter. If something occurs naturally, leave it.

# events

| | |
|---|---|
| **March** | Carmel Kite Festival, (831) 620–2020 |
| **April** | Chateau Julien Wine & Art Festival, (831) 624–2600 |
| **May** | Robinson Jeffers Tor House Garden Party, Carmel, (831) 624–1813 |
| | Pebble Beach Spring Horse Show, (831) 624–2756 |
| | Carmel Art Festival, (831) 624–9035 |
| | Memorial Day Regatta, Pebble Beach, (831) 625–8507 |
| **June** | Art & Wine Festival at The Barnyard, Carmel, (831) 624–8886 |
| | Friday Concerts in the Park, Carmel, (831) 620–2020 |
| **July** | Carmel Bach Festival, (831) 624–2046 |
| **August** | Carmel Valley Fiesta, (831) 659–4502 or 659–4000 |
| | Carmel Shakespeare Festival, (831) 622–0700 |
| | Pebble Beach Concours D' Elegance, (831) 622–1700 |
| **September** | Labor Day Regatta, Pebble Beach, (831) 625–8507 |
| | Carmel Outdoor Art Festival, (831) 624–3996 |
| | Strides & Tides Horse Show, Pebble Beach, (831) 624–2756 |
| | Fiesta De San Carlos Borromeo, Carmel, (831) 624–1271 |

## events cont.

| | |
|---|---|
| **October** | Carmel Sand Castle Contest, (831) 620–2020 |
| | Robinson Jeffers Tor House Festival & Poetry Walk, Carmel, (831) 624–1813 |
| **November** | Pebble Beach Equestrian Championships, (831) 624–2756 |
| | Homecrafter's Marketplace, Carmel, (831) 620–2020 |
| | Carmel-by-the-Sea's Annual Tree Lighting, (831) 620–2020 |

Along the 6 miles of coastline in the reserve are many tidepools, rock formations, coves, and headlands to explore. There are picnic areas and places to observe the plentiful wildlife, which includes seabirds, harbor seals, sea lions, sea otters, and even occasional blue and minke whales.

Diving is permitted in the reserve, but only at Whalers and Bluefish coves. No more than ten pairs of divers per day are allowed in the reserve, and permits—available at the gate—are required.

The reserve is usually open from 9:00 A.M. to 5:00 P.M., but it often remains open later in the summer. Guides and maps are available as are docent-led tours.

Carmel River State Beach, west of Highway 1, off Scenic Road, is a favorite place for hiking and picnicking and a good area for watching and photographing birds. The Carmel Submarine Canyon, just offshore, creates some dangerous currents, however, so this is not a good swimming area.

Swimming and surfing conditions are better at Carmel City Beach, west of Highway 1 at the foot of Ocean Street. This is also a popular picnic spot.

Opportunities for hiking, picnicking, exploring tidepools, and photographing exciting coastal scenery and marine wildlife are around every bend of 17-Mile Drive at Pebble Beach. The gate guard who takes your toll will provide you with a map and guide to more than two dozen attractions and points of interest.

Binoculars and telephoto lenses come in handy along this route. Sea otters frequent the area and are easy to spot in the kelp beds. Seals and sea lions haul out on offshore rocks. Seabirds are plentiful on shore and off. And on cool mornings you are sure to see plenty of black-tailed deer.

# Golf

**The Links at Spanish Bay,** 2700 17-Mile Drive, P.O. Box 1418, Pebble Beach 93953; (831) 647–7495; www.pebblebeach.com. An eighteen-hole, par-seventy-two, 6,820-yard Scottish-style course with spectacular ocean views. Driving range, practice greens, pro shop, resident pro, clubhouse, club and cart rental, restaurants, and bar.

**Pebble Beach Golf Links,** P.O. Box 658, Pebble Beach 93953; (831) 622–8723 or (800) 654–9300; www.pebblebeach.com. At The Lodge on 17-Mile Drive, overlooking Carmel Bay and Pebble Beach. An eighteen-hole, par-seventy-two, 6,737-yard course open to the public. Driving range, practice greens, club and cart rental. Pro shop, resident pro, restaurants, and cocktail lounges.

**Peter Hay Par 3 Golf Course,** P.O. Box 658, Pebble Beach 93953; (831) 622–8723; www.pebblebeach.com. At The Lodge, on 17-Mile Drive, overlooking Carmel Bay and Pebble Beach. Public nine-hole, par-twenty-seven course. Driving range, practice greens, club and cart rental. Restaurants and cocktail lounges nearby.

**Rancho Canada Golf Club,** P.O. Box 22590, Carmel 93922; (831) 624–0111 or (800) 536–9459; www.carmel-golf.com. One mile east of Highway 1 on Carmel Valley Road. Two lovely public courses in the Carmel River Valley. East course, eighteen holes, par seventy-one, 6,109 yards; west course, eighteen holes, par seventy-two, 6,349 yards. Driving range, practice greens, club and cart rental. Huge pro shop, resident pro, restaurant, bar, and cocktail lounge.

**Spyglass Hill Golf Course,** P.O. Box 658, Pebble Beach 93953; (831) 625–8563; www.pebblebeach.com. On Spyglass Hill Road. A tough eighteen-hole, par-seventy-two, 6,862-yard course with driving range, practice greens, pro shop, resident pro, clubhouse, and equipment rental. Restaurant and bars nearby.

# Winery

**Chateau Julien Winery,** 8940 Carmel Valley Road, Carmel; (831) 624–2600; www.chateaujulien.com. In Carmel Valley, 5 miles east of Highway 1. Wine tasting, 8:30 A.M. to 5:00 P.M. Monday through Friday and 11:00 A.M. to 5:00 P.M. Saturday and Sunday; winery tours, 8:00 A.M. and 2:30 P.M. Monday through Friday; weekends 12:30 and 2:00 P.M. Tour the winery and sample the award-winning wines. T.G.I.F. tour limited to eight persons and includes wine tasting and evaluation.

# Other Attractions

**Carmel Mission,** 3080 Rio Road, P.O. Box 2235, Carmel 93921; (831) 624–1271; museum, (831) 624–3600; www.carmelmission.org. West of Highway 1 via Rio Road, south end of Carmel. Monday through Saturday, 9:30 A.M. to 4:30 P.M.; Sunday, 10:30 A.M. to 4:30 P.M. Founded in 1770 by Father Junípero Serra as the second California mission. After secularization in 1833, the mission fell into disrepair and languished for a century before being fully restored. Father Serra and Father Crespi are interred at the basilica.

**Tor House,** 26304 Ocean Avenue, P.O. Box 1887, Carmel 93921; (831) 624–1813; www.torhouse.org. West of Highway 1, on Carmel Point, Ocean View Avenue at Stewart Way. Friday and Saturday, 10:00 A.M. to 4:00 P.M. Home of poet Robinson Jeffers and his family. Docent-led tours of the Tor House, Hawk Tower, and Old World gardens limited to six persons per hour.

## Travel Information

**Carmel Chamber of Commerce,** San Carlos between Fifth and Sixth, P.O. Box 4444, Carmel 93921; (831) 624–2522 or (800) 550–4333; www.carmelcalifornia.org

**Point Lobos State Reserve,** Route 1, Box 62, Carmel 93923; (831) 624–4909; www.pt-lobos.parks.state.ca.us; e-mail: ptlobos@mbay.net

# Monterey / Pacific Grove

**Location:** Monterey is on California Highway 1, about 32 miles north of Big Sur, 99 miles north of San Simeon, and 95 miles south of Half Moon Bay; adjacent Pacific Grove is at the northwest tip of the Monterey Peninsula.

**Population:** Monterey 30,000; Pacific Grove 15,444

When the Spanish named the Big Sur River *El Rio Grande del Sur,* or "The Big River of the South," they meant south of Monterey, which was California's capital during its Spanish and Mexican periods. When the Mexicans gave up the Monterey Peninsula to the Americans in 1846, Monterey retained its importance as a political and cultural center. In fact, the California Constitutional Convention was held in 1849 at Colton Hall, which is now a Monterey museum. The following year, California became the thirty-first state.

Industries here have flourished and vanished, beginning with the brisk hide and tallow trade with English and Americans in the early 1800s. The first pier was built on the bay in 1846 to service trading vessels. In the 1850s it became part of a Portuguese whaling station. At the beginning of the twentieth century, a commercial fishery for Pacific sardines burgeoned and soon mushroomed as seining and canning technology improved. Annual landings of the tiny fish grew from a few thousand tons in the early 1900s to a quarter-million tons in the mid-1940s. Such harvests continued until the sardines "mysteriously disappeared" in 1951.

During the heyday of the sardine fishery, twenty-three canneries and nineteen reduction plants were strung along the shore of Monterey Bay. Known as Cannery Row and immortalized in the John Steinbeck novel of that title, the area deteriorated after the sardine fishery collapsed, but it was revived and refurbished in the 1970s. It's now a major tourist attraction, with seven hotels and inns; ten candy and pastry shops; four wine-tasting rooms; nine clubs, pubs, and watering holes; twenty-eight restaurants, delis, and pizzerias; more than sixty-five stores, shops, and galleries; and such attractions as the Steinbeck Museum and the Monterey Bay Aquarium.

Near downtown and just a few blocks southeast of Cannery Row is the famed Fisherman's Wharf, crowded with browsers, shoppers, diners, sightseers, and anglers. Among the gift shops and galleries are fish markets, delis, and restaurants selling all sorts of seafood. This is also where the sportfishing fleet is moored. Those who aren't interested in angling but who would like to explore the bay can board one of the vessels offering sightseeing and whale-watching excursions.

The natural beauty of the bay and peninsula led to the development of tourism in the late nineteenth century. Tourism is now Monterey's leading industry, and the city has an abundance of superior accommodations and superb restaurants to serve its many visitors—something for everyone's budget and appetite.

Next door is Monterey's sister city, Pacific Grove—a late bloomer, but charming nonetheless. Founded in 1875 as a Methodist retreat, it stayed straitlaced for nearly a century, prohibiting the sale of alcohol within city limits, except for medicinal purposes, until 1969.

Reminders of Pacific Grove's Victorian past are everywhere, including more than 250 houses built before 1910. A number of these handsome structures are now bed-and-breakfast inns.

Tourists aren't the only ones drawn regularly to the pleasant climate and tranquility of Pacific Grove. Monarch butterflies begin arriving in October and overwinter in the groves of Monterey cypress, Monterey pine, and eucalyptus trees.

Pacific Grove is easy to reach from Highway 1 by taking the State Route 68 exit west, or by driving through Monterey past Cannery Row. From Carmel and Pebble Beach, 17-Mile Drive also leads to Pacific Grove.

# Lodging

**The Gosby House Inn,** 643 Lighthouse Avenue, Pacific Grove; (831) 375–1287 or (800) 527–8828; www.gosbyhouseinn.com. West of Highway 1 via Route 68 and Forest Avenue to Lighthouse Avenue, then left 3 blocks. Built as a private dwelling in 1887 but began accommodating guests in 1894. The beautiful Queen Anne has 22 rooms, some with fireplaces, most with private baths. Hors d'oeuvres and fresh fruits served with sherry or tea each afternoon. Breakfast served in the parlor. Near golf courses, bay, and other peninsula attractions. Moderate to expensive.

**Lighthouse Lodge and Suites,** 1150 Lighthouse Avenue, Pacific Grove; (831) 655–2111 or (800) 858–1249; www.lhls.com. Three miles west of Monterey. Queen and king beds in 64-room lodge and one- and two-bedroom suites, all with cable TV and some with fireplaces, ocean views, kitchenettes, wet bars, and microwaves. Heated pool, hot tub in suites, complimentary afternoon wine and cheese in lodge, free barbecue buffet dinner, and complimentary continental breakfast. Three blocks to the ocean. Moderate to extremely expensive.

**Monterey Bay Inn,** 242 Cannery Row, Monterey; (831) 373–6242; in California, (800) 424–6242; elsewhere, (800) 225–2902; www.montereybayinn.com. West of Highway 1, between downtown Monterey and Pacific Grove, on Cannery Row. King beds in 47 rooms and 3 suites, all with sleeper sofas, private balconies, snack bars, refrigerators, and remote-control cable TV. Suites also have desks and easy chairs. Whirlpool, sauna, and health club. Special facilities for divers include outside showers and gear lockers. Walk to shops, restaurants, and aquarium. Expensive to very expensive.

**Monterey Plaza Hotel,** 400 Cannery Row, Monterey; (831) 646–1700 or (800) 334–3999; www.montereyplazahotel.com. West of Highway 1 and downtown, on the bay. Twin, sofa-queen, and king beds in 290 rooms and 20 suites, many with bay views, most with patios or balconies. Ristorante Delfino, on premises, serves breakfast, lunch, and dinner. Delfino Lounge overlooks the bay. Walk to shops and aquarium. Moderate to very expensive.

**Sand Dollar Inn,** 755 Abrego Street, Monterey; (831) 372–7551 or (800) 982–1986; www.sanddollarinn.com. West of Highway 1 via Munras Avenue, which becomes Abrego Street. Queen and king beds in 63 rooms and suites with remote-control cable TV, some with fireplaces, some with wet bars, and some with private balconies. Two-bedroom suites also have minirefrigerators. Heated pool, exercise room, and whirlpool. Inexpensive to moderate.

**Seven Gables Inn,** 555 Ocean View Boulevard, Pacific Grove; (831) 372–4341; www.pginns.com. West of Highway 1 via Route 68 and Forest Avenue to Ocean View, then right 2 blocks. Queen beds in 14 rooms in a beautiful Victorian bed-and-breakfast inn on the edge of Monterey Bay. Each room has a private bath and ocean view. Furnished with fine antiques. Afternoon wine and hors d'oeuvres, full breakfast each morning. Expensive to very expensive.

**Victorian Inn,** 487 Foam Street, Monterey; (831) 373–8000 or (800) 232–4141; www.victorianinn.com. West of Highway 1, 2 blocks from Cannery Row, between Hoffman and McClellan. Remote-control cable TV, cable movies, and fireplaces in 68 rooms with private patios or balconies, some with ocean view. Each bathroom with second phone and shower massage. Hot tub. Afternoon wine and cheese, continental breakfast. Moderate to expensive.

## Campgrounds and RV Parks

**Laguna Seca Recreation Area,** Monterey County Parks, 1025 Monterey Road, P.O. Box 5279, Salinas 93915; (831) 755–4899 or (888) 588–2267; www.co.monterey.ca.us. Eight miles east of Highway 1 via Route 68 (Salinas exit). Has 102 developed campsites. Water and electrical hookups available. Tent sites available; sites are in the hills among the oaks. Showers and tank dump. Expensive.

# Food

**Bubba Gump Shrimp Company Restaurant & Market,** 720 Cannery Row, Monterey; (831) 373–1884; www.bubbagump.com. West of downtown Monterey. Lunch and dinner daily. From the appetizer menu, choose from peel-and-eat shrimp, garlic-bread basket, hush pups, calamari fritti, among others. New England clam chowder, Caesar salad, or shrimp salad. Among the sandwiches are burgers, fish, barbecued pork, and grilled chicken. Shrimp specialties include fried, barbecued, with coconut, steamed in beer, in bourbon sauce, scampi, or in dipping sauce with French bread. Try such entrees as fish-and-chips, mahimahi, baby back ribs, salmon, ribeye steak, and veggie plate. Full bar. Moderate.

**Bullwacker's Restaurant and Pub,** 653 Cannery Row, Monterey; (831) 373–1353; www.canneryrow.com. Breakfast, lunch, and dinner daily. A casual English-style eatery and watering hole that serves omelets, burgers, steaks, seafood, fish-and-chips, pasta dishes, sandwiches, and vegetarian dishes. Full bar. Moderate.

**Chart House,** 444 Cannery Row, Monterey; (831) 372–3362; www.chart-house.com. West of downtown Monterey. Dinner daily. For starters, choose from more than a half-dozen appetizers, such as coconut shrimp or seared peppered ahi tuna. Try the New England clam chowder or house-signature Caesar salad. House seafood specialties include sesame-crusted salmon, mahimahi, Alaskan king crab legs, and fresh fish of the day. From the grill come such entrees as filet mignon with cracked black-peppercorn crust and New York strip. For dessert, try the chocolate lava cake. Full bar. Moderate.

**Sardine Factory,** 701 Wave Street, Monterey; (831) 373–3775; www.sardinefactory .com. Dinner daily in the elegant surroundings of four dining areas and the cocktail lounge. Generous and tasty appetizers include whole Dungeness crab with vinaigrette dressing or mustard sauce, baked abalone and oysters Rockefeller, seared sea scallops, smoked king salmon and sardines, Gulf prawns with chili salsa, steamed clams or mussels, and escargot. Sensational soups include the house-famous abalone bisque or such offerings as lobster bisque, forest mushroom soup, or artichoke bisque. Try the house Caesar salad or Carmel Valley tomato salad. In addition to vegetarian, chicken, veal, beef, and pork entrees are such seafood specialties as abalone steak, grilled Monterey sanddabs, bay prawns, king salmon, and Cannery Row cioppino. Catch of the day might include sea bass, halibut, or tuna. Wine list features more than 1,000 domestic and imported selections. Full bar. Expensive to very expensive.

# Shopping and Browsing

Both Monterey and Pacific Grove have stores, shops, and galleries scattered throughout downtown areas and concentrated in plazas, malls, and shopping centers, as well as in such places as Cannery Row and Fisherman's Wharf. And if that's not enough, a short drive will put you in Carmel, where shopping and browsing were invented.

**American Tin Cannery Premium Outlets,** 125 Ocean View Boulevard #110, Pacific Grove; (831) 372–1442. West of Highway 1 via Route 68 and Forest Avenue, then right on Ocean View Boulevard, or west through Monterey, 1 block past the Monterey Bay Aquarium. More than a half-dozen restaurants and more than fifty stores, boutiques, and specialty shops. Among the shops are those specializing in clothing, jewelry, kitchenware, crystal, china, gifts, and decorating items.

# Museums and Aquarium

**Maritime Museum of Monterey,** 5 Custom House Plaza, Monterey; (831) 372–2608. Downtown Monterey, near Fisherman's Wharf. Open every day except Wednesday from 10:00 A.M. to 5:00 P.M. A large collection of navigational instruments, ship models, scrimshaw, paintings, and nautical hardware and memorabilia.

**Monterey Bay Aquarium,** 886 Cannery Row, Monterey; (831) 648–4888; www .montereybayaquarium.org. Northwest of downtown, at Cannery Row. Daily, except Christmas, 9:30 A.M. to 6:00 P.M. More than 6,000 specimens representing nearly 600 species of sea creatures inhabit the tanks at this spectacular $50-million aquarium. Dazzling undersea and above-sea, indoor and outdoor exhibits—nearly one hundred in all. Deep-sea, tidepool, seashore, marsh, and creek exhibits. The Kelp Forest exhibit is an amazing tank three stories high, containing 335,000 gallons of seawater. The Monterey Bay Habitats exhibit is 90 feet long and inhabited by sharks, rays, salmon, and other species. Elsewhere are marine mammals, birds, shellfish, and touch pools. Feeding times are posted and provide exciting shows. Also on the premises are a Cannery Museum, a Marine Mammal Gallery with life-size models of whales and porpoises, a gift shop, and restaurant. Classified *must see.*

**Monterey State Historic Park,** 20 Custom House Plaza, Monterey; (831) 649–7118; www.parks.ca.gov. Downtown, near Fisherman's Wharf. Daily, 10:00 A.M. to 4:00 P.M. Ten historic adobe buildings and museum displays. Maps available at park headquarters next to the Custom House. Custom House, Pacific House, and Cooper Store open most days; others open for guided tours at various times. Check at park headquarters for schedule.

**Pacific Grove Museum of Natural History,** 165 Forest Avenue, Pacific Grove; (831) 648–5716; www.pgmuseum.org. West of Highway 1 via Route 68 and Forest Avenue to Central Avenue. Tuesday through Saturday, 10:00 A.M. to 5:00 P.M. Considered the best of its size in the United States. Collection includes more than 400 mounted bird specimens from Monterey County, as well as an interpretive display devoted to monarch butterflies. Traveling exhibits also on display.

**Steinbeck's Spirit of Monterey Wax Museum,** 700 Cannery Row, Monterey; (831)

375–3770; www.wax-museum.com. On the bay, northwest of downtown. Open 10:30 A.M. to 7:00 or 8:00 P.M.; extended summer hours. More than one hundred life-size and lifelike wax figures in various scenes representing 400 years of California history. Also depictions of Steinbeck's *Cannery Row* scenes and characters.

# Beaches, Parks, Trails, and Waysides

A string of sandy beaches extends northeasterly from the vicinity of Monterey's Municipal Wharf. There's swimming at Monterey Beach Park, next to the wharf, but at Monterey State Beach, off Del Monte via Park Avenue, the currents and surf are dangerous. West of the Municipal Wharf, Fisherman's Shoreline Park, between Fisherman's Wharf and the Coast Guard Pier, is a pleasant park offering a sidewalk, bike path, and benches as well as a good place for waterfront photography. There are usually pelicans, harbor seals, and sea lions in the area.

The city of Pacific Grove owns the shoreline within the city limits, so the coast along the bay and ocean is just one park after another, with plenty of space to hike, explore tide-pools, watch sunsets, and photograph the spectacular scenery.

From Point Cabrillo northwest to Point Pinos, Shoreline, Berwick, Lover's Point, and Perkins parks are on the bay, along the bluffs beside Ocean View Boulevard. Bike paths and hiking trails course through patches of ice plants, which bloom from April through August, adding great swatches of magenta to the already-stunning seascape.

At the tip of the Monterey Peninsula lies the Point Pinos Lighthouse Reservation. The attractive lighthouse, built in 1855, is now the oldest operating light station on the West Coast. The reservation is open to the public from 1:00 to 4:00 P.M. on weekends.

Near Point Pinos, Ocean View Boulevard becomes Sunset Drive, a fitting name for a road flanking the Pacific shoreline. Here Asilomar State Beach offers dunes and tide-pools to explore and sandy beaches to hike. Although this is a popular diving area, swimmers should look elsewhere, as the area is subject to dangerous riptides.

# Water Sports and Activities

Monterey Bay and nearby waters attract scuba divers from afar and offer excellent diving opportunities. There are dive shops in the area and charter operators catering to divers' needs. The beach on the northwest side of the Coast Guard Pier in Monterey is a popular staging area for divers.

Although fishermen ply the surf east of the Municipal Wharf, most of the fishing on Monterey Bay is from private, party, and charter boats. Anglers towing boats will find launching facilities near the Coast Guard Pier. Party and charter boats are at Fisherman's Wharf.

**Aquarius Dive Shop,** 2040 Del Monte Avenue, Monterey; (831) 375–1933; www.aquariusdivers.com. Weekdays 9:00 A.M. to 6:00 P.M.; weekends 7:00 A.M. to 6:00 P.M.

Fully equipped dive shop. Equipment sales, service, and rentals. Professional instruction, guided tours, dive packages, videotaped dives.

**Monterey Bay Kayaks,** 693 Del Monte Avenue, Monterey; (831) 373–5357 or (800) 649–5357; www.montereybaykayaks.com. West of Highway 1, in town. Sea-kayak rentals, instructions, and tours. Clinics and classes on such topics as basic skills, the Eskimo roll, kayaking in the surf zone, and rough-water rescues. Tours of Monterey Bay, Carmel Bay, Elkhorn Slough, and Big Sur. Also sunset tours.

**Randy's Fishing Trips,** 66 Fisherman's Wharf #1, Monterey; (831) 372–7440 or (800) 251–7440; www.randysfishingtrips.com. Four boats running deep-sea fishing trips for salmon and albacore. Party trips and private charters. Bait furnished. Tackle, licenses, sack lunches, and fish cleaning available.

# Rentals

**Adventures by the Sea,** 299 Cannery Row, Monterey; (831) 372–1807 or (831) 648–7236; www.adventuresbythesea.com. Northwest of downtown. Daily 9:00 A.M. to sunset. Rents mountain bikes, beach cruisers, four-wheel surreys, and kayaks by the hour, half-day, day, and longer. Free delivery and pickup.

**Monterey Moped Adventures,** 1250 Del Monte Avenue, Monterey; (831) 373–2696. West of Highway 1, Del Monte Avenue at Sloat Avenue. Rents single- and double-seat mopeds with baskets. Provides free lessons and tour maps.

# Travel Information

**Monterey County Convention and Visitors Bureau,** 150 Oliver Street, Monterey; (831) 649–1770 or (888) 221–1010; www.montereyinfo.com

**Monterey Peninsula Chamber of Commerce,** 380 Alvarado Street, P.O. Box 1770, Monterey 93940; (831) 648–5360; www.mpcc.com; e-mail: info@mpcc.com

**Pacific Grove Chamber of Commerce,** Forest and Central Avenues, P.O. Box 167, Pacific Grove 93950; (831) 373–3304 or (800) 656–6650; www.pacificgrove.org

# events

| | |
|---|---|
| **January** | Annual Great Taste of Pacific Grove, (831) 642–4943 |
| **February** | Indian Arts and Crafts Show, (650) 856–6622 |
| **April** | Dixieland Monterey, (888) 349–6879 |
| | Monterey Wine Festival, (831) 649–6690 |
| | Wildflower Show, Pacific Grove, (831) 648–5716 |
| | Good Old Days Celebration, Pacific Grove, (831) 373–3304 |
| **May** | Block Party on Cannery Row, (831) 644–9399 |
| **June** | Monterey Blues Festival, (831) 394–2652 |
| **July** | Fourth of July Celebration and Fireworks, (831) 646–3427 |
| | Feast of the Lanterns, (831) 649–8737 |
| **August** | Monterey Historic Automobile Races, (800) 327–7322 or (831) 647–6355 |
| **September** | Triathlon at Pacific Grove, (831) 373–0678 |
| | Monterey Jazz Festival, (831) 373–3366 |
| | Gem and Mineral Show, Monterey, (831) 659–4156 |
| **October** | Butterfly Parade, Pacific Grove, (831) 373–3304 |
| **December** | Christmas at the Inns, Pacific Grove, (831) 373–3304 |

Northern
California

# Northern California

Goose Lake

395

OREGON
CALIFORNIA

SIERRA NEVADA

Lassen
Volcanic
National
Park

36

CASCADE RANGE

Mount
Shasta

Redding

5

5

KLAMATH MOUNTAINS

299

36

COAST RANGES

199

Smith River

Jedediah Smith
Redwoods State Park
Del Norte Coast
Redwoods State Park

Point St. George
Crescent City

Prairie Creek Redwoods
State Park

Redwood
National
Park

Patricks Point
State Park

Trinidad

Arcata

Eureka

Fortuna

Ferndale

Cape Mendocino

101

Pepperwood

Redcrest

Weott

Humboldt Redwoods
State Park

Myers Flat

Miranda

Phillipsville

Garberville

Richardson Grove
State Park

Leggett

Shelter Cove

Sinkyone Wilderness
State Park

1

MacKerricher
State Park

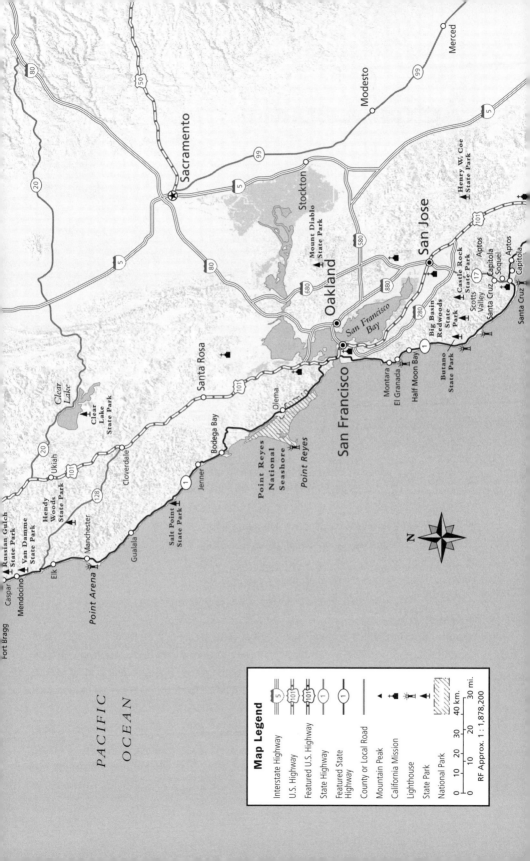

PACIFIC OCEAN

Fort Bragg
Caspar
Mendocino
Elk
Gualala
Manchester
Point Arena
Russian Gulch State Park
Van Damme State Park
Hendy Woods State Park
Salt Point State Park
Jenner
Bodega Bay
Cloverdale
Ukiah
Clear Lake
Clear Lake State Park
Point Reyes National Seashore
Point Reyes
Olema

Santa Rosa

Sacramento
Stockton
Mount Diablo State Park
Oakland
San Francisco Bay
San Francisco

San Jose
Henry W. Coe State Park
Aptos
Aptos
Capitola
Capitola
Soquel
Santa Cruz
Santa Cruz
Scotts Valley
Castle Rock State Park
Big Basin Redwoods State Park
Butano State Park
Montara
El Granada
Half Moon Bay

Modesto
Merced
Stockton

80
50
20
5
99
5
80
680
580
880
280
101
128
1
17

**Map Legend**

Interstate Highway
U.S. Highway
Featured U.S. Highway
State Highway
Featured State Highway
County or Local Road
Mountain Peak
California Mission
Lighthouse
State Park
National Park

RF Approx. 1 : 1,878,200

0   10   20   30   40 km.
0   10   20   30 mi.

N

# Aptos / Capitola

**Location:** Aptos lies along California Highway 1, 33 miles north of Monterey and 4 miles southeast of Capitola; Capitola, just seaward of Highway 1, is 4 miles east of Santa Cruz.

**Population:** Aptos 27,000; Capitola 10,800

At the northern end of the great crescent of Monterey Bay, the Pacific shoreline sweeps westerly, taking Highway 1 with it. Here beaches and surf lie south of the highway, with inland farms and mountains to the north.

Aptos—said to be a Spanish corruption of the Indian word *awotos,* meaning "meeting of the streams"—is the name of an unincorporated village that serves chiefly as a bedroom community for Santa Cruz. With its interesting restaurants, fine bed-and-breakfast inns, and nearby beaches and parks, it's also a pleasant stopover for travelers and destination for vacationers.

Capitola, founded in 1869 by lumber baron Frederick A. Hihn, is purportedly California's oldest seaside resort. By all appearances, it's also the birthplace of the adjective *charming.* It's the kind of clean and perfect little village normally found only in model-railroad layouts.

Compact Capitola is made for walking, so park your vehicle and enjoy strolling along the Esplanade or investigating the many shops and galleries. You can take a sailboat trip or rent a skiff at the Capitola Wharf, or you can swim at any of the sandy beaches that stretch from here east and south along Monterey Bay.

## Lodging

**Apple Lane Inn,** 6265 Soquel Drive, Aptos; (831) 475–6868 or (800) 649–8988. Just north of Highway 1. Five guest rooms with double and queen beds in a lovely restored Victorian farmhouse with private and shared baths. Many antiques and period furnishings and fixtures. Afternoon sherry and full breakfast served in the parlor. Moderate to expensive.

**Best Western Seacliff Inn,** 7500 Old Dominion Court, Aptos; (831) 688–7300 or (800) 367–2003; www.seacliffinn.com. Off Highway 1 via Seacliff Beach exit. Has 149 large, comfortably appointed rooms and suites with extra-long double and king beds and cable TV. Each suite has two bathrooms and an extra-large whirlpool spa. Heated pool, whirlpool, fitness center, and putting green. Severino's Restaurant on premises. Cocktail lounge with live entertainment and dancing on weekends. Moderate to expensive.

**Mangels House,** 570 Aptos Creek Road, P.O. Box 302, Aptos 95003; (831) 688–7982 or (800) 320–7401. North of Highway 1, off Soquel Drive. Six guest rooms, one with a marble fireplace, in the historic Mangels house, built in the 1880s and meticulously restored. Private and shared baths. Complimentary afternoon sherry and full breakfast. Beautiful wooded setting. Expensive.

**Rio Sands Motel,** 116 Aptos Beach Drive, Aptos; (831) 688–3207 or (800) 826–2077; www.riosands.com. South of Highway 1 via Rio del Mar exit and Rio del Mar Boulevard, then right 1 block on Stephen Road. Queen and king beds or waterbeds in 52 rooms and suites, each with patio or deck, cable TV, and coffeemaker. Heated pool, hot tub, continental breakfast, and barbecue area. Two blocks to the beach. Moderate.

## Campgrounds and RV Parks

**New Brighton State Beach,** 1500 Park Avenue, Capitola; (831) 464–6330 or (800) 444–7275; www.parks.ca.gov. South of Highway 1, between Aptos and Capitola, via the Park Avenue exit, on a bluff overlooking Monterey Bay. Has 112 campsites with tables and fire pits, but no hookups. Showers and firewood available. Beach access. Moderate.

**Santa Cruz KOA Kampground,** 1186 San Andreas Road, Watsonville; (831) 722–0551 or 722–2377 or (800) 562–7701; www.santacruzkoa.com. South of Aptos off Highway 1 at Larken Valley Road, then 3 miles south on San Andreas Road. Has 230 full-hookup sites and 21 tent sites. Showers, laundry, tank dump, heated pool, and whirlpools. Store with RV supplies, propane, ice, and gasoline. Video games, basketball, volleyball, and horseshoes. One mile to Manresa State Beach. Moderate to expensive.

**Seacliff State Beach,** State Park Drive, Aptos; (831) 429–2850 or (800) 444–7275; www.parks.ca.gov. South of Highway 1 via Seacliff exit. Has 26 premium, full-hookup campsites right on the beach, with tables and fire pits. Showers, easy beach access, nearby fishing pier, snack bar, and bait shop. Expensive.

**Sunset State Beach,** 201 Sunset Beach Road, Watsonville; (831) 763–7062 or (800) 444–7275; www.parks.ca.gov. Between Aptos and Watsonville via San Andreas Road. Has 90 campsites with tables and fire pits, but no hookups. En route campsites also available. Showers, access to dunes and beach, summer campfire programs. Moderate.

# Food

**Cafe Rio,** 131 Esplanade, Rio del Mar, Aptos; (831) 688–8917. South of Highway 1 via Rio del Mar Boulevard. Dinner daily; oyster bar and cocktails from 3:00 P.M. daily. Enjoy cocktails with oysters on the half-shell, shrimp or crab cocktail, smoked salmon, steamed mussels or clams, and fresh artichoke or calamari appetizer. Dinners include grilled sanddabs, charbroiled swordfish, broiled or poached salmon, sautéed scallops, broiled halibut, Alaskan king crab, grilled trout, steak, chicken, and rack of lamb. Full bar. Moderate.

**Cafe Sparrow,** 8042 Soquel Drive, Aptos; (831) 688–6238; www.cafesparrow.com. East of Highway 1, between Rio Del Mar Boulevard and State Park Drive. Breakfast, lunch, and dinner daily; Sunday brunch. Hearty breakfast offerings include traditional egg dishes, scrambles, and omelets, as well as flapjacks and Sparrow French Toast: cinnamon-raisin bread in spiced batter and topped with toasted almonds. Appetizers and salads include chicken-liver pâté made with herbs and cognac, roasted garlic with melted Brie and croutons, cockles steamed in seasoned white wine and served with drawn butter, pan-fried oysters with lemon-caper crème, goat cheese salad with toast points, and classic Caesar salad for two. French-influenced entrees include vegetarian pasta, stir-fry, ragout, and omelet, as well as chicken breast, rack of lamb, sautéed chicken livers, calamari picatta, and several renditions of filet mignon, cut from Angus beef. House-made desserts include crème caramel, apricot-walnut cake, chocolate truffle cake, warm bread pudding with lemon cream, and pecan-brownie sundae with caramel sauce. Beer and wine. Moderate.

**Shadowbrook Restaurant,** 1750 Wharf Road, Capitola; (831) 475–1222 or (800) 975–1511; www.shadowbrook-capitola.com. South of Highway 1, Wharf Road at Capitola Road, on Soquel Creek. Daily dinner and weekend brunch. A local favorite since 1947. Appetizers include grilled artichokes, calamari strips, and baked Brie. Dinners offer choice of artichoke soup, soup of the day, or salad, plus homemade breads and such entrees as scampì, scallops, rack of lamb, veal, steaks, teriyaki brochette of beef, and breast of chicken. Chef's specials served nightly. Full bar, excellent wine list, live entertainment, and dancing. Moderate to expensive.

# Shopping and Browsing

Agriculture is one of the major contributors to the economy of Santa Cruz County. In addition to all the quaint seaside shops and galleries in the vicinity are many roadside stands and farm stores where you can buy the freshest produce and other farm products at unbelievably low prices—imagine, a buck a bag for artichokes. Whether you're stocking a refrigerator, ice chest, or picnic basket, you'll have plenty of opportunities to buy great locally grown products. Boutiques, antiques shops, stores, and art galleries are scattered here and there, between and in Aptos and Capitola.

**The Craft Gallery,** 126 San Jose Avenue, Capitola; (831) 475–4466 or (800) 331–4467; www.craftgallery.net. San Jose Avenue at Capitola Avenue. Daily, 10:00 A.M. to 7:00 P.M. A large selection of handcrafted gift items and souvenirs. Jewelry, jewelry boxes, pottery, stained glass, T-shirts, leather goods, and cards.

**Sally Bookman Gallery,** 109 Capitola Avenue, Capitola; (831) 464–3838. Featuring many local artists, the gallery is open daily 10:30 A.M. to 5:00 P.M.

## Beaches, Parks, Trails, and Waysides

From the Santa Cruz County line at the Pajaro River north to Capitola are several long and broad sandy beaches with good public access. Some offer excellent beachcombing, while others are good for swimming, exploring tidepools, or hiking.

San Andreas Road runs roughly parallel to Highway 1 but nearer the beach, and leads to other roads with beach access. Use San Andreas Road to reach Palm Beach (via Beach Road), Sunset State Beach (via Sunset Beach Road), and Manresa State Beach.

Rio del Mar Boulevard and State Park Road, respectively, lead to Rio del Mar Beach and Seacliff State Beach. Between Aptos and Capitola, take the Park Avenue exit to New Brighton State Beach. Park Avenue also leads to Monterey Avenue and the Esplanade at Capitola. The popular City Beach is adjacent.

The Forest of Nisene Marks State Park lies 4 miles north of Soquel Drive, via Aptos Creek Road. Within its boundaries are 10,000 acres of mostly second-growth timber, unpaved roads, picnic areas, and about 30 miles of trails. It's managed as a semiwilderness area and is among Central California's largest state parks.

## Water Sports and Activities

Several species of clams reside along the surf of Monterey Bay, from Sunset State Beach to Seacliff State Beach. Manresa State Beach is the most popular spot to dig for pismo clams, and Seacliff Beach is the northern limit for this clam's range. The season for pismo clams runs from September through April.

These are also good surf-fishing beaches, where anglers take a variety of species, including surfperch, flounder, and the occasional shark. The larger creeks entering the bay support runs of coho salmon and steelhead trout.

The old supply ship *Palo Alto* is scuttled at the end of the pier at Seacliff State Beach, providing habitat for a great assortment of fish, including surfperch, seaperch, halibut, flounder, sole, and white croaker. Offshore, anglers take the same species, as well as salmon, sea bass, and several species of shark.

The Capitola Wharf is another popular place to fish and is a good place to launch a boat or rent one. Anglers are allowed to drive onto the pier to launch and haul out boats and load or unload gear and catch, but they are limited to a twenty-minute stay. Parking is available nearby.

## events

| | |
|---|---|
| **February** | Village Sidewalk Sale, Capitola, (831) 475–6522 |
| **April** | Easter Egg Hunt at Capitola Beach, (831) 475–6522 |
| **May** | Capitola Kite Classic, (831) 475–6522 |
| | Santa Cruz Blues Festival, Aptos, (831) 479–9814 |
| **June** | Festival at the Cement Ship, Aptos, (831) 685–4444 |
| **July** | Wharf to Wharf Race, Capitola, (831) 475–2196 |
| **August** | Fine Art Festival, Soquel, (831) 475–2258 |
| **September** | Capitola Begonia Festival, (831) 475–6522 |
| | Sand Castle Contest, Capitola, (831) 475–6522 |
| | Fishing Derby, Capitola, (831) 475–6522 |
| | Rowboat Races, Capitola, (831) 475–6522 |
| | Capitola Art and Wine Festival, (831) 475–6522 |
| **October** | Village Halloween Parade, Capitola, (831) 475–6522 |

**Capitola Boat & Bait,** 1400 Wharf Road, Capitola; (831) 462–2208. At the end of Capitola Wharf. Open daily at sunrise. Rents 16-foot wooden skiffs with 8-horsepower outboards. Boat-launching facilities. Bait, tackle, licenses, equipment rental, reef maps, food, snacks, ice, and beverages. A good source of information about local fishing and weather and water conditions.

# Golf

**Aptos Seascape Golf Course,** 610 Clubhouse Drive, Aptos; (831) 688–3213; restaurant, (831) 688–3254. South of Highway 1 via Rio del Mar Boulevard. An eighteen-hole, par-seventy-two course with driving range, pro shop, equipment rentals, and resident pro. Restaurant on premises.

# Winery

**Bargetto Winery,** 3535 North Main, Soquel; (831) 475–2258 or (800) 422–7438; www.bargetto.com. Northeast of Highway 1. Tasting, noon to 5:00 P.M. daily. Largest winery in the area, established in 1933. Both fruit and varietal wines. White wines include chardonnay, Riesling, and gewürztraminer. Pinot noir and cabernet sauvignon are red-wine specialties. Tours available.

# Travel Information

**Aptos Chamber of Commerce,** Redwood Village, 7605–A Old Dominion Court, Aptos; (831) 688–1467; www.aptoschamber.com

**Capitola Chamber of Commerce,** 716–G Capitola Avenue, Capitola; (831) 475–6522; www.capitolachamber.com; e-mail: capinfo@capitolachamber.com

# Santa Cruz

**Location:** On California Highway 1, at the junctures of State Routes 9 and 17, about 70 miles south of San Francisco, 42 miles south of Half Moon Bay, and about 43 miles north of Monterey.

**Population:** 54,262

Santa Cruz has been attracting vacationers and weekend visitors to its rough-hewn coastline, intriguing pocket beaches, and moderate climate since its early days of bayside camps and bathhouses. By the late nineteenth century, it was widely known and highly regarded as a resort community, a reputation it has enjoyed through the twentieth century.

Not even the mighty rumblings of the San Andreas Fault have been able to shake the city's appeal or cause tourism to waver. The same earthquake that tumbled buildings and brought down bridges and freeways in San Francisco on October 17, 1989, caused extensive damage to downtown Santa Cruz, but it left most outlying areas and shoreline attractions and neighborhoods relatively unscathed, or at least reparable.

Santa Cruzans proceeded carefully and thoughtfully with reconstruction of the city's core, where most of the damage occurred. Now, many new shops, boutiques, galleries, and cafes have renewed downtown Santa Cruz's charm and appeal.

Most of the area's natural attractions are along the shore of Monterey Bay and in the forests and foothills of the Santa Cruz Mountains. There are plenty of opportunities for outdoor recreation, many restaurants offering a wide range of cuisines, and a variety of fine accommodations—from graceful old Victorian bed-and-breakfast inns to modern, full-service resorts. The atmosphere is casual and relaxed, and the people are friendly and helpful.

## Lodging

**The Babbling Brook Inn,** 1025 Laurel Street; (831) 427–2437 or (800) 866–1131; www.innsbythesea.com. Two blocks south of Highway 1 on Laurel, between California and Walti Streets. Queen and king beds and fireplaces in 13 guest rooms in this secluded inn with French country decor. Set amid lush gardens with trees, creek, and waterfalls. Most rooms have whirlpool baths. Some have decks, some open-beam ceilings, all private baths. Full breakfast; afternoon wine and cheese and teas. Expensive.

**Best Western Inn,** 126 Plymouth Street; (831) 425–4717 or (800) 528–1234; www .bestwestern.com. South of Highway 1 via Ocean Avenue exit. Queen and king beds in 26 rooms and suites with cable TV and coffeemakers. Suites have whirlpool baths and wet bars. Sauna. Moderate to expensive.

**Chateau Victorian,** 118 First Street; (831) 458–9458; www.chateauvictorian.com. South of Highway 1 via Bay Street, then left on West Cliff. One block north of Beach Street, near the boardwalk. Queen beds in 7 rooms with private baths and fireplaces. Complimentary beverages with cheese and crackers each afternoon, continental breakfast each morning. Easy walk to beach, boardwalk, wharf, shops, and restaurants. Moderate to expensive.

**The Inn at Pasatiempo,** 555 Highway 17; (831) 423–5000 or (800) 834–2546; www .innatpasatiempo.com. North of Highway 1. Cable TV, armoires, quilts, and open-beam ceilings in 54 rooms and suites. Suites have canopy beds, French doors, VCRs, and stocked refrigerators. Pool and whirlpool. Adjacent golf course. Peachwood's Grill & Bar on premises. Room service. Moderate to very expensive.

## Campgrounds and RV Parks

**Big Basin Redwoods State Park,** 21600 Big Basin Way, Boulder Creek; (831) 338–8860 or (800) 444–7275; www.bigbasin.org; horse-camp reservations, (831) 425–1218. Located 23 miles northeast of Santa Cruz via State Route 9 off Highway 1. Has 147 developed campsites with tables, fire pits, and food lockers. Showers. Six trail camps for backpackers. Horse-trail camp just east of Highway 1, near Waddell Beach. Hiking trails. Moderate.

**Henry Cowell Redwoods State Park Campground,** 101 North Big Trees Park Road, P.O. Box 53, Felton 95018, (831) 438–2396 or (800) 444–7275; www.parks.ca.gov. The park is 3 miles north of Santa Cruz via State Route 9. From park headquarters, drive north to Felton, then right on Graham Hill Road to the campground. Has 113 developed campsites with tables and stoves to accommodate RVs to 36 feet. Piped water near all sites, showers, and laundry tubs. Trails for hiking and horseback riding. Moderate.

## Food

**The Crow's Nest Restaurant,** 2218 East Cliff Drive; (831) 476–4560; www.crows nest-santacruz.com. South of Highway 1, at the small-craft harbor, with a great view of Monterey Bay. Lunch and dinner daily. Luncheon appetizers include chilled artichokes, ahi, and spring rolls. Luncheon entrees feature crab Louis, enchiladas, seafood thermidor, burgers, steak sandwich, and crab-salad sandwich. Dinner entrees include broiled lobster tail, tempura prawns, and scallop and prawn fettucine. At the oyster bar and lounge, choose from more than a dozen offerings, such as oys-

ter shooters, shrimp cocktail, stuffed artichokes, stuffed potato skins, and fried calamari. Full bar. Great outdoor deck overlooking the ocean. Live entertainment nightly.
Inexpensive to moderate.

**Peachwood's Steakhouse,** 555 Highway 17; (831) 426–6333; www.peach
woods.com. North of Highway 1, at the Inn at Pasatiempo. Lunch and dinner daily.
Enjoy such appetizers as crisp-fried artichoke hearts with tarragon mayonnaise,
coconut prawns, or grilled *passilla* peppers filled with Jack cheese. Try the soup of the
day or the black bean and smoked sirloin soup with sour cream and salsa. Meal-size
salads, big burgers, deli-style sandwiches, and deep-fried catfish. Entrees include
chicken, smoked pork tenderloin, baby back ribs, steaks, prime rib, rack of lamb, and
rotisserie duckling, all roasted over peachwood for a mildly smoky flavor. Full bar.
Moderate to expensive.

## Shopping and Browsing

Downtown Santa Cruz is a shopper's delight, where travelers will want to park and stroll
along its clean, tree-lined streets and visit the handsome buildings where the city's businesses flourish. All manner of shops and boutiques, specialty stores and art galleries,
restaurants and cafes invite visitors to pause, linger, and enjoy the casual hospitality that
characterizes this gem of the central California coast.

Spring, summer, and fall, merchants join for seasonal sidewalk sales; in winter they
conduct their annual clearance sale. All year long, the Downtown Association sponsors
the Antique and Collectibles Faire, from 9:00 A.M. to 4:00 P.M. on the second Sunday of
every month.

## Beaches, Parks, Trails, and Waysides

Highway 1 veers inland as it approaches Santa Cruz, and in the center of town it trans-
forms from freeway to city street. Head for the bay to avoid midday and rush-hour con-
gestion.

East Cliff Drive and West Cliff Drive cling to the coastal bluffs and provide many sce-
nic overlooks and access to beaches, tidepools, and other seaside attractions. From
Capitola, take Cliff Drive west from the village. Travelers arriving from the south via
Highway 1 can take Forty-first Avenue to East Cliff Drive. Those arriving from the north
should turn right on Mission Street, then right on Natural Bridges Drive, left on Delaware
Avenue, and right on Swanton Boulevard to West Cliff Drive. Bay Street also meets West
Cliff, near the Santa Cruz Beach and Boardwalk. It's possible to travel along the coast all
the way from Capitola to Natural Bridges State Beach, at the opposite end of Santa Cruz.

Mile-long Santa Cruz Main Beach is probably the area's most popular, especially with
swimmers. It's in the heart of the city's bayside recreation area, with the municipal wharf
at one end and the boardwalk flanking it.

Santa Cruz Surfing Museum *Courtesy of Robert Holmes/CalTour*

About a mile west of the Santa Cruz Municipal Wharf is Point Santa Cruz and Lighthouse Field State Beach. The cliffs here overlook a popular surfing area known as Steamer Lane. This is also a good spot for watching whales and sea lions.

The Mark Abbott Memorial Lighthouse stands atop a cliff, with parking nearby. It functions as the Santa Cruz Surfing Museum and is open to the public every day but Tuesday, from noon to 4:00 P.M.

Westward, sheer cliffs are interrupted by pocket beaches, the largest of which is Natural Bridges State Beach. Although it was named after the naturally eroded sandstone bridges in the area, all but one have collapsed. The park is better known now for a eucalyptus grove that is the largest monarch-butterfly wintering area in the nation. A ¾-mile nature trail leads through the grove.

At Henry Crowell Redwoods State Park, north of Santa Cruz on State Route 9, are 4,000 acres of forest containing Douglas fir, madrone, tanbark oak, coast redwoods, and ponderosa pine. In addition to picnic areas and river bottoms are 15 miles of trails for hikers and equestrians.

Big Basin Redwoods State Park, 23 miles northeast of Santa Cruz via Highways 1 and 9, was established in 1902 and is the oldest in the California system. The 14,000-acre park sprawls from the Santa Cruz Mountains to the coast and has more than 100 miles of hiking and riding trails through the coast redwoods.

# Water Sports and Activities

Because of its east-west orientation, the coastline of the Santa Cruz area is ideal for surfing. Pleasure Point Beach—along East Cliff Drive, in Live Oak, between Forty-first and Thirty-second Avenues—is a popular surfing area. Steamer Lane, between Point Santa Cruz and the municipal wharf, is one of the best surfing spots on the California coast.

Several of the larger creeks in the Santa Cruz vicinity support runs of coho salmon and steelhead trout during the fall and winter. The San Lorenzo River gets the biggest runs of any stream south of San Francisco Bay. Fishing is best on the upper river. Some favorite spots are within Henry Cowell Redwoods State Park, north of town, via State Route 9.

Virtually any place that provides parking and beach access offers surf- or rock-fishing opportunities for a variety of species, including surfperch, flounder, and rockfish. The east jetty at the entrance to the small-craft harbor is a good fishing area, reached by way of Twin Lakes State Beach, Seventh Avenue at East Cliff Drive.

The Santa Cruz Municipal Wharf attracts anglers who take bonito, croaker, flounder, halibut, lingcod, and shark. Crabbing is also good here at times.

Charter- and party-boat operators work from the wharf and from the Santa Cruz Small Craft Harbor, Eaton Street at Lake Avenue. For those towing boats, the harbor provides launching facilities, as well as marine service, supplies, and repairs.

**Aqua Safari Scuba Center,** 6896 Soquel Avenue, Santa Cruz; (831) 479–4386; www.aquasafaris.com. Rents and sells scuba equipment and offers dive tours, boat charters, diving classes, and kayak rentals.

**Pacific Yachting & Sailing,** 790 Mariner Park Way, Santa Cruz; (831) 423–7245 or (800) 374–2626; www.pacificsail.com. At the Santa Cruz Yacht Harbor. Sailing lessons available: basic, intermediate, and advanced sailing; seamanship; cruising; navigation and piloting; and other courses and instructional vacations, all taught aboard modern 25- to 43-foot yachts.

**Shamrock Charters, Inc.,** Fisherman's Supply, 2210 East Cliff Drive, Santa Cruz; (831) 476–2648; www.scurfslanding.com. At the Santa Cruz Yacht Harbor. Charter fishing trips for salmon, lingcod, and rockfish. Whale-watching trips in season. Full line of tackle, bait, and fuel available at the tackle shop. Ocean skiffs for rent.

# Tours and Trips

**Santa Cruz, Big Trees & Pacific Railway Company,** P.O. Box G–1, Felton 95018; (831) 335–4484; www.roaringcamp.com. Board at Santa Cruz Beach Boardwalk or at Felton, north of Highway 1 via State Route 9. Steam and diesel locomotives pull trains of vintage passenger and open observation cars between Felton and the Santa Cruz Beach Boardwalk. Round-trips take about two hours, not counting layovers. (One-way trip available as well.) Roaring Camp & Big Trees Narrow-Gauge Railroad provides passenger service from Felton on trains pulled by early twentieth-century steam locomotives up the steepest narrow-gauge grades in North America into forests of great coastal redwoods. The round-trip takes about an hour and a quarter.

# Golf

**Pasatiempo Golf Club,** 18 Clubhouse Road, P.O. Box 535, 95061; (831) 459–9155; www.pasatiempo.com. A half-mile north of Santa Cruz on State Route 17. An eighteen-hole, par-seventy-one, 6,600-yard course in the hills above Santa Cruz. Ranked in the top one hundred courses in America. Driving range, putting greens, pro shop, equipment rentals, golf lessons, restaurant, and bar.

# Wineries

**Bonny Doon Vineyard,** 10 Pine Flat Road, P.O. Box 8376, 95061; (831) 425–3625 or (831) 425–4518; www.bonnydoonvineyard.com. North of Highway 1, west of Santa Cruz. Tasting, 11:00 A.M. to 5:00 P.M. daily. Among the wines produced are chardonnay, grenache, and muscat canelli.

**David Bruce Winery,** 21439 Bear Creek Road, Los Gatos; (408) 354–4214 or (800) 397–9972; www.davidbrucewinery.com. North off Highway 1 on State Route 9, then east on Bear Creek Road. Tasting, noon to 5:00 P.M. daily. Specializes in cabernet sauvignon, Pinot noir, and chardonnay. Picnic area.

**Hallcrest Vineyards,** 379 Felton-Empire Road, Felton; (831) 335–4441; www.hallcrestvineyards.com. Northwest of Santa Cruz via State Route 9. Tasting, noon to 5:00 P.M. daily. Specialties include cabernet sauvignon, chardonnay, and Riesling.

# Other Attractions

**Santa Cruz Beach Boardwalk,** 400 Beach Street; (831) 423–5590; www.beachboardwalk.com. South of Highway 1 via Bay Street, or follow signs to Santa Cruz Beach. Boardwalk opens 11:00 A.M. daily from Memorial Day through Labor Day; open weekends the rest of the year. Casino Arcade is open daily, except Thanksgiving and Christmas. In operation since 1907, now California's only oceanside amusement park, situated on the beautiful, mile-long Santa Cruz Beach. More than twenty major rides, including a famous carousel and Big Dipper roller coaster, which are National Historic Landmarks. Facilities at adjacent Coconut Grove accommodate many events, including trade shows, concerts, Sunday brunch, and big-band dances. Plenty of places to eat, and gift shops galore.

# Travel Information

**Downtown Association of Santa Cruz,** 1347 Pacific Avenue, Suite 201, P.O. Box 1384, 95061; (831) 429–8433; www.downtownsantacruz.com; e-mail: info@shop santacruz.com

**Santa Cruz County Conference and Visitors Council,** 1211 Ocean Street; (831) 425–1234 or (800) 833–3494; www.santacruzca.org

# events

For information about any of the events listed below, or to learn about events recently added to the Santa Cruz calender, write or call the Santa Cruz County Conference and Visitors Council, or visit the Downtown Association's Web site (see above).

| | |
|---|---|
| **February** | Clam Chowder Cookoff |
| **April** | Ducky Derby at Harvey West Park |
| **May** | Great Salsa Taste-off at the Wharf |
| | Celebrate Santa Cruz: Art, Wine, and Jazz Festival |
| | Santa Cruz Longboard Club Invitational at Steamers Lane |
| **June** | Woodies on the Wharf |
| **July** | Shakespeare Santa Cruz |
| **August** | Shakespeare Santa Cruz continues |
| | Cabrillo Music Festival |
| | Aloha Outrigger Races and Polynesian Festival |
| **September** | Shark Festival & Sanctuary Celebration |
| **October** | Santa Cruz Fireworks Spectacular |
| **November** | Community Tree Lighting |
| **December** | Downtown Holiday Parade |

# Half Moon Bay

**Location:** On California Highway 1 at the juncture of Route 92, 42 miles north of Santa Cruz, 95 miles north of Monterey, and 28 miles south of San Francisco.

**Population:** 12,143

Half Moon Bay is the social and economic hub of a collection of small towns and villages clustered along the Pacific and known locally as Coastside. The surrounding marine terraces, creek bottoms, and rolling foothills were inhabited for centuries by Costanoan Indians. Spanish immigrants settled the area in the 1840s, followed by Mexican and Chilean laborers, which accounts for Half Moon Bay's earlier name: Spanishtown.

The first American settlers came after the war with Mexico ended in 1848. During the latter half of the nineteenth century, the area flourished as more immigrants arrived. Rail was laid from San Francisco to just beyond Half Moon Bay, sparking a boom that died with the failure of the railroad, a lingering demise that took from 1906 to 1920.

The Volstead Act of 1919 and consequent Eighteenth Amendment to the U.S. Constitution brought Prohibition to the nation and another boom to the shores of Half Moon Bay. Numerous pocket beaches and coves made ideal landings for the rumrunners. Bordellos and roadhouses served locals and travelers alike, while bootleggers sped nightly along winding coastal and mountain roads, hauling their precious cargo to the San Francisco Bay Area. When Prohibition was revoked in 1933, Half Moon Bay had to settle in and await the next boom.

Rich agricultural lands flank the coast, and the climate is ideal for growing a variety of crops, such as artichokes, brussels sprouts, peas, pumpkins, kiwifruit, and berries. Agriculture is a major contributor to the area economy, with a countywide annual harvest running to $206 million.

Pillar Point Harbor is west of Highway 1, about 4 miles north of Half Moon Bay. In addition to slips and facilities for recreational boaters and anglers, the harbor is also home to a commercial-fishing fleet of more than 200 vessels. The commercial catch includes white croaker, sanddab, several species of sole, rockfish, halibut, salmon, swordfish, Dungeness crab, and red abalone and amounts to more than five million pounds a year.

Today, Half Moon Bay's boom is largely in the form of tourism. Across the county, annual revenues from travel and tourism are approaching $700 million. Many of those dollars are spent along this stretch of the coast, where fine restaurants, superb accommodations, sandy beaches, and other attractions await the traveler.

# Lodging

**Cypress Inn,** 407 Mirada Road, Miramar Beach; (650) 726–6002 or (800) 832–3224. West of Highway 1 via Medio or Magellan, between Half Moon Bay and Pillar Point Harbor. Contemporary bed-and-breakfast inn with 18 rooms, each individually decorated and each with private bath, fireplace, private whirlpool spa, and private deck with ocean view. On the beach. Afternoon wine and hors d'oeuvres. Full gourmet breakfast. Expensive to very expensive.

**Harbor View Inn,** 51 Avenue Alhambra, P.O. Box 127, El Granada 94018; (650) 726–2329 or (800) 886–6997; www.harbor-view-inn.com. Just east of Highway 1, 4 miles north of Half Moon Bay. Double and queen beds in 17 rooms, each with cable TV and a bay-window seat overlooking the harbor and ocean. Complimentary continental breakfast. Comfortable, tastefully decorated rooms at reasonable rates. Inexpensive to moderate.

**Mill Rose Inn,** 615 Mill Street; (650) 726–8750 or (800) 900–7673; www.mill roseinn.com. West of Main Street, south of Half Moon Bay Road (Route 92), and east of Highway 1. Country English elegance at an exquisitely appointed bed-and-breakfast inn with 6 flower-filled rooms and suites, each with private bath, private entrance, fireplace, view of lovely gardens, phones, cable TV, coffeemaker, and well-stocked refrigerator. Queen and king beds. Whirlpool spa. Full champagne breakfast delivered to guests' rooms or served in dining room. Expensive to very expensive.

**Old Thyme Inn,** 779 Main Street; (650) 726–1616 or (800) 720–4277; www.old thymeinn.com. In town. A Victorian house built in 1898, fully restored, with 7 guest rooms, all with private baths. Garden suite has private entrance, whirlpool tub, refrigerator, skylight, some fireplaces, TV, VCR, videotapes, and complimentary beverages. Double and queen beds. Complimentary wine and sherry. Full breakfast. Seasonal rates. Moderate to very expensive.

**The Pillar Point Inn,** 380 Capistrano Road, P.O. Box 388, Princeton-By-The-Sea 94018; (650) 728–7377 or (800) 400–8281; www.pillar-point.com. Four miles north of Half Moon Bay, just west of Highway 1. A bed-and-breakfast inn overlooking the harbor, with 11 rooms, each with private bath, fireplace, featherbed, TV, VCR, and refrigerator. Some have private steam baths. Ocean and harbor views from all rooms. Complimentary afternoon tea. Breakfast served in guests' rooms or in breakfast room. Next to Shore Bird Restaurant. Walk to harbor. Moderate to expensive.

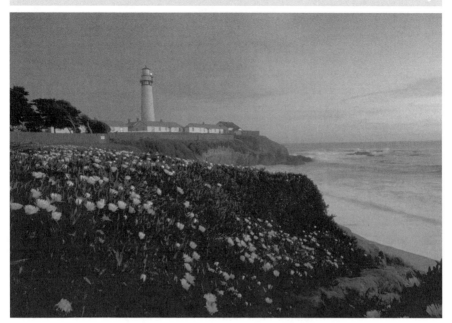

Pigeon Point Half Moon Bay *Courtesy of Robert Holmes/CalTour*

## Campgrounds and RV Parks

**Butano State Park,** P.O. Box 9, Pescadero 94060; (650) 879–2040 or (800) 444–7275; www.parks.ca.gov. Three miles east of Highway 1, 5 miles south of Pescadero on Cloverdale Road, south off Pescadero Road or north off Gazos Creek Road. A 2,200-acre park in the redwoods with 18 drive-in and 21 walk-in campsites. Hiking trails. Summer nature walks and campfire programs. Inexpensive.

**Francis Beach Campground,** Half Moon Bay State Beach, 95 Kelly Avenue; (650) 726–8819 or (800) 444–7275; www.parks.ca.gov. At the foot of Kelly Avenue, west of Highway 1 about ¼ mile south of Route 92. Has 52 campsites near the beach for tents and RVs. Tables, showers, and beach access.

**Pelican Point RV Park,** 1001 Miramontes Point Road, P.O. Box 65, 94019; (650) 726–9100. A tree-shaded and grassy park overlooking the ocean, with 75 full-hookup sites and 19 tent sites. Tables, cable TV, showers, laundry, tank dump, and beach access. Store and gift shop. Ice and propane available. Expensive.

## Food

**The Miramar Beach Restaurant & Bar,** 131 Mirada Road; (650) 726–9053; www .miramarbeach.com. Just west of Highway 1, at Magellan Avenue and Mirada Road, on the beach. A delightful restaurant with a spectacular ocean view and checkered past, the Miramar was designed and built during Prohibition to function as a roadhouse and speakeasy. Daily lunch and dinner; Sunday champagne brunch. Start with

Dungeness crab cakes, Bonzai oysters, buffalo-style prawns, Castroville artichoke, prawn cocktail, or calamari picante. Try the soup du jour or the creamy seafood chowder, made with crab, shrimp, clams, and a dollop of sherry. Meal-size salads include a seafood Caesar, blackened chicken Caesar, and seafood Louis. Lunch offerings include pasta dishes, fish-and-chips, burgers, and such specialty sandwiches as the Miramar crab melt on toasted sourdough bread or blackened salmon on a sourdough roll. Among the dinner entrees are steaks, rack of lamb, chicken piccata, Coquille St. Jacques, salmon en croute, and more than a half-dozen pasta dishes. Beer, wine, and cocktails. Piano lounge. Moderate.

**Moss Beach Distillery,** 140 Beach Way, Moss Beach; (650) 728–5595; www.moss beachdistillery.com. North of Half Moon Bay, at Beach Way and Ocean Street, west of Highway 1. Lunch and dinner daily; Sunday brunch. Fresh seafood is done to perfection and served within view of the ocean. Also prime rib, rack of lamb, hardwood-smoked ribs and chicken. Oyster bar and salad bar. Moderate.

**Spanishtown Mexican Restaurant & Market,** 515 Church Street; (650) 726–7357. East of Highway 1, west of Main Street, south of Half Moon Bay Road (Route 92). Lunch and dinner daily. Home-style Mexican food. Tacos, enchiladas, burritos, flautas, chimichangas, *chiles rellenos,* fajitas, and more. Combination plates for lunch and dinner. Mexican-style seafood. Inexpensive to moderate.

## Shopping and Browsing

The various communities that make up the Coastside area have a variety of shops and galleries. Half Moon Bay's historic downtown area is a pleasant place to stroll, browse, and shop. But another kind of shopping opportunity awaits travelers to this area—a number of produce stands and "you-pick" farms where you can buy the freshest fruits and vegetables at the lowest prices. Stop by and stock your ice chest or refrigerator, or just pick up some fresh produce for your next hike or picnic or to munch on as you head down the road.

**G. Berta's,** Half Moon Bay Road; (650) 726–4922. One mile east of Half Moon Bay on Route 92. Summer, 9:00 A.M. to 6:30 P.M. daily; winter, 10:00 A.M. to 5:00 P.M. daily. Produce stand offering a variety of fruits and vegetables in season, such as peas, green beans, beets, lettuce, carrots, broccoli, cauliflower, leeks, escarole, endive, artichokes, and pumpkins.

**Farmer's Daughter,** El Granada; (650) 728–8660. On Highway 1, between El Granada and Moss Beach, 5 miles north of Half Moon Bay. Friday, Saturday, and Sunday, 10:00 A.M. until dark; daily during pumpkin season. Weekend produce stand offering fresh, locally grown peas, corn, potatoes, chard, brussels sprouts, artichokes, fruits, pistachio nuts, pumpkins, and honey.

**Phipps Ranch,** 2700 Pescadero Road, Pescadero; (650) 879–0787. South of Half Moon Bay, east of Highway 1, just past Stage Road. Summer, 10:00 A.M. to 7:00 P.M. daily; winter, 10:00 A.M. to 6:00 P.M. daily. Roadside market and nursery with fresh fruits and vegetables available all year; large selection of dried beans, fresh herbs, dried herbs, herbal vinegars, and potpourri. Pick your own berries in summer.

**Tom & Pete's Produce and Half Moon Bay Fish Market,** Highway 1; (650) 726–2561. Highway 1 at Route 92. Daily, 9:00 A.M. to 7:00 P.M. Indoor vegetable and fruit stand and adjacent seafood market offering fresh fish and shellfish, including lobsters and crabs, live or cooked.

# Beaches, Parks, Trails, and Waysides

At the extreme southern end of San Mateo County, west of Highway 1, lies Ano Nuevo Point, the site of a 1,500-acre state reserve known for its abundant wildlife. This is an excellent spot for watching and photographing migratory birds in the spring and fall. Gray whales pass near the point in January and March. And from December through April, huge elephant seals come ashore to give birth and breed, during which time the reserve near the rookery is open only to guided tours, for which reservations are necessary. Information, (650) 879–0227; reservations, (650) 393–6914.

Pigeon Point Lighthouse stands 115 feet tall atop a 35-foot cliff, 18½ miles south of Half Moon Bay. The light began operating in 1872 and is the second tallest lighthouse on the West Coast. Its beacon, automated in 1972, is visible 20 miles out. The lighthouse is open every Sunday for tours at 10:00 and 11:15 A.M., and at 12:30, 1:45, and 3:00 P.M. Saturday tours given summer only, starting in June.

Pescadero Marsh Natural Preserve lies east of Highway 1 off the north side of Pescadero Road and is the largest coastal marsh between San Francisco Bay and Monterey Bay. An interpretive trail along Highway 1 and dirt levees off Pescadero Road offer opportunities for watching and photographing the plentiful bird life.

Half Moon Bay State Beach—encompassing Francis, Venice, and Dunes Beaches—is west of Highway 1 at Half Moon Bay. Francis Beach is at the foot of Kelly Avenue. Venice Boulevard leads west off Highway 1 to Venice Beach. Dunes Beach is at the foot of Young Avenue, west off Highway 1. Hiking, kite flying, horseback riding, and picnicking are among the possible activities.

Point Montara Lighthouse, about 2 miles north of Pillar Point Harbor, is not open for public tours, but the picturesque point with its immaculately kept buildings offers an excellent spot for photography and good seaward views. Although a fog station was established here in 1875, the current lighthouse wasn't built until 1928.

## Water Sports and Activities

Miramar Beach, at the foot of Magellan Avenue, west off Highway 1, is a popular surfing area, as are two places farther north. Broad, sandy El Granada Beach runs along Highway 1 near Pillar Point Harbor; surfers like the area near the east breakwater. North of Point Montara Lighthouse, surfing is good at ½-mile-long Montara Beach.

Surf and rock fishing is often good along the coast here, with surfperch, white croaker, starry flounder, and rockfish the species most often taken. South of Half Moon Bay, both Pomponio and San Gregorio state beaches are good spots. Martin's Beach, 6 miles south of Half Moon Bay, is a private beach where a nominal fee is charged. There's good surf fishing here and smelt netting. Rental nets are available.

Half Moon and El Granada state beaches are other favorite surf-fishing areas. The east breakwater at El Granada Beach is a good rock-fishing spot.

Pillar Point Harbor provides boat-launching facilities and other services for anglers. Anglers take rockfish, starry flounder, and other species at Johnson Pier, which is open twenty-four hours a day. Party and charter boats are also moored at the harbor.

**Huck Finn Sportfishing,** (mailing address) 1016 Bancroft Avenue; (650) 726–7133 or (800) 572–2934; www.huckfinnsportfishing.com. At Pillar Point Harbor, 4 miles north of Half Moon Bay, west of Highway 1 via Capistrano Road. Check in, 5:15 A.M.; departure, 6:15 A.M.; returns between 2:30 and 3:00 P.M. Open-party and charter trips for salmon and rockfish. Also whale-watching trips in season. Bait, tackle, and rental gear available.

## Bike Rentals

**The Bicyclery,** 101B Main Street; (650) 726–6000. In town. Monday through Friday, 9:30 A.M. to 6:30 P.M.; Saturday, 10:00 A.M. to 5:00 P.M.; Sunday, 11:00 A.M. to 5:00 P.M. Rents mountain and touring bikes.

## Golf

**Half Moon Bay Golf Links,** 2 Miramontes Point Road; (650) 726–4438; www.halfmoon baygolf.com. Located off Highway 1, 3 miles south of Route 92. Beautiful eighteen-hole course designed by Arnold Palmer. Pro shop, equipment sales and rentals, restaurant, and bar.

## Winery

**Obester Winery,** 12341 San Mateo Road, Route 1, Box 2–Q, 94019; (650) 726–9463; www.obesterwinery.com. Two miles east of Half Moon Bay on Route 92. Tastings daily, 10:00 A.M. to 5:00 P.M. Tasting room in the rolling hills east of Highway 1. Grapes grown in Mendocino County are made into award-winning wines here. Specialties are chardonnay, Riesling, and sauvignon blanc.

# Other Attractions

**Sea Horse and Friendly Acres Horse Ranches,** P.O. Box 279, 94019; (650) 726–2362 or 726–9903; www.horserentals.com. On Highway 1, 1 mile north of Half Moon Bay. Daily, 8:00 A.M. to dark. More than 200 horses and ponies. Ride the beaches and trails on your own or in a guided group.

# Travel Information

**Half Moon Bay Coastside Chamber of Commerce,** 520 Kelly Avenue; (650) 726–8380; www.coastsidelive.com

## events

| April | Pacific Coast Dream Machines, Half Moon Bay Airport, (650) 726–2328 |
|---|---|
| May | Pescadero Chamarita Festival, (650) 726–5701 |
| June | Half Moon Bay Chamarita Festival, (650) 726–2729 |
| July | Old Fashioned Fourth of July Parade, Half Moon Bay, (650) 726–7969 |
| | Tours de Fleurs, Coastside, (650) 726–8380 |
| August | Pescadero Arts and Fun Festival, (650) 879–0848 |
| October | The Great Pumpkin Weigh-off, Half Moon Bay, (650) 726–9652 |
| | Half Moon Bay Art & Pumpkin Festival, (650) 726–9652 |
| December | Christmas Tree Lighting, Half Moon Bay, (650) 726–8380 |
| | Harbor Lights Ceremony, Pillar Point Harbor, (650) 726–5723 |

# Bodega Bay / Point Arena

**Location:** Bodega Bay is on California Highway 1, about 60 miles north of San Francisco and about 23 miles west of U.S. Highway 101 at Santa Rosa; Point Arena, also on California Highway 1, lies 63 miles north of Bodega Bay and 35 miles south of Mendocino.

**Population:** Bodega Bay 1,423; Point Arena 478

---

North of San Francisco Bay along the coast is another California, this one characterized by environmental diversity, a sparse and far-flung population, the absence of freeway noise, and a pace dictated by a tortuous Highway 1. The area from northwestern Marin County, just south of Bodega Bay, to southwestern Mendocino County, in the vicinity of Point Arena, is one of the least developed regions in the state.

The main geologic feature here is the San Andreas Fault, and evidence of upheaval abounds. The famous fault zone begins in south-central California and extends northwesterly from the Salton Sea for about 650 miles, then swings westerly into the ocean near Shelter Cove. The fault lies parallel to and near the coast from south of Bodega Bay northward. Just south of Fort Ross, the fault swings offshore, where the ancient landslide mass has created cliffs that drop 1,000 sheer feet to the surf.

The broad marine terraces and rolling pastureland near Bodega Bay begin to narrow north of the Russian River, with the rocky coastline becoming a series of steep cliffs and tiny pocket beaches. Many sea stacks, offshore rocks, and islets add drama to the seascape and provide havens and rookeries for countless seabirds, seals, and sea lions.

Natural features more than compensate for the lack of man-made attractions along this expanse of fractured coastline, but they also retard the pace of travel. With all its curves, switchbacks, and changes in elevation, Highway 1 allows an average speed of only about 30 miles per hour. So relax and enjoy it.

## Lodging

**Blackthorne Inn,** 266 Vallejo Avenue, P.O. Box 712, Inverness 94937; (415) 663–8621; www.blackthorneinn.com. Located in Inverness Park, 2 miles south of Inverness, off Sir Francis Drake Boulevard, near Point Reyes National Seashore. A bed-and-breakfast inn offering queen beds in 5 guest rooms with balconies. Private and shared baths, huge sundeck, hot tub. Unusual architecture in an interesting inn built of redwood, cedar, and Douglas fir. Full buffet-style breakfast. Very expensive.

**Bodega Bay Lodge & Spa,** 103 Coast Highway 1; (707) 875–3525 or (800) 368–2468; www.bodegabaylodge.com. At the south end of Bodega Bay. King and queen beds in 84 well-appointed rooms and 6 luxurious suites. All rooms have cable TV with on-command movie systems, private balconies or terraces with views, fireplaces, wet bars, stocked refrigerators, and large tile baths. Each suite is 565 square feet and features a comfortably furnished living area with fireplace, king bed with down comforter, two televisions, four telephones, entertainment center, CD stereo, wet bar, refrigerator, whirlpool tub for two, vaulted ceilings, custom lighting and chandeliers, private view terrace, and more. Beach and bay views, ocean-view pool, full-service spa, nightly complimentary wine hour, and guest library. Restaurant on premises. Specials and package deals available. Expensive to very expensive.

**The Inn at the Tides,** 800 Coast Highway, P.O. Box 640, Bodega Bay 94923; (707) 875–2669 or (800) 541–7788; www.innatthetides.com. On Highway 1, overlooking the harbor. Twin, queen, and king beds in 86 spacious rooms with remote-control cable TV, refrigerators, and coffeemakers. Robes and daily newspapers provided. Complimentary continental breakfast. Heated indoor/outdoor pool, whirlpool, sauna, fireplaces, and bay view. Lounge on premises. Tides Restaurant serves breakfast, lunch, and dinner. Gourmet dining at the Bay View Room. Package plans available. Expensive.

**Jenner Inn and Cottages,** Box 69, Jenner 95450; (707) 865–2377 or (800) 732–2377; www.jennerinn.com. On Highway 1, 11 miles north of Bodega Bay. Double, queen, and king beds in 16 guest rooms, 4 suites, and 4 cottages with private baths. Kitchens available. River and ocean views, private decks, hot tubs, and private entrances. Furnished with wicker and antiques. No television, some phones, kitchens. Restaurant on premises. Wholesome extended continental breakfast. Expensive.

**Point Reyes Seashore Lodge,** 10021 Coast Highway 1, P.O. Box 39, Olema 94950; (415) 663–9000; www.pointreyesseashore.com. At Olema, about 33 miles south of Bodega Bay. Has 21 rooms, some with fireplaces, most with whirlpool tubs, all with private baths. Three suites also have wet bars, refrigerators, and bedroom lofts with European featherbeds. Continental breakfast. Moderate to expensive.

# Campgrounds and RV Parks

**Bodega Dunes Campground,** Sonoma Coast State Beach, Bodega Bay; (707) 875–3483 or (800) 444–7275; www.parks.ca.gov. Off Highway 1, about ½-mile north of Bodega Bay. Has 99 developed campsites with tables and fire pits. Showers, tank dump, dunes and beach access, and a 5-mile trail system for hikers and equestrians. More than 10 miles of beach in this 5,000-acre park. Moderate.

**Doran County Park,** Doran Beach Road, P.O. Box 372, Bodega Bay 94923; (707) 875–3540; www.sonoma-county.org/parks. West of Highway 1 at the south end of town. Has 138 campsites with tables and fire pits, but no hookups. Tank dump, fishing pier, fish-cleaning facilities, boat ramp, and access to beach and dunes. Moderate.

**Manchester Beach KOA Kampground,** P.O. Box 266, Manchester 95459; (707) 882–2375. Five miles north of Point Arena, 1 mile north of Manchester, west of Highway 1, via Kinney Road. Has 75 RV and tent sites, full hookups, cable TV, Kamping Kabins, showers, laundry, heated pool, hot tub, store, and campground. Beach access. Expensive.

**Salt Point State Park,** 25050 Coast Highway 1, Jenner; (707) 847–3221 or (800) 444–7275; www.parks.ca.gov. Off Highway 1, 20 miles north of Jenner. Has 109 campsites located near the shore with tables, fire pits, and water nearby; on east side of the highway are tables, stoves, and water; but no showers. There are also walk-in sites and hiker/biker sites. Moderate.

**Wright's Beach Campground,** Sonoma Coast State Beach, Bodega Bay; (707) 875–3483 or (800) 444–7275; www.parks.ca.gov. Off Highway 1, about 6 miles north of Bodega Bay. Has 30 developed sites, with tables and fire pits, located along the edge of the beach. No showers, no hookups. Ocean view, beach access. Reservations suggested. Moderate.

# Food

**Bay View Room,** 800 Coast Highway, P.O. Box 640, Bodega Bay 94923; (707) 875–2751 or (800) 541–7788; www.innatthetides.com. At The Inn at the Tides, south end of town. Dinner Wednesday through Sunday. Five-course dinners include such appetizers as crab cakes and pork ribs; choice of chowder, soup, or salad; pasta; such entrees as filet mignon, veal steak, and salmon *en croute;* and sumptuous desserts—Grand Marnier soufflé, double-chocolate almond tart, and poached pear with caramel sauce. Dinner prix fixe or a la carte. Cocktails. Large wine list. Expensive.

**The Duck Club Restaurant,** 103 Coast Highway 1; (707) 875–3525. At the Bodega Bay Lodge & Spa, south end of town. Daily breakfast, lunch, and dinner. Breakfast offerings include the traditional egg dishes, omelets, eggs Benedict, Belgian waffles, blueberry buttermilk pancakes, and French toast. For smaller appetites, fresh fruits, cereals, bagels, croissants, and muffins. For lunch or dinner, start with the chef's seafood sampler, duck confit spring rolls, Dungeness crab cakes, or polenta torta. Try the soup of the day or creamy clam chowder. Caesar salads, spinach salad and warm goat cheese, and mixed greens round out the salad offerings. Order a pizza or a burger with fries. The crisp-roasted duck with orange sauce is served with wild rice pilaf and vegetable medley. The marinated pork tenderloin comes with apple-sherry sauce, gnocchi, butternut squash puree, and braised greens with roasted shallots. Other choices include filet mignon, sea bass with wild mushrooms, seafood pasta, vegetarian plate, daily lamb special, and fresh seafood catch of the day. Desserts include crème brûlée, warm chocolate cake with vanilla ice cream, and Key lime pie. Full bar. Moderate.

# Museum

**Point Arena Lighthouse & Museum,** Point Arena Lighthouse Keepers, 45500 Lighthouse Road, P.O. Box 11, Point Arena 95468; (707) 882–2777 or (877) 725–4448; www.pointarenalighthouse.com. Located 2⁹⁄₁₀ miles west of Highway 1, on Point Arena headland. Open daily 10:00 A.M. to 4:30 P.M. (April through September) and to 3:30 P.M. (October through March). Point Arena Lighthouse is open to the public year-round, with guided tours available. Housed in the adjacent fog-signal house, the museum contains photographs and maritime artifacts. The great earthquake of 1906 that destroyed much of San Francisco and the town of Point Arena also toppled the original brick lighthouse that stood here. The present structure was built of steel-reinforced concrete by the Concrete Chimney Company of San Francisco, which accounts for its resemblance to a smokestack.

## Beaches, Parks, Trails, and Waysides

About 33 miles south of Bodega Bay, at Olema, take Bear Valley Road west to reach the Point Reyes National Seashore, a great natural area with abundant wildlife, a variety of landforms, and both saltwater and freshwater areas, as well as estuarine habitat.

More than 360 species of birds have been recorded here. Sea lions frequent the offshore rocks near Point Reyes, and harbor seals haul out on the beaches. The point is also a good place to watch migrating gray whales. Near Tomales Point, you'll find elk, and anywhere in the area you might encounter the native black-tailed deer or fallow deer, transplanted years ago from the Mediterranean, easily distinguished by their splayed antlers. Some fallow deer are dusky brown, others white as mountain goats.

The seaward beaches are fine for hiking, but stay out of the water there because the surf is treacherous and the undertow dangerous. Several beaches east of the point are safe for swimming. Be sure to check tide tables before venturing onto any of the beaches, to avoid being stranded—or worse.

Visitor centers are on Bear Valley Road, on Drake's Bay, and at the Point Reyes Lighthouse. There you'll find maps, guides, and books to help you enjoy your visit.

North from Olema and Point Reyes Station, Highway 1 parallels mile-wide Tomales Bay for much of its 13-mile length. This shallow bay is a drowned rift valley that lies along the San Andreas Fault. Its great diversity of bottom sediments, sand, and gravel encourages the growth of hundreds of species of invertebrates and shellfish, which in turn attract shorebirds, waterfowl, and fish.

Fort Ross *Courtesy of Diane Martin*

At the northern end of Bodega Bay, Bodega Head is a popular spot for whale watching and for panoramic views of the Pacific. To reach it, take Bay Flat Road west off Highway 1, then Westside Road to road's end.

From Bodega Head north, Sonoma Coast State Beach stretches past Jenner to Russian Gulch. This 16-mile expanse of sand and gravel beaches, rocky bluffs, tidepools, and trails is accessible to hikers, beachcombers, picnickers, and others at more than a dozen points along Highway 1.

This area attracts more than 300 species of birds, among them several endangered species, such as peregrine falcon, California brown pelican, and snowy plover. The marshes near the mouth of Salmon Creek, 2½ miles north of Bodega Bay, are particularly good for observing migrating and wintering waterfowl, including the magnificent tundra swan, which is normally found farther inland. The shallow Russian River estuary also attracts a great number of shorebirds and waterfowl.

Fort Ross State Historic Park, 11 miles north of Jenner, is where early nineteenth-century Russian fur traders erected fortifications and dwellings—and nearly exterminated every sea otter on the north coast. Only one of the original buildings remains standing, but replica structures within a stockade provide an idea of what life was like here in the 1830s.

Seven miles of shoreline at the 4,000-acre Salt Point State Park include sheltered coves beneath sandstone cliffs where there are many tidepools to explore. Hiking and horseback trails along the bluffs lead to some excellent vantage points for observing the abundant bird life and migrating gray whales.

Adjacent Kruse Rhododendron State Reserve comprises 317 acres of second-growth forest with 5 miles of hiking trails through stands of redwood, Douglas fir, and, of course, rhododendrons.

On the east side of Highway 1, 3½ miles south of Gualala, is an interesting but different kind of wayside—a small, nondenominational chapel that is a pleasant wonder of art and architecture. Built in 1985 mainly of redwood, the unusual structure has teak doors, a cedar roof with copper crown, and walls made of local stone. It's a good place to take five and admire the work of local artisans.

In the vicinity of the Gualala River, which parallels Highway 1 near the ever-growing community of Gualala, bald eagles spend the winter months. Egrets, herons, loons, ospreys, and other shorebirds, seabirds, and waterfowl also frequent the area, as do such mammals as raccoons and river otters.

The Garcia River estuary, adjacent to the Point Arena headland, attracts a variety of migratory shorebirds and waterfowl, including both diver ducks and puddle ducks, as well as tundra swans.

A mile north of Manchester, take Kinney Road west of Highway 1 to reach Manchester State Beach. Here you'll find access to a fine beach and nearby dunes. The beach extends south almost to the Garcia River and north to Alder Creek.

## Water Sports and Activities

Surf and rock anglers find plenty of places to fish here, with surfperch, greenling, rockfish, and flounder the main quarry. The estuaries of rivers and large creeks also offer fishing for salmon and steelhead trout.

Shallow Tomales Bay offers good fishing for surfperch, seaperch, flounder, and sanddab. This is also a popular place with crabbers. The mudflats give up gaper, hard-shell, and littleneck clams.

Bodega Bay is another favorite fishing area, with the catch consisting mainly of rockfish, greenling, and surfperch. Crabbers harvest both Dungeness and rock crabs, and diggers take gaper and hard-shell clams on the mudflats. Offshore, fishing is for salmon, bottom fish, and albacore.

North of Bodega Bay to the Point Arena area, the Russian, Gualala, Garcia, and Navarro Rivers support sizable runs of coho salmon and steelhead trout in the fall and winter. The lower reaches of these rivers also offer fishing for a number of saltwater species.

**The Boat House,** 1445 Highway 1, Bodega Bay; (707) 875–3495. At the harbor. Open-party and charter trips for salmon and rockfish. Bait included. Rod rental, tackle, and licenses available. Whale-watching cruises January through April.

# Golf

**Bodega Harbour Golf Links,** 21301 Heron Drive, P.O. Box 368, 94923; (707) 875–3538 or (800) 503–8158; www.bodegaharborgolf.com. South of town and just off Highway 1, via South Harbor Way. An eighteen-hole, par-seventy, 6,220-yard, Scottish-style course with pro shop, clubhouse, driving range, practice greens, and club and cart rental.

# Travel Information

**Bodega Bay Chamber of Commerce,** 850 Highway 1, Bodega Bay; (707) 875–3422; www.bodegabay.com

**Bodega Bay Visitors Center,** 900 Highway 1, Bodega Bay; (707) 875–3866

**Point Reyes National Seashore,** Point Reyes; (415) 663–1092; www.nps.gov/pore

## events

| | |
|---|---|
| **January** | Crab Cioppino Feed, Bodega Bay, (707) 875–3022 |
| **April** | Bodega Bay Fisherman's Festival and Blessing of the Fleet, (707) 875–3286 |
| **May** | Memorial Weekend Barbecue and Disco, Jenner, (707) 875–3866 |
| **August** | Seafood, Art, and Wine Festival, Bodega Bay, (707) 824–8717 |
| **September** | Whale of a Gala, (707) 865–2310 |

# Mendocino

**Location:** On California Highway 1, 10 miles south of Fort Bragg, 2 miles north of Little River, 5 miles north of Albion, 7 miles north of the Route 128 junction, and about 150 miles north of San Francisco.

**Population:** 824

Rocky coastal bluffs rise 50 feet above the surf to a marine terrace where the nineteenth-century buildings of Mendocino stand amidst a scattering of pine and cypress trees. Even to the casual observer, the quaint seaside village is at once reminiscent of another era, another place, from the Eastlake Victorians surrounded by picket fences to the sharply spired steeple of the old Presbyterian church, now a State Historical Landmark.

If the place looks more down east than out west, rest assured others have made the same observation. In fact, millions who have never been to the northern coast of California know the town as Cabot Cove, Maine, the fictional hometown of Jessica Fletcher, the supersleuth played by Angela Lansbury on the television series *Murder She Wrote.* Jessica's lovely Victorian home turns out to be one of Mendocino's many fine bed-and-breakfast inns.

Mendocino, founded in the early 1850s, was first known as Meiggsville, after Harry Meiggs, a San Francisco entrepreneur who built the first redwood mill here. Early settlers came from the eastern United States by ship around Cape Horn and built houses and commercial buildings similar to those they had left behind. When the timber industry declined in the 1930s and local mills shut down, Mendocino languished. In the 1950s it began attracting the attention of artists who moved here and transformed the old lumber town into an artists' colony. Today, evidence of the residents' creativity and craftsmanship is everywhere in this town.

Two miles south of Mendocino is the town of Little River, site of the Little River Inn; the inn and, basically, the town were created by shipbuilder and lumberman Silas Coombs. Caspar is a tiny village located west of Highway 1 and 3 miles north of Mendocino. Like Mendocino, many of the early settlers in Caspar and Little River came from New England, and the architecture of the inn and of several of the older homes in Caspar is similar in style to that found in Mendocino. Caspar and Little River are great sites for diving, hiking, feeling the beauty and serenity of the Mendocino coast, and experiencing a spectacular sunset over the ocean.

Mendocino, along with neighboring Caspar and Little River, has more than its share of quaint and comfortable accommodations, fine restaurants, shops, and galleries. It's a pleasure to poke around in the compact downtown area, browsing through a gallery one moment, breathing crisp salt air the next, then checking out a neighboring shop, eatery, or watering hole.

# Lodging

**Agate Cove Inn,** 11201 North Lansing Street, P.O. Box 1150, 95460; (707) 937–0551 or (800) 527–3111; www.agatecove.com. West of Highway 1 via Lansing Street exit, on the north end of town. An 1860s farmhouse and cottages with a total of 10 rooms, some with fireplaces, some with private decks. Private baths, queen and king beds, and comforters. Ocean view. Full country breakfast served. Moderate to very expensive.

**Blair House Inn,** 45110 Little Lake Street, P.O. Box 1608, 95460; (707) 937–1800 or (800) 699–9296; www.blairhouse.com. West of Highway 1 via Little Lake Road. A Victorian bed-and-breakfast inn built in 1888, offering 5 guest rooms. Private and shared baths. Rooms with fireplaces and ocean views available. Exterior familiar to millions of TV viewers as the home of Jessica Fletcher on *Murder She Wrote*. Moderate to expensive.

**Little River Inn,** 7750 North Highway 1, Drawer B, Little River; (707) 937–5942 or (888) 466–5683; www.littleriverinn.com. On Highway 1, 2 miles south of Mendocino. Built in 1853. Has 55 lodge rooms and cottages, some with kitchens, some with fireplaces. Breakfast and dinner served daily in the dining room, where seafood and steaks are house specialties. Full bar and renowned weekend brunch. Regulation nine-hole golf course, day spa, and lighted tennis courts on premises. Moderate to expensive.

**MacCallum House Inn,** 45020 Albion Street, P.O. Box 206, 95460; (707) 937–0289 or (800) 609–0492; www.maccallumhouse.com. West of Highway 1, downtown, between Lansing and Kasten. King and queen beds in 19 rooms or suites, all with private baths, in a stunning old Victorian built in 1882. Unique structures, including a barn, gazebo, and water tower. Claw foot tubs for two. Restaurant and Grey Whale Bar on premises. Continental breakfast. Moderate to very expensive.

**Mendocino Hotel & Garden Suites,** 45080 Main Street, P.O. Box 587, 95460; (707) 937–0511 or (800) 548–0513; www.mendocinohotel.com. West of Highway 1, downtown. Twin, double, queen, and king beds in 50 rooms and suites with private and shared baths, some with fireplaces, some with balconies. Built in 1878 and decorated with Victorian antiques. Room service. Dining rooms and lounges on premises. Moderate to very expensive.

**Mendo Coast Reservations,** 1000 Main Street, Mendocino; (707) 937–5033 or (800) 262–7801; www.mendocinovacations.com. Arranges for rental of private homes in and around Mendocino. Moderate to very expensive.

# Campgrounds and RV Parks

**Caspar Beach RV Campground,** 14441 Point Cabrillo Drive, P.O. Box 189, 95460; (707) 964–3306; www.casparbeachrv.com. West of Highway 1, 2 miles north of Mendocino, via exit for Russian Gulch State Park. Has 114 sites with tables and stoves. Full and partial hookups and cable TV available. Showers, laundry, tank dump, fish-cleaning facilities, horseshoe pits, video arcade, and convenience store. Expensive.

**Russian Gulch State Park,** Mendocino District, P.O. Box 440, 95460; (707) 937–5804 or (800) 444–7275; www.parks.ca.gov. Two miles north of Mendocino, west side of Highway 1. Has 30 developed sites with tables, fire pits, and food lockers for tents, trailers, and motor homes. Also a horse camp with 4 tent sites. Hiking and biking trails, nature trails, and showers. Moderate.

**Schooner's Landing RV Park & Marina,** P.O. Box 218, Albion 95410; (707) 937–5707. Five miles south of Mendocino, 2 miles north of Route 128, east off Highway 1, near the mouth of the Albion River. A fishing camp with 27 full-hookup sites, 4 sites with water and electricity, 3 tent sites. Boat launch, boat docks, trailer storage, fish-cleaning facilities, showers, and tank dump. Moderate.

**Van Damme State Park,** Mendocino District, P.O. Box 440, 95460; (707) 937–5804 or (800) 444–7275; www.parks.ca.gov. On Highway 1 at Little River, 3 miles south of Mendocino. Has 74 developed and 10 hike-in campsites with tables and fire pits and 24 en-route sites at the beach parking lot. Showers, hiking and nature trails, beach, and beautiful wooded setting. Moderate.

# Food

**Bay View Cafe,** 45040 Main Street, Mendocino; (707) 937–4197; www.bayview cafe.com. West of Highway 1. Breakfast, lunch, and dinner daily. Breakfast includes *huevos* California, various omelets, eggs Benedict or Florentine, blintzes, and crepes. Great seafood salads, burgers, and deli-style sandwiches. Seafood hors d'oeuvres, seafood crepes with Mornay sauce, charbroiled chinook salmon steaks, roast duckling, pasta dishes, and steaks. Excellent view. Full bar. Moderate.

**Hill House Inn,** 10701 Palette Drive, P.O. Box 625, Mendocino 95460; (707) 937–0554 or (800) 422–0554; www.hillhouseinn.com. West of Highway 1 via Little Lake Road exit, then right 1 block on Lansing. Dinner daily. Mostly Italian cuisine. Appetizers include escargot, coquille St. Jacques, and veal pâté. Clam chowder, shrimp bisque, and soup of the day. Entrees include chicken, quail, filet mignon with artichoke hearts, and veal dishes. Full bar. Appetizers served in the lounge, downstairs. Moderate to expensive.

Mendocino Village *Courtesy of Robert Holmes/CalTour*

**The Ledford House,** 3000 North Highway 1, Albion; (707) 937–0282; www.ledford house.com. Just south of Mendocino. Dinner Wednesday through Sunday. Delicious appetizers include Pacific oysters on the half-shell, black mussels baked with Italian sausage, and grilled asparagus tart. Among the entrees are New York steak, rack of lamb, pepper-encrusted ahi tuna, braised halibut, and roasted half duckling with strawberry-rhubarb sauce. Moderate.

**Little River Restaurant,** 7901 North Highway 1, Little River; (707) 937–5942 or (888) 466–5683. Gourmet breakfasts, dinners, and bar menu. Innovative restaurant specializing in fresh seafood, local organic produce, and seasonal specialties. Menu items change constantly. Moderate to expensive.

**MacCallum House Restaurant,** 45020 Albion Street, P.O. Box 500, 95460; (707) 937–5763; www.maccallumhouse.com. West of Highway 1, downtown, between Lansing and Kasten Streets. Dinner daily. From the cafe menu choose a double burger with caramelized onions and white cheddar on a poppyseed bun, grilled day-boat scallop and asparagus salad, potato gnocchi with wild mushroom-sherry sauce, or the nightly hand-rolled pasta special. From the dinner menu try such appetizers as steamed mussels in coconut-ginger broth with lemongrass or oysters on the half-shell in champagne-shiitake mushroom glaze with black pepper brioche and alder-smoked salmon roe. Main courses include roast thyme-scented chicken, roast duck leg confit, grilled loin lamb chops, grilled steak, Chilean sea bass, and north coast rockfish— all served with tantalizing accompaniments. Desserts include a tangerine soufflé, chocolate brownie mousse, and an assortment of house-made ice creams. Full bar. Moderate to expensive.

## Shopping and Browsing

**Highlight Gallery,** 45052 Main Street, P.O. Box 1515, Mendocino 95460; (707) 937–3132; www.thehighlightgallery.com. West of Highway 1, between Lansing and Kasten. Daily, 10:00 A.M. to 5:00 P.M. One of the best galleries on the north coast with many fine wooden items and exquisite furniture—all handcrafted. An excellent collection of paintings, ceramics, sculpture, jewelry, scrimshaw, and gift items. A large and pleasing gallery.

**Out of This World,** 45–100 Main Street, Mendocino; (707) 937–3324 or (800) 485–6884; www.discounttelescopes.com. Albion at Lansing Street. Daily, 10:00 A.M. to 6:00 P.M. An unusual and interesting shop selling telescopes, microscopes, binoculars, celestial and terrestrial maps, celestial mobiles, and many other items related to astronomy and science fiction.

**Papa Birds,** 45040 Albion Street, P.O. Box 2380, Mendocino 95460; (707) 937–2730. West of Highway 1. Daily, 10:00 A.M. to 5:00 P.M. An interesting specialty shop for anyone who likes and wants to care for wild birds. Handmade birdhouses and feeders, books, and gift items.

**William Zimmer Gallery,** 45101 Ukiah Street, Mendocino; (707) 937–5121; www.williamzimmergallery.com. At Kasten and Ukiah Streets. Wonderful collection of hand-blown, playful and unique martini glasses, handcrafted wood furniture and watercolors and oil paintings by the finest local and California artists. Open 10:30 A.M. to 5:00 P.M.

## Beaches, Parks, Trails, and Waysides

Van Damme State Park has a small sandy beach at the mouth of the Little River. Nature trails in the park lead through pygmy forests of dwarf cypress no more than 1 foot tall and pines of 6 feet or so that are more than fifty years old. Despite the nearly perfect tree-growing climate here, poor soils have retarded the growth of these trees.

In Mendocino take Lansing Street north to Heeser Drive, turn left, and drive to Mendocino Headlands State Park, where you can hike or bike along bluff-top trails overlooking the spectacular seascape.

North of Mendocino, 1½ miles beyond Caspar, is Jughandle State Reserve. Here you'll find about 5 miles of nature trails, a beach, and a series of terraces called an "ecological staircase." The terraces were formed during the Pleistocene period as sea levels fluctuated.

## Golf and Tennis

**Little River Inn Golf & Tennis Club,** 7751 North Highway 1, Drawer B, Little River; (707) 937–5942; www.littleriverinn.com. Nine-hole golf course and lighted tennis courts. Pro shop, resident pro, driving range, putting green, motel, and restaurant.

## Other Attractions

**Mendocino Theater Company,** Helen Schoeni Theatre, 45200 Little Lake Street, P.O. Box 800, Mendocino 95460; (707) 937–4477; www.mcn.org. Performances Thursday through Sunday, 8:00 P.M. sharp. A variety of stage productions offered throughout the year.

## Travel Information

**Fort Bragg–Mendocino Coast Chamber of Commerce,** 332 North Main Street, P.O. Box 1141, Fort Bragg 95437; (707) 961–6300; www.mendocino.org or www.go mendo.com

| | |
|---|---|
| **January** | Crab & Wine Days Festival, (707) 462–7417 or (800) 726–2780 |
| **March** | Mendocino Whale Festival, (707) 961–6300 |
| **May** | Historic House & Building Tour, Mendocino, (707) 937–5791 |
| | Arts & Crafts Market, Little River, (707) 937–5791 |
| **June** | Mendocino Coast Garden Tour, Mendocino, (707) 937–5818 or (800) 653–3328 |
| | Mendocino Village Walking Tour, (707) 937–5818 or (800) 653–3328 |
| **July** | Mendocino Music Festival, (707) 937–2044 |
| | Summer Art Fair, Mendocino, (707) 937–5818 |
| **November** | Mendocino Coast Mushroom Festival, (707) 462–7417 |
| **December** | Candlelight Inn Tours, Mendocino, (707) 964–1228 |

# Fort Bragg

**Location:** On California Highway 1, 42 miles southwest of Leggett, 135 miles south of Eureka, 44 miles north of Point Arena, and 180 miles north of San Francisco.

**Population:** 6,867

At the business end of the Mendocino Coast stands Fort Bragg, the largest north coast city between San Francisco and Eureka. The area was settled in the mid-nineteenth century, shortly after the Mendocino Indian Reservation was created in 1856. The following year, the U.S. Army established a post near the reservation and named it after Colonel Braxton Bragg, who later rose to the rank of general in the Confederate army. The fort was abandoned in 1864, and the reservation followed suit in 1867.

After the Indians were moved to various California reservations, the area was opened to settlement and incorporated as a city in 1889. The building of the Union Lumber Company in the 1880s and the subsequent establishment of a steamship company and railroad did much to secure Fort Bragg's position as the economic hub of the Mendocino Coast, a role it retains today.

The Noyo Harbor, near the mouth of the Noyo River, is home port to the largest commercial-fishing fleet between Eureka and San Francisco. The fleet harvests rockfish (marketed as snapper or rockcod), sablefish (marketed as black cod), salmon, sole, shrimp, Dungeness crab, and sea urchin.

The harbor is a busy, bustling place with several good seafood restaurants and fish markets. A parking area near the jetty provides a vantage for watching boat traffic and photographing the activities. One of the best places to watch and photograph the harbor is from one of the balconies at the Harbor Lite Lodge, at the north end of the bridge.

## Lodging

**Grey Whale Inn,** 615 North Main Street; (707) 964–0640 or (800) 382–7244; www.grey whaleinn.com. On Highway 1, downtown. Twin, double, queen, and king beds in 14 rooms with private baths, some with ocean views. A beautiful old inn near shops and restaurants. Recreation room with TV, VCR, and billiards. Fireside Rendezvous Room with many books and magazines. Buffet-style breakfast with homemade baked goods. Moderate to expensive.

**Harbor Lite Lodge,** 120 North Harbor Drive; (707) 964–0221 or (800) 643–2700; www.harborlitelodge.com. Just east of Highway 1, overlooking the harbor. Satellite TV in 79 rooms with queen and king beds. Some ocean-view rooms with private balconies that overlook the harbor. Watch the fishing fleet come and go. From November through March, watch migrating gray whales. Moderate.

**Howard Creek Ranch Bed & Breakfast Inn,** 40501 North Highway 1, P.O. Box 121, Westport 95488; (707) 964–6725; www.howardcreekranch.com. Three miles north of Westport on Highway 1, north of Fort Bragg. Twelve rooms, suites, and cabins, some with kitchens, some with fireplaces, some with ocean view, and most with private baths, on a ranch settled in 1867. Ranch house was built in 1871. Furnished with antiques and collectibles. Wood-heated hot tub, sauna, and pool. Daily breakfast. Massage available by appointment. Cottages available. Moderate to expensive.

**Super 8 Motel,** 888 South Main Street; (707) 964–4003 or (800) 206–9833. On Highway 1, just north of the harbor. Cable TV in 53 rooms with queen beds. Some rooms have ocean view. Restaurant on premises serves breakfast, lunch, and dinner. Inexpensive to moderate.

## Campgrounds and RV Parks

**MacKerricher State Park,** Mendocino District, P.O. Box 440, Mendocino 95460; (707) 964–9112 or (800) 444–7275; www.parks.ca.gov. On Highway 1, 3 miles north of Fort Bragg. Has 150 developed sites and 11 walk-in sites with tables, fire rings, and food lockers. Showers, tank dump, beach, hiking trails, and a freshwater lake with a trail around it for bird-watching and fishing. Moderate.

**Pomo Campground,** 17999 Tregoning Lane; (707) 964–3373; www.infortbragg.com. On Highway 1, 1½ miles south of Route 20 junction. Has 110 campsites with tables, fire rings, full hookups, and cable TV. Showers, laundry, tank dump, fish-cleaning station, horseshoe pits, and convenience store. Propane and firewood available. Expensive.

**Wages Creek Beach Campground,** 37700 North Highway 1, Westport; (707) 964–2964. On Highway 1, ½ mile north of Westport. Has 175 campsites, but no hookups. Showers, tank dump, and beach access. Warm, potable water; dogs allowed, and you can camp by the creek or on the beach. Moderate.

**Woodside RV Park & Campground,** 17900 North Highway 1; (707) 964–3684 or (800) 207–8772; www.infortbragg.com. Two miles south of Fort Bragg on Highway 1. A nine-acre wooded park with 104 campsites, full hookups, partial hookups, cable TV, showers, tank dump, horseshoe pits, fish-cleaning table, beach access, and minimarket. Moderate to expensive.

# Food

**Egghead's Restaurant,** 326 North Main Street; (707) 964–5005. On Highway 1, downtown. Breakfast and lunch daily. In addition to pancakes, French toast, waffles, and other breakfast favorites, a selection of more than forty omelets with such fillings as cream cheese, Jack cheese, cheddar, sour cream, bell pepper, green chilis, onions, black olives, sprouts, spinach, mushrooms, avocado, zucchini, Polish sausage, ham, bacon, ground beef, and crab in a variety of combinations. Also deli-style sandwiches and half-pound burgers. Moderate.

**North Coast Brewing Company,** 444 North Main Street; (707) 964–2739; www.north coastbrewing.com. On Highway 1, downtown. Lunch and dinner daily. Large salads, nachos, deli-style sandwiches, burgers, grilled sausages, chili, Cajun black beans and dirty rice, and fish-and-chips. Ten varieties of beer are brewed here, among which are Scrimshaw (pale pilsner style), Red Seal Ale (copper-red pale ale), and Old No. 38 (a dry, full-bodied stout). Moderate.

**North Coast Sports Cafe,** 118 East Redwood Avenue; (707) 964–1517. Downtown, just east of Main Street (Highway 1). Lunch and dinner daily; Sunday brunch. Menu includes salad, beef, ham, chicken, and fresh local seafood. Homemade soups. Freshly baked rolls and muffins. Beer and wine. Moderate.

# Shopping and Browsing

**For the Shell of It Et Cetera,** 344 North Main Street; (707) 961–0461. On Highway 1, downtown. Daily, 9:00 A.M. to 6:00 P.M. Not just a shell shop, but much more. Jewelry, baskets, ceramics, folk art, marine art, collectibles, Christmas ornaments, gift items, and, of course, lots of shells.

**Tangents,** 368 North Main Street; (707) 964–3884; www.tangentsonline.com. At the corner of Laurel. Open daily from 10:00 A.M. to 5:30 P.M. This store has a unique collection of original art and cards, ethnic crafts, clothing, furniture, and jewelry from all over the world, as well as creations of local artists and writers.

# Museum

**Guest House Museum,** 343 North Main Street; (707) 961–2840. On Highway 1, downtown. Wednesday through Sunday, 10:00 A.M. to 4:00 P.M. A three-story Victorian structure built of redwood in 1892 as the residence of T. L. Johnson, whose brother C. R. Johnson founded the Union Lumber Company. In 1912 the building became a guest house for lodging customers and others associated with the lumber company. Inside are photos of and artifacts from early Fort Bragg and the Mendocino Coast logging days. Outside are steam donkeys, locomotives, and other vintage logging equipment.

# Beaches, Parks, Trails, and Waysides

Two miles south of Fort Bragg, on the west side of the highway, you'll find Mendocino Coast Botanical Gardens, a 47-acre park with thousands of native and introduced plants, including trees and shrubs, roses, camellias, succulents, ivies, heathers, and rhododendrons. Trails lead past dwarf and hybrid species as well.

MacKerricher State Park, 3 miles north of Fort Bragg, is a 1,600-acre park containing dunes, wetlands, and 10 miles of coastline. Horse and hiking trails lead to a great variety of flora and fauna for study and photography.

# Water Sports and Activities

Noyo River estuary is popular with anglers who take surfperch, starry flounder, and various bottom species, as well as salmon and steelhead.

At MacKerricher State Park, north of Fort Bragg, Lake Cleone is regularly stocked with rainbow trout. Surf anglers work the rocky shore near Laguna Beach for cabezon, lingcod, and rockfish. This is also both a good spot for dipping smelt and an access area for abalone divers.

**Lady Irma II,** 780 North Harbor Drive, P.O. Box 103, 95437; (707) 964–3854; www.ladyirmacharters.com. At Noyo Harbor. Charter fishing and party-boat trips for salmon and rock cod. Two five-hour trips daily, from 6:30 A.M. to noon and from 1:00 to 6:00 P.M. Two-hour whale-watching trips from December through April.

**Noyo Fishing Center,** 32440 North Harbor Drive; (707) 964–3000; www.fortbragg fishing.com. At Noyo Harbor. A well-stocked bait and tackle shop offering a complete line of fishing tackle and bait, as well as one-day licenses and tags. Also books charter and party-boat trips.

**Sub-Surface Progression,** 18600 North Highway 1; (707) 964–3793. This establishment sells and rents wet suits, tanks, and diving equipment and organizes trips for abalone diving.

# Tours and Trips

**California Western Railroad,** P.O. Box 907, 95437; (707) 964–6371 or (800) 866–1690; recorded information, (415) 399–1194; www.skunktrain.com. West off Main Street (Highway 1) at the foot of Laurel Avenue or Pine Street. Train trips through the redwoods in passenger cars and open-observation cars pulled by diesel or steam locomotives, or in self-powered motorcars known as "skunks," so called because they were originally powered by gas engines that emitted unpleasant fumes. Trips are between Fort Bragg and Willits at US 101, and between Fort Bragg and Northspar, which is halfway to Willits. On the 40-mile trip to Willits, trains cross thirty bridges and trestles and pass through two deep-mountain tunnels. Spectacular mountain and forest scenery. One of Fort Bragg's biggest attractions and certainly *a must* for every rail buff.

## events

| | |
|---|---|
| **January** | Crab & Wine Days Festival, (707) 462–7417 or (800) 726–2780 |
| **March** | Fort Bragg Whale Festival, (707) 961–6300 |
| **May** | Mendocino Coast Furniture Makers Exhibition, (707) 541–0220 |
| | Prime Time Rhododendron Tours, Fort Bragg, (707) 964–4352 |
| | Fort Bragg Rhododendron Show, (707) 964–4352 |
| | Great Rubber Ducky Race, Westport, (707) 964–2872 |
| | Fort Bragg Quilt Show, (707) 964–5279 |
| **July** | World's Largest Salmon Barbecue, Fort Bragg, (707) 964–2781 |
| | Fireworks Extravaganza, Fort Bragg, (707) 961–6300 |
| **August** | Art in the Gardens, Fort Bragg, (707) 964–4352 |
| **September** | Paul Bunyon Days, Fort Bragg, (707) 961–6300 |
| | Winesong! At The Mendocino Coast Botanical Gardens, (707) 961–4688 |
| | Portuguese Festa, Fort Bragg, (707) 964–4971 |
| **November** | Mendocino Coast Mushroom Festival, (707) 462–7417 |
| **December** | Craft Show & Sale, Fort Bragg, (707) 964–0807 |

## Other Attractions

**The Fort Bragg Footlighters,** Footlighters Little Theatre, 248 East Laurel Street, P.O. Box 575, 95437; (707) 964–8050. East of Main Street (Highway 1), downtown. Wednesday and Saturday, 8:00 P.M., from Memorial Day weekend through Labor Day weekend. Original comedy and melodrama in the tradition of the 1890s.

**Gloriana Opera Company,** 721 North Franklin Street, between Bush and Spruce, downtown; (707) 964–7469; www.gloriana.org. Musical theater and opera, performed by local talents, many of whom are professional and world-renowned musicians and opera singers.

**Lari Shea's Ricochet Ridge Ranch,** 24201 North Highway 1; (707) 964–7669 or (888) 873–5777; www.ricochetranch.com. North of town. Horseback riding on the beach or in the redwoods. Western or English tack.

## Travel Information

**Fort Bragg–Mendocino Coast Chamber of Commerce,** 332 North Main Street, P.O. Box 1141, 95437; (707) 961–6300; www.mendocino.com or www.visitfortbragg.com

# Garberville / Shelter Cove

**Location:** Garberville is on U.S. Highway 101, 68 miles south of Eureka, 24 miles north of Leggett, and 200 miles north of San Francisco; Shelter Cove is on the coast, about 24 miles west of Garberville.

**Population:** Garberville 2,200; Shelter Cove 350

Rugged terrain forces highway travelers well inland in this part of northern California, but local roads and thoroughfares carry them through country that rivals the coast for scenic splendor. Magnificent redwoods are the attraction here, and from Garberville north are some of the greatest stands of these trees remaining on the planet.

Although US 101 cuts through the redwoods as it heads north and becomes one of the most scenic stretches of freeway in the state, remnants of the old Coast Highway remain intact and afford the traveler a much more pleasant and intimate relationship with these magnificent trees. Known as the Avenue of the Giants, this two-lane, paved road begins at Sylvandale (via the Phillipsville exit), about 6 miles north of Garberville, and meanders northward for 33 miles, much of the way along the banks of the Eel River and the South Fork of the Eel. It stays fairly near the freeway and in fact crosses over or under it several times. A number of freeway exits lead to the avenue, so it's possible to enjoy this scenic route in sections.

Between Sylvandale to the south and Stafford at the north end of the Avenue of the Giants lie the small communities of Phillipsville, Miranda, Myers Flat, Weott, Redcrest, and Pepperwood, separated from one another by roughly 6 miles. In addition to the state parks and many groves along the avenue are small motels and lodges, campgrounds and RV parks, several restaurants, convenience stores, and gift shops.

Garberville makes an excellent headquarters for exploring the redwoods north and south. Those who require frequent doses of salt air can drive over the hump to Shelter Cove for a quick fix. A two-lane paved road leads west from Redway over the mountains to Shelter Cove, King Range National Conservation Area, and what's known as California's "Lost Coast." Although the road is narrow and curvy, often steep, and full of switchbacks through the mountains, it is a year-round road, suitable for travel trailers, motor homes, and vehicles towing boats. But it's not a route for people in a hurry. Those in cars, vans, or pickup trucks not towing anything should plan at least forty-five minutes for the one-way trip, not counting stops.

Shelter Cove is a tiny community on a grassy marine terrace overlooking the Pacific. North and south of it are steep mountains sloping sharply to the sea. Mariners have used the natural harbor here for many years. Today, it mainly attracts commercial and sport fishermen. There are overnight accommodations, an RV park, marina, and several restaurants in town and primitive camping areas in the King Range.

# Lodging

**Benbow Inn,** 445 Lake Benbow Drive, Garberville; (707) 923–2124 or (800) 355–3301; www.benbowinn.com. Just west of US 101, 2 miles south of Garberville. Cable TV in 55 rooms in a beautiful inn opened in 1926 and recently restored and remodeled. Some rooms with fireplaces, some with VCRs. Elegant, with many amenities and nice touches, such as complimentary English tea and scones every afternoon, mulled wine on chilly afternoons, and hors d'oeuvres from 5:00 to 7:00 P.M. in the lounge. A basketful of mystery novels in each room, along with coffee, tea, and sherry. Nearby tennis courts, stables, golf course, and exercise trail. Dining room on premises. Expensive to very expensive.

**Best Western Humboldt House Inn,** 701 Redwood Drive, Garberville; (707) 923–2771 or (800) 528–1234. East of US 101, downtown. Queen and king beds in 76 rooms with cable TV, most rooms offering private balconies or patios. Heated pool, whirlpool, and laundry facilities. Continental breakfast. Easy walk to shops and restaurants. Moderate.

**Dean Creek Resort Motel,** 4112 Redwood Drive, P.O. Box 157, Redway 95560; (877) 923–2555; www.deancreekresort.com. East of US 101, 3 miles north of Garberville. Queen beds in 9 rooms and suites with cable TV. Kitchen units available. Whirlpool. Inexpensive to moderate.

**Redcrest Resort,** 26459 Avenue of the Giants, P.O. Box 235, Redcrest 95569; (707) 722–4208; www.redcrestresort.com. On the Avenue of the Giants, between Weott and Pepperwood, north of Garberville. Double and king beds in 10 cottages with kitchens. Laundry facilities on premises. Inexpensive to moderate.

**Shelter Cove Beachcomber Inn,** 412 Machi Road, Shelter Cove; (707) 986–7551 or (800) 718–4789. Queen and twin beds in 6 units, each with private entrance and private bath. Three have fireplace woodstoves; all have TV, coffeemakers, and either full or minikitchens. Ocean-view deck, easy beach access. Picnic tables and barbecue areas. Inexpensive to moderate.

**Shelter Cove Inn of the Lost Coast,** 205 Wave Drive, Shelter Cove; (707) 986–7521 or (888) 570–9676; www.innofthelostcoast.com. King and queen beds in 16 rooms and suites with Direct TV and VCR, ocean views, microwave ovens, refrigerators, coffeemakers, and hair dryers. Private balconies with ocean view. Laundry facilities and barbecue available. Moderate to expensive.

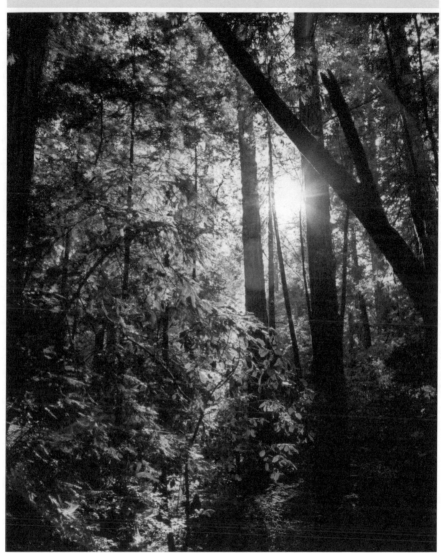

Avenue of the Giants *Courtesy of Dorothy Dean*

**Sherwood Forest Motel,** 814 Redwood Drive, Garberville; (707) 923–2721; www.sherwoodforestmotel.com. East of US 101, downtown. Queen beds, cable TV, and cable movies in 32 rooms and suites with refrigerators and microwaves. Heated pool, hot tub, and barbecue area. Cribs and roll-aways available. Easy walk to shops and restaurants. Inexpensive to moderate.

**Whispering Pines Lodge,** 6582 Avenue of the Giants, P.O. Box 246, Miranda 95553; (707) 943–3182 or (800) 626–6835. On the Avenue of the Giants, north of Garberville. Queen beds in 17 rooms and suites with satellite TV. Kitchens available. Set amid three acres of redwoods. Heated pool, table tennis, horseshoes, shuffleboard, and badminton. Picnic tables and barbecue grills. Recreation room with pool table, games, books, and fireplace. Moderate.

## Campgrounds and RV Parks

**Albee Creek Campground,** Humboldt Redwoods State Park, P.O. Box 100, Weott 95571; (707) 946–2409 or (800) 444–7275; www.humboldtredwoods.org. Five miles west of US 101 and Avenue of the Giants, on Bull Creek Flats Road. Has 40 developed campsites with tables, stoves, and food lockers. Piped water and showers. Sites available on first-come, first-served basis. Closed October to mid-May. Moderate.

**Benbow Lake State Recreation Area,** 1600 U.S. Highway 101, Garberville; (707) 923–3238, summer; (707) 247–3318, winter; (800) 444–7275, reservations; www .parks.ca.gov. Has 76 developed campsites with tables and fire rings. Showers. Open spring and summer. Moderate.

**Burlington Campgrounds,** Humboldt Redwoods State Park, P.O. Box 100, Weott 95571; (707) 946–2409 or (800) 444–7275. On the Avenue of the Giants, near park headquarters. Has 57 developed campsites with tables, stoves, and food lockers. Piped water, showers, laundry tubs, and tank dump. Moderate.

**Dean Creek Resort RV Park,** 4112 Redwood Drive, P.O. Box 157, Redway 95560; (707) 923–2555; www.deancreekresort.com. East of US 101, 3 miles north of Garberville. Has 64 campsites—some with full hookups, some with water and electricity, and 6 with no hookups. Cable TV, tables, stoves, showers, laundry, tank dump, whirlpool, and sauna. Store with ice, propane, and firewood available. Moderate.

**Giant Redwoods RV & Camp,** 455 Boy Scout Camp Road, P.O. Box 222, Myers Flat 95554; (707) 943–3198. On the Avenue of the Giants and the Eel River, north of Garberville. Has 82 campsites—14 with full hookups, 43 with water and electricity, and 25 with no hookups. Drive-through sites available. Tables, showers, laundry, tank dump. Camping in the redwoods. Store on premises. Propane and ice available. Moderate.

**Hidden Springs Campground,** Humboldt Redwoods State Park, P.O. Box 100, Weott 95571; (707) 946–2409 or (800) 444–7275. East of US 101, on the Avenue of the Giants, near Myers Flat. Has 154 developed campsites with tables, stoves, and food lockers. Piped water, showers, and laundry tubs. Closed mid-October to mid-May. Moderate.

**Redcrest Resort,** 26459 Avenue of the Giants, P.O. Box 235, Redcrest 95569; (707) 722–4208; www.redcrestresort.com. On the Avenue of the Giants, between Weott and Pepperwood, north of Garberville. Has 19 full-hookup campsites. Showers, laundry, cable television, playground, and store on premises. Moderate.

**Richardson Grove State Park,** 1600 Highway 101, Garberville; (707) 247–3318, 946–2311, or (800) 444–7275; www.parks.ca.gov. Has 170 developed campsites with tables, fire rings, and food lockers. Showers and tank dump. Reservations accepted during spring and summer; open October through April on a first-come, first-served basis. Moderate.

**Shelter Cove Campground,** 492 Machi Road, Whitehorn; (707) 986–7474. Across the road from the marina. Has 105 campsites—52 with full hookups, 53 with no hookups. Showers, laundry, tank dump, deli, and store with propane available. Moderate.

**Trailer Life's Benbow Valley RV Resort,** 7000 Benbow Drive, Garberville; (707) 923–2777 or (866) BENBOWRV; www.benbowrv.com. Just east of US 101, 2 miles south of Garberville. Has 112 full-hookup sites with cable TV. All roads and pads paved. Pull-through sites available. Grassy sites with trees, set in beautiful rolling hills. Showers, laundry, and heated pool. Recreation room and nine-hole golf course. Convenience store with ice and propane available. Expensive.

# Food

**Benbow Inn,** 445 Lake Benbow Drive, Garberville; (800) 355–3301; www.ben bowinn.com. Located 2 miles south of Garberville, this Tudor-style inn serves some of the very best food in southern Humboldt County; exquisite appetizers. The food is California style with a French twist. Open daily for breakfast and dinner; patio dining. Moderate to expensive.

**Sicilito's Casa De Linda,** 445 Conger Street, Garberville; (707) 923–2814. Behind the Humboldt House Inn, downtown. Lunch and dinner daily in summer, dinner only in winter. Mexican and Italian-American food. Mexican appetizers include nachos or guacamole and chips. Such dinners as steak ranchero, Vera Cruz–style fish, enchiladas, *chiles rellenos,* burritos, tostadas, tacos, and combinations. Pizza, Italian sandwiches, and pasta with shrimp, scallops, or chicken. Beer and wine. Carryout service available, with free delivery in Garberville and Redway. Inexpensive to moderate.

**The Waterwheel Restaurant & Gift Shop,** 924 Redwood Drive, Garberville; (707) 923–2031. East of US 101, downtown. Breakfast, lunch, and dinner daily. Hearty breakfasts with large portions, served all day. Eggs with bacon, sausage, ham, steak, half-pound hamburger steak, or corned-beef hash come with biscuits, gravy, and potatoes. Soups, chowder, salads, French dip, burgers, and other sandwiches, as well as spaghetti and ravioli. Dinner entrees include sole Monterey, scampi, calamari, honey-raisin ham, chicken, steaks, and pasta dishes. Mexican food Thursday and Friday. Domestic and imported beers and wines. Inexpensive to moderate.

## Shopping and Browsing

**Ancient Redwood Resort,** 28101 Avenue of the Giants, P.O. Box 254, Redcrest 95569; (707) 722–4396. North end of the Avenue of the Giants. Daily, 9:00 A.M. to 5:00 P.M.; closed October through March. Large selection of redwood carvings, toys, kitchen items, desk accessories, clocks, mirrors, furniture, slabs, table bases, wood signs, and more.

## Beaches, Parks, Trails, and Waysides

Shelter Cove has several sandy beach areas, as well as rocky shoreline with tidepools. In all, more than 4 miles of beach are accessible and open to the public. The beaches provide good places for hiking and beachcombing, and the bluffs in the Shelter Cove area offer excellent vantage points for whale watching.

Nearby King Range National Conservation Area reaches as much as 6 miles inland and extends along 35 miles of coastline. It contains 47,000 acres of paved, graveled, and dirt roads, some of them impassable during wet winter months. Hiking and backpacking are popular along beaches and bluffs and on mountain trails. A guide with map is available from the Bureau of Land Management in Ukiah or Arcata. Hiking can be very difficult along the mountain trails between November and April, due to frequent floods and landslides.

Seven miles south of Garberville, on US 101, lies Richardson Grove State Park, comprising more than 1,000 acres of forest and river bottoms. Hikers and nature enthusiasts enjoy miles of trails. Guided hikes and interpretive programs are conducted in the summer.

Two miles south of Garberville is Benbow Lake State Recreation Area. A dam on the South Fork of the Eel River creates a summer lake where swimming is popular. A park along the sandy riverbank near the Benbow Inn provides access and has picnic tables. There are hiking trails and summer interpretive activities, including nature hikes, canoe hikes on the lake, and paddleboat rentals.

Along the length of the Avenue of the Giants are many redwood groves with trails, picnic areas, and some phenomenal specimens of the mighty coast redwood. For much of the length of the avenue and well west of the road is the huge Humboldt Redwoods State Park. At more than 51,000 acres, it ranks third in size among California's state parks, and it continues to grow, thanks to the efforts of the Save-the-Redwoods League. Within the park proper are more than 100 miles of hiking and backpacking trails and six trail camps.

## Water Sports and Activities

A summer fishery draws a few anglers to the banks of the Eel River and its South Fork, but the water is warm and low then, with the catch consisting of small trout and rough fish. Summer river activities are mainly swimming and floating the river in inner tubes.

Fall and winter rains signal the anadromous salmon and steelhead, which move up

## events

| | |
|---|---|
| **May** | Antique Fair, Benbow, (707) 923–2613 |
| | Cinco de Mayo Celebration, Garberville, (707) 923–2613 |
| **June** | Summer Arts Fair and Music Festival, Benbow Lake State Recreation Area, (707) 923–3238 |
| | Jazz on the Lake, Benbow Lake State Recreation Area, (707) 923–4599 |
| | Garberville Rodeo, (707) 923–2613 |
| **July** | Shakespeare Festival, Benbow Lake State Recreation Area, (800) 923–3238 |
| **August** | Reggae on the River, (707) 923–4583 |
| **October** | Humboldt Redwood Marathon, Humboldt Redwoods State Park, (707) 946–1814 |
| **December** | Winter Arts Fair, Redway, (707) 923–3368 |

the rivers to spawn. Both coho (silver) and chinook (king) salmon use the Eel River system and draw many anglers each year. Steelhead trout also enter the river system in the fall, and some are still present as late as March and April.

Saltwater recreation will require a trip to Shelter Cove, where surfing, diving, fishing, and crabbing are popular. Surf anglers take surfperch and several species of bottom fish. Offshore, people troll for salmon and jig for lingcod, rockfish, cabezon, and other bottom fish.

*Annika* **Sport Fishing,** Shelter Cove; (707) 986–7836 or (916) 686–1507. The 28-foot *Annika* accommodates up to four anglers on half-day and full-day trips for salmon, halibut, lingcod, and rockfish. Bait and tackle furnished. Also offers whale-watching trips.

# Golf

**Benbow Valley Golf Course,** 7000 Benbow Drive, Garberville; (707) 923–2777. Just east of US 101, 2 miles south of Garberville, at Benbow Valley RV Park. A nine-hole, par-thirty-five course with driving range, pro shop, cart and club rental.

**Shelter Cove Golf Links,** 1555 Upper Pacific Drive, Shelter Cove; (707) 986–7000. Next to the airport. A nine-hole, par-thirty-three, 2,465-yard course with great ocean views. Pro shop, clubhouse, club and cart rental. Missing Links Pub serves food and beverages.

# Other Attractions

**The Chimney Tree,** 1111 Avenue of the Giants, P.O. Box 86, Phillipsville 95559; (707) 923–2265; www.chimneytree.com. One mile south of Phillipsville, 8 miles north of Garberville on Avenue of the Giants. Daily, 8:00 A.M. to 8:00 P.M. (closed mid-September through March). In 1914 an unextinguished campfire near this redwood set fire to the great tree and burned inside it for days, hollowing out its interior. Later, a severe storm blew off the top of the tree. Not only did the mighty redwood survive, but for years it also provided shelter to hunters, whose campfire smoke rose through the tree and out the top—hence the name. At one time the tree was further hollowed out and shelves were installed when it was used as a gift shop. The amazing tree has healed itself and sprouted much new growth. When last measured, in 1978, it stood 78 feet tall, more than 14 feet in diameter, and more than 50 feet in circumference. Gift shop and restaurant on premises.

# Travel Information

**Garberville/Redway Chamber of Commerce,** 773 Redwood Drive, P.O. Box 445, Garberville 95442; (707) 923–2613 or (800) 923–2613; www.garberville.org; e-mail: info@garberville.org

# Ferndale

**Location:** 17 miles southwest of Eureka, 5 miles southwest of U.S. Highway 101 via Route 211.

**Population:** 1,388

Take the Ferndale exit off US 101, and the short drive becomes a trip in a time machine to a quaint Victorian village in the heart of a rich farming area sometime in the nineteenth century. Founded in 1852, Ferndale became the hub of a prosperous dairy-farming community, with many ornate Victorian mansions, known then as the "Butterfat Palaces."

The Victorians are still standing, either meticulously preserved or painstakingly restored, and several now function as bed-and-breakfast inns. Churches, the public library, and various business establishments also seem frozen in time. The face of Main Street has gone nearly unchanged. There are even a general store that still sells penny candy, a blacksmith shop where you can buy handmade weather vanes, and a bank that looks the way it did when a dollar was a dollar.

Something else carefully preserved is the town's sense of humor. You'll find it expressed in many ways, such as the whimsical names of some of the businesses, or the zany works and collections of Hobart Brown at Hobart Galleries, or Stan Bennett's wild and wonderful "motion sculpture."

Even the village's best-known annual event takes on a proportion of humor and level of high jinks unrivaled anywhere. What started simply with one of Hobart Brown's nutty inventions—a modified tricycle called the "pentacycle"—that was then challenged by the nutty inventions of other artists and artisans to a race down Main Street has grown considerably over the years. The World Championship Great Arcata to Ferndale Cross-Country Kinetic Sculpture Race now takes three days to run and covers 38 miles of land, sand, mud, water, bog, and marsh—all in homemade, people-powered contraptions. The major networks and several national magazines have covered the event, and there's no telling what it might eventually grow into.

Ferndale is a pleasant place to visit, as much for its friendly and witty inhabitants as for its idyllic beauty. The entire village has been designated a State Historical Landmark.

# Lodging

**The Fern Motel,** 332 Ocean Avenue, P.O. Box 121, 95536; (707) 786–5000; www.fern-motel.com. Queen beds in 8 rooms and suites with cable TV and refrigerators; suites also have full kitchens. Laundry facilities on premises. Easy walk to all in-town attractions. Moderate.

**The Gingerbread Mansion Inn,** 400 Berding Street; (707) 786–4000 or (800) 952–4136; www.gingerbread-mansion.com. One block southeast of Main Street. Eleven rooms and suites in one of the most elegant Victorian mansions in coastal California. Not just private baths here, but the Fountain Suite has his-and-her claw-foot tubs on a raised platform by the fireplace. Many amenities, such as bathrobes, hand-dipped chocolates at bedside, complimentary afternoon tea, and morning coffee tray. Four parlors and English garden. Lavish full breakfast served in formal dining room. Bicycles available. One block to Main Street shops and galleries. Expensive to extremely expensive.

**The Shaw House Inn,** 703 Main Street, P.O. Box 1125, 95536; (707) 786–9958 or (800) 557–SHAW; www.shawhouse.com. Built in 1854 in the Carpenter gothic style of architecture, the first structure in Ferndale, now on the National Register of Historic Places. Six rooms and two suites with private baths. Double and queen beds. Furnished with antiques, memorabilia, and original art. A short walk to all the village attractions. Continental breakfast. Moderate to expensive.

# Campgrounds and RV Parks

**Humboldt County Fairgrounds Campground,** (707) 786–9511. Van Ness Avenue at Fifth Street, ⅗₀ mile north of Main Street, via Van Ness. Has 100 grassy sites with hookups and tank dump. Near town. Inexpensive.

# Food

**Curly's Grill,** 460 Ocean Street; (707) 786–9696. Downtown. Specializes in grilled foods and California cuisine with an Asian accent. Local art adorns the walls. Good food in pleasant surroundings. Moderate.

# Shopping and Browsing

**Foggy Bottoms Antiques,** 563 Main Street, Suite 3, P.O. Box 998, 95536; (707) 786–9188. Monday through Saturday, 10:00 A.M. to 5:00 P.M.; Sunday, 10:00 A.M. to 4:00 P.M. Antiques and collectibles include a good selection of jewelry, glass, porcelain, and furniture.

**Golden Gait Mercantile,** 421 Main Street; (707) 786–4891. Monday through Saturday, 10:00 A.M. to 5:00 P.M.; Sunday, noon to 5:00 P.M. Step back more than a few decades as you walk across creaky wooden floors past the counter where the penny candy is sold. A great old general store offering antiques, collectibles, and modern goods, such as kitchenware and cookware. A good browse.

**Hobart Galleries,** 393 Main Street; (707) 786–WAKY. Main Street at Brown Street. Monday through Saturday, 11:00 A.M. to 5:16 P.M.; Sunday, noon to 5:16 P.M. Closed Monday in winter. Objets d'art—from semiserious to outrageous. A fascinating place to browse and buy. This is a *must stop,* and if you comport yourself with all due dignity, you might be invited to see the upstairs museum. If you're not invited, save yourself the embarrassment of asking why. This is a small town, and word spreads fast.

## Museum

**Ferndale Museum,** 515 Shaw Avenue, P.O. Box 431, 95536; (707) 786–4466. Just west of Main Street at Third and Shaw. June through September, 11:00 A.M. to 4:00 P.M. on Tuesday through Saturday and 1:00 to 4:00 P.M. on Sunday; October through May, 11:00 A.M. to 4:00 P.M. on Wednesday through Saturday and 1:00 to 4:00 P.M. on Sunday; closed in January. A fine country museum with a surprising array of tools, farm implements, antiques, and artifacts. Many items are set up in specific kinds of rooms: kitchen, dining room, bedroom, parlor, and such. Many changing displays as well. Also on premises is an operating Bosch-Omori seismograph with an interesting history.

## Beaches, Parks, Trails, and Waysides

A half mile east of Main Street via Ocean Avenue and Bluff Street is Russ Park, where trails lead through a forest of Sitka spruce and fir. Guided nature hikes are conducted Saturday morning, spring and summer, from 9:00 to 11:00 A.M.

Take Ocean Avenue west, instead, and it becomes Centerville Beach Road, which will take you past magnificent Fern Cottage to Centerville Beach, about 5 miles from town. There's a county park with meager facilities. Activities include surf fishing, beachcombing, and hiking on the beach and in the dunes. Currents are dangerous, so don't swim here.

Just south of the beach parking lot stands a white concrete cross that commemorates the loss of thirty-eight lives when the side-wheel steamer *Northerner* went down off the beach in 1860 after striking an uncharted reef.

Farther south, Wildcat Road rises into rugged but lush and beautiful ranchlands where sheep and cattle graze. This is the northern extreme of California's "Lost Coast." Seaward views are spectacular, with whale watching an added bonus.

## Other Attractions

**Fern Cottage,** 2121 Centerville Road, P.O. Box 36, 95536; (707) 786–4835 or 786–4735. About 3 miles west of Ferndale on Centerville Beach Road. The magnificent Russ family home, open for tours. Write or call for days and times.

## Travel Information

**Ferndale Chamber of Commerce,** P.O. Box 325, 95536; (707) 786–4477; www.victorianferndale.org/chamber

## events

| | |
|---|---|
| **April** | Spring Concert, (707) 786–4477 |
| **May** | Cinco de Mayo Folkloric Festival, (707) 786–9668 |
| | World Championship Great Arcata to Ferndale Cross–Country Kinetic Sculpture Race, (707) 786–4477 |
| | Memorial Day Parade, (707) 786–4477 |
| **June** | Portuguese Holy Ghost Celebration, (707) 786–9640 |
| | Scandinavian Mid Summer Festival, (707) 444–8444 |
| | Pet Parade, (707) 786–4477 |
| | Garden Tour, (707) 786–4477 |
| **August** | Humboldt County Fair and Horse Races, (707) 786–9511 |
| **September** | Tastes of Ferndale and Friends, (707) 786–4477 |
| **October** | Octoberfest, (707) 786–4477 |
| **December** | Lighting America's Tallest Living Christmas Tree, (707) 786–4477 |
| | Portuguese Linguica & Beans Dinner, (707) 786–4222 |
| | Hospitality Night Open House, (707) 786–4477 |
| | Lighted Tractor Parade, (707) 786–4477 |

# Eureka

**Location:** On U.S. Highway 101, 80 miles south of Crescent City, 65 miles north of Garberville, 287 miles north of San Francisco, and 150 miles west of Redding.

**Population:** 25,808

That a California town called Eureka could trace its history to the gold rush and the era of the forty-niners shouldn't surprise anyone, but the growth and success of this city had less to do with gold dust than with sawdust. The town of Arcata, 8 miles to the north, was in fact nearer the goldfields in the Trinity Mountains and was outgrowing Eureka in the early 1850s. But when mine activity waned in 1856, it was Eureka, with its deepwater port, that was destined to become the largest city on Humboldt Bay.

Lumber is the area's major industry, as it always has been. When the city was incorporated in 1856, there were already seven sawmills operating here. Even then Eureka had the capability of turning out two million board feet of lumber a month, southbound by schooner for booming and lumber-starved San Francisco.

As the bay area developed and the forest-products industry flourished, Eureka grew into the largest coastal California city north of San Francisco, situated on the second-largest deepwater port in the state.

The 500 boats of the Humboldt Bay commercial-fishing fleet annually land the largest catch on the California coast. The cold, nutrient-rich Pacific waters beyond the harbor entrance give up chinook and coho salmon, halibut, rockfish (marketed as snapper and cod), albacore, lingcod, perch, sole, Dungeness crab, and shrimp. Most of the same species are included in the sport catch.

Eureka's most popular attraction is the original town site, known as Old Town. To get there, turn toward the bay from US 101 (Fourth Street southbound, Fifth Street northbound) between C and M Streets. Old Town lies along First, Second, and Third Streets, where you will find various types of Victorian architecture well represented: Queen Anne, Eastlake, Italianate, Greek Revival, and Stick Style.

Second Street is the heart of Old Town, at the head of which stands the district's doyenne, the grande dame of venerable Victorians—the Carson Mansion. Built of redwood in the mid-1850s by lumber baron William McKendrie Carson, this three-story structure combines a variety of architectural styles and displays an abundance of adornments.

Although now a private men's club and closed to the public, the mansion is easily photographed from M or Second Streets.

Carson also built the beautiful pink-and-white Queen Anne across the street. It was a wedding gift for his eldest son, J. Milton Carson.

Old Town also houses some of the area's best restaurants and most interesting shops and galleries. Maps and guides are available at the chamber of commerce visitor center.

# Lodging

**Abigail's Elegant Victorian Mansion,** 1406 C Street; (707) 444–3144. C Street at Fourteenth Street, near Old Town. A beautifully preserved and restored architectural treasure, this fine old Victorian functions as a bed-and-breakfast inn where elegance is the watchword and guests are pampered. Three guest rooms with three shared baths, one suite with private bath. Opulent French breakfast includes fresh-brewed coffee, assorted teas, juice, fresh fruits, and homemade breads, followed by a main course that changes daily. Views of city, bay, and mountains. Sauna and laundry facilities on premises. Secured parking behind locked gates. Moderate to expensive.

**Best Western Humboldt Bay Inn,** 232 West Fifth Street; (707) 443–2234 or (800) 528–1234; www.humboldtbayinn.com. On US 101, in town, near Old Town. Queen and king beds in 115 rooms and suites with cable TV and cable movies. Heated pool, whirlpool, electronic-game room, and coffee shop on premises. Inexpensive.

**Carter House Inns,** 301 L Street; (707) 444–8062 or (800) 404–1390; www.carter house.com. Full restaurant on premises. Four of the most handsome Victorian structures in Old Town, based on designs by Samuel and Joseph Newsom, architects who also designed the Carson Mansion. Thirty-two rooms and suites, plus a cottage with private and shared baths. Full breakfast served, considered among the best in the state. Limousine service in a 1958 Bentley available to and from airport. Moderate to very expensive.

**The Eureka Inn,** 518 Seventh Street; (707) 442–6441 or (800) 862–4906; www.eurekainn.com. At Seventh and F Streets. An English Tudor–style inn built in 1922, now a National Historic Landmark. Has 110 rooms and suites. Luxury suites have fireplaces and whirlpool spas. Heated pool, whirlpool, and two saunas. Restaurant, coffee shop, cocktail lounge, and pub on premises. Limousine and concierge service available. Moderate to very expensive.

**Old Town Bed & Breakfast Inn,** 1521 Third Street; (707) 443–5235 or (888) 508–5235; www.oldtownbnb.com. Third Street at P Street, 1 block from the Carson Mansion. Twin, double, queen, and king beds in 4 rooms with private and shared baths in a Greek Revival–Victorian house built in 1871 and once the residence of the William Carson family. Evening social hour and full breakfast. Moderate.

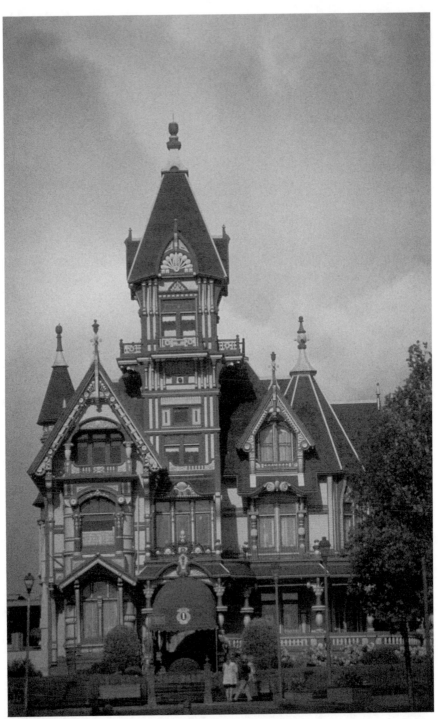

Carson Mansion, Eureka *Courtesy of Robert Holmes/CalTour*

## Campgrounds and RV Parks

**E-Z Landing RV Park & Marina,** King Salmon Resort, 1875 Buhne Drive; (707) 442–1118. Four miles south of Eureka, 1 mile west of US 101, via King Salmon Avenue. Has 45 full-hookup sites with cable TV for trailers and motor homes; 20 drive-through sites available. Fishing tackle, docks, boat rentals, and full-service marina on premises. Moderate.

**Johnny's RV Park & Marina,** King Salmon Resort, 1821 Buhne Drive; (707) 442–2284. Four miles south of Eureka, 1 mile west of US 101, via King Salmon Avenue. Has 53 sites with full hookups. Showers and laundry facilities. Full-service marina on premises. Moderate.

**KOA Kampground,** 4050 North Highway 101; (707) 822–4243; www.koa.com. Four miles north of Eureka. Has 165 full-hookup sites and 29 grassy tent sites with tables and grills. Kamping Kabins, showers, laundry facilities, hot tub, grocery store, recreation room, and snack bar. Propane and ice available. Moderate to expensive.

## Food

**Samoa Cookhouse,** 79 Lookhouse Lane, Samoa; (707) 442–1659. West of US 101 via the Samoa Bridge (Route 255), then left on Samoa Road, and left again at the first road. Breakfast, lunch, and dinner daily. The last of the great lumber-camp cookhouses, where fresh, wholesome food is served camp style. The menu varies according to availability but always includes the freshest meats, vegetables, fruits, and butter. Homemade bread, pastries, and pies. Meals are made to satisfy loggers' appetites. Nobody leaves hungry. This is an eating experience you won't want to miss. Moderate.

**The Sea Grill,** 316 E Street; (707) 443–7187. In Old Town. Lunch, Tuesday through Friday; dinner, Monday through Saturday. French dip, burgers, and such seafood sandwiches as grilled crab and Jack cheese on sourdough, grilled shrimp and cheddar on sourdough, and calamari steak on French roll. For dinner, try the Cajun-style cod, beer-batter prawns, orange roughy amandine, scallops, clams, oysters, or combination plate. Full bar. Moderate.

## Shopping and Browsing

**Abraxas Jewelry & Leather,** 425 Third Street; (707) 443–4638. In Old Town, next to the Ritz. Monday through Saturday, 10:00 A.M. to 5:30 P.M. Gold and silver jewelry, large selection of earrings, custom leather goods, pottery, craft items, jewelry boxes, and leaded glass.

**American Indian Art & Gift Shop,** 241 F Street; (707) 445–8451 or (800) 566–2381. In Old Town. Monday through Saturday, 10:00 A.M. to 6:00 P.M. A large selection of Indian arts and crafts. Exquisite baskets, fine silver and turquoise jewelry and accessories, moccasins, and beadwork.

**Antiques & Goodies,** 1128 Third Street; (707) 442–0445. Upper end of Old Town, next to Hotel Carter. Monday through Saturday, 10:00 A.M. to 5:00 P.M.; Sunday, 10:00 A.M. to 2:00 P.M. A large and interesting shop with 5,000 square feet of fine Old World antiques, oak furniture, crockery, china, cloisonné, paintings, and prints.

**Old Town Art Gallery,** 233 F Street; (707) 445–2315; www.oldtowngalleryeureka.com. In Old Town. Monday through Sunday, 10:00 A.M. to 5:00 P.M. A lovely gallery with good selection and variety. Landscapes, seascapes, and wildlife art. Stained glass, sculpture, pottery, drawings, old paintings, acrylics, watercolors, batiks, and craft items.

**Restoration Hardware,** 417 Second Street; (707) 443–3152; www.restoration hardware.com. In Old Town. Monday through Saturday, 10:00 A.M. to 6:00 P.M.; Sunday, 11:00 A.M. to 5:00 P.M. Victorian fixtures of all kinds—door, garden, plumbing, lighting, and electrical. Clocks, lamps, artwork, mailboxes, sundials, and bathroom accessories. A great shop for the fixer-upper or for anyone looking for unusual gifts.

## Museums

**Clarke Memorial Museum,** 240 Third Street; (707) 443–1947. In Old Town. At Third and E Streets. Tuesday through Saturday, noon to 4:00 P.M. Built in 1911–12 to house the Bank of Eureka, the beautiful Italian Renaissance structure that now functions as a museum is itself a valuable piece of local history. Excellent collection of American Indian artifacts—especially fine baskets. More than 1,200 Indian artifacts on display. Firearms, glassware, nineteenth-century paintings, models, and exhibits of logging, lumber, shipbuilding, and maritime trades. Pioneer memorabilia, Victorian furniture, textiles, and decorative pieces.

**Humboldt Bay Maritime Museum,** 423 First Street; (707) 444–9440. Behind the Carson Mansion. Daily, 11:00 A.M. to 4:00 P.M. Artifacts depicting the maritime history of Humboldt Bay. Models of ships and boats, plus many photographs of the Humboldt Bay area. An interesting little museum.

## Beaches, Parks, Trails, and Waysides

The vicinity of Eureka and Humboldt Bay isn't famous for broad beaches, lush green parks, and abundant hiking trails; areas to the north and south are better choices for such outdoor attractions. The region does, however, offer ocean beaches and dunes along the North Spit, as well as areas for camping and picnicking there. To reach the spit, take the Samoa Bridge, Route 255, west from Eureka to Samoa, and turn left on New Navy Base Road.

As industrialized as the north arm of Humboldt Bay is, much of the south arm is a wildlife refuge, where egrets, herons, waterfowl, and shorebirds are seasonally abundant. Fields Landing and King Salmon Resort, south of Eureka, provide access to the south bay.

In town the Eureka Mooring Basin, at Commercial and First Streets, is where most of the local fishing boats and pleasure craft are moored. This is a good place for a picnic and for watching harbor traffic, birds, seals, and sea lions.

# Water Sports and Activities

Boaters and anglers who tow boats will find several launching facilities in and near Eureka. There's a one-lane concrete ramp at the Eureka Mooring Basin, at First and Commercial Streets. At the foot of Railroad Avenue in Fields Landing, south of town, is a two-lane concrete ramp on the bay. Nearby King Salmon Resort has two full-service marinas with hoists.

Much of the sportfishing activities center on the King Salmon Resort. The beach and breakwaters here serve as popular fishing spots, the catch consisting mainly of surfperch and various bottom species.

Offshore fishing is seasonally good for coho and chinook salmon, and bottom fishing is excellent much of the year, weather and water conditions permitting.

Crabbers take Dungeness, red, and rock crabs from the bay. On minus tides, clam diggers ply the mudflats for gaper, littleneck, and hard-shell clams.

**Bucksport Sporting Goods,** 3650 South Broadway; (707) 442–1832. On US 101, south end of town. Monday through Saturday, 9:00 A.M. to 5:30 P.M. A fine sport shop with a large selection of top-quality outdoor clothing, fishing tackle, crab pots, and more. Sells fishing licenses.

**E-Z Landing RV Park & Marina,** King Salmon Resort, 1875 Buhne Drive; (707) 442–1118. On Humboldt Bay, 4 miles south of Eureka, west of US 101, via King Salmon Avenue. Electric boat launch for vessels to two tons and 22 feet. Marine gas and oil, bait, tackle, and rental boats and motors.

**Johnny's RV Park & Marina,** King Salmon Resort, 1821 Buhne Drive; (707) 442–2284. On Humboldt Bay, 4 miles south of Eureka, west of US 101, via King Salmon Avenue. Electric boat launch, boat repairs, marine supplies, and boat rentals.

# Tours and Trips

**Humboldt Bay Harbor Cruise;** (707) 445–1910. Enjoy narrated cruises aboard the beautiful M/V *Madaket,* launched in 1910 and owned by the Humboldt Bay Maritime Museum. March through October, Wednesday through Saturday sightseeing cruises depart at 1:00, 2:00, 4:00, and 5:30 P.M. Friday and Saturday dinner cruises leave at 7:30 P.M. Sunday brunch cruises sail at 11:00 A.M. All departures from the foot of C Street in Old Town.

## events

| | |
|---|---|
| **March** | Daffodil Show, Fortuna, (707) 725–2281 |
| **April** | Redwood Coast Dixieland Jazz Fest, (707) 445–3378 |
| | Rhododendron Festival, (707) 442–3738 |
| **May** | Avenue of the Giants Marathon, (707) 443–1226 |
| **June** | U.S. Coast Guard Days, (707) 443–5097 |
| | Redwood Acres Fair & Rodeo, (707) 445–3037 |
| **July** | The Sea Hunt Archery Tournament, (707) 839–7600 |
| | Humboldt Bay Fourth of July Festival, (707) 442–9054 |
| | Blues by the Bay Music Festival, (707) 443–3378 |
| **September** | Festival on the Bay, (707) 445–3801 |
| **November** | Gem & Mineral Show, (707) 445–3037 |
| | Holiday Craft Bazaar, (707) 443–2874 |
| **December** | Truckers Christmas Convoy, (707) 442–5744 |

# Golf

**Eureka Municipal Golf Course,** 4750 Fairway Drive; (707) 443–4808. Follow F Street to the south end of town, where F Street turns into Fairway Drive. An exceptionally beautiful eighteen-hole public course. Driving range, pro shop, resident pro, cart and club rentals.

## Weather and Tide Information

**National Weather Service;** recorded message, (707) 443–7062

## Travel Information

**Eureka Chamber of Commerce,** 2112 Broadway; (707) 442–3738 or (800) 356–6381; www.eurekachamber.com; e-mail: eurekacc@northerncoast.com

# Arcata / Trinidad

**Location:** Arcata is on U.S. Highway 101, 8 miles north of Eureka; Trinidad lies west of US 101, 13 miles north of Arcata, 19 miles south of Orick, and 59 miles south of Crescent City.

**Population:** Arcata 16,891; Trinidad 311

Arcata began in the early 1850s as a supply depot for the gold mines in the Trinity Mountains. It was the county's first seat of government, a post Eureka took over in 1856. As mining activity decreased, agriculture and logging gained importance in and near Arcata.

Like its neighbor across the bay, Arcata has dozens of Victorian houses, mansions, and other structures, many of which are well preserved and lovingly cared for. The downtown area is built around a plaza. In the hills above downtown is the campus of Humboldt State University.

Every town with an eye on tourism claims to be a county's, region's, or state's "best-kept secret." The phrase is so often used it's a cliché and so often abused it's usually a lie. But it might just fit Trinidad, a tiny town and teacup harbor just far enough north of San Francisco and south of Portland that most people "driving the Pacific Coast" seem to drive right by.

Don't make the same mistake. Take the Trinidad exit and visit the spotless town and nearby beaches and headlands. Fish out of the harbor aboard your own boat or one of the charter craft. Stay at one of the beautiful bed-and-breakfast inns or bargain-priced motels. If you're camping, pitch a tent or plug in the RV at one of several campgrounds and RV parks.

## Lodging

**Bishop Pine Lodge,** 1481 Patrick's Point Drive, Trinidad; (707) 677–3314; www.bishop pinelodge.com. West of US 101 on Main Street, via Trinidad exit, then north 2 miles on Patrick's Point Drive. Double, queen, and king beds in 13 1-, 2-, and 3-bedroom cottages with cable TV and cable movies, most with fully equipped kitchens. Two rooms share outdoor hot tub. Two deluxe suites have kitchen, microwave, refrigerator, and phones with bathroom extensions. Hair dryers in all units. Barbecue area. Cribs, rollaways, and waterbeds available. Inexpensive to moderate.

**The Lady Anne Victorian Inn,** 902 Fourteenth Street, Arcata; (707) 822–2797. West of US 101, Fourteenth at I Street. Five rooms in a Victorian mansion built in 1888, furnished

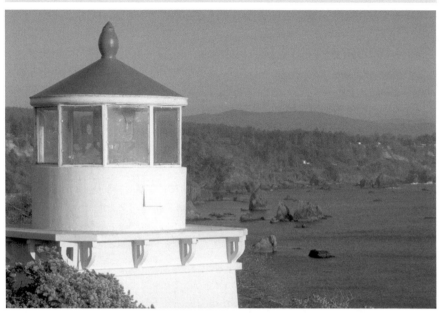

Trinidad Memorial Lighthouse *Courtesy of Robert Holmes/CalTour*

with antiques. Shared and private baths. Music room. Bicycles available. Full breakfast. Walking distance to several restaurants. Near the university. Moderate.

**The Lost Whale Bed & Breakfast Inn,** 3452 Patrick's Point Drive, Trinidad; (707) 677–3425; www.lostwhaleinn.com. West of US 101 via Seawood Drive exit or Patrick's Point Drive exit. Five ocean-view rooms with private baths in a contemporary inn offering one of the best views on the coast. The building is uniquely designed and set up with families in mind, featuring sleeping lofts for kids and a two-story playhouse; babysitting provided. Private path to private beach. Afternoon cappuccino, sherry, and homemade pastries. Full breakfast served in bright and cheerful dining area. Lots of deck space and a big backyard. Moderate to expensive.

**Trinidad Bay Bed & Breakfast,** 560 Edwards Street, P.O. Box 849, Trinidad 95570; (707) 677–0840; www.trinidadbaybnb.com. West of US 101, Edwards at Trinity, overlooking harbor and lighthouse. King beds in 2 rooms with private baths in a Cape Cod house affording ocean and harbor view. Walk to shops, restaurants, and beaches. Continental breakfast. Moderate to expensive.

**Trinidad Inn,** 1170 Patrick's Point Drive, Trinidad; (707) 677–3349; www .trinidadinn.com. West of US 101, 2 miles north of town. One of those sleeper bargains (no pun intended), with 11 spotless rooms and suites, tastefully decorated. Large honeymoon suite with wicker furniture and lots of white and muted pastels. Family suite on two floors sleeps six to eight persons. Kitchen units available. Cable TV, queen beds. Quiet, wooded setting. Inexpensive to moderate.

# Campgrounds and RV Parks

**Mad River Rapids RV Park,** 3501 Janes Road, Arcata; (707) 822–7275; www .madriverrv.com. West of US 101 via Guintoli Lane, just north of Arcata. Has 92 full-hookup sites with cable TV. Barbecue grills, showers, laundry, tank dump, VCR equipment and movie rentals, heated pool, hot tub, horseshoe pits, video arcade, pool tables, table tennis, and basketball court. Grocery store, restaurant, and sports bar. Moderate.

**Midway RV Park,** P.O. Box 830, Trinidad, 95570; (707) 677–3934. West of US 101 via Trinidad exit and Main Street, then north ½ mile on Patrick's Point Drive. Has 72 full-hookup sites with cable TV and tables. Showers, tank dump, recreation room, fish-cleaning facilities, smokehouse, canning facilities, and boat and RV storage. Moderate.

**Patrick's Point State Park,** 4150 Patrick's Point Drive, Trinidad; (707) 677–3570 or (800) 444–7275; www.parks.ca.gov. West of US 101, 5 miles north of Trinidad. Has 124 developed campsites with tables, stoves, and cupboards. Piped water and showers. Trails to the beach. Summer camp-fire program. Moderate.

**Sounds of the Sea RV Park,** 3443 Patrick's Point Drive, Trinidad; (707) 677–3271. One mile south of Patrick's Point. Has 52 full-hookup sites with tables, some with ocean view. Showers, laundry, horseshoes, volleyball, and croquet. Store with ice and camping supplies. Moderate.

# Food

**Humboldt Brewery,** 856 Tenth Street, Arcata; (707) 826–2739; www.humbrew.com. West of US 101, downtown. Monday through Wednesday, 4:00 P.M. to midnight; Thursday through Saturday, 11:30 A.M. to 2:00 A.M.; Sunday, 2:00 to 10:00 P.M. Pub food includes spicy or mild Buffalo chicken wings, Cajun chicken sandwiches, Cajun burgers, bacon cheeseburgers, "chainsaw" chili cheeseburgers, beer-batter fish-and-chips, and pasta dishes. Fine English-style brews are Gold Rush Ale, Red Nectar Ale, Storm Cellar Porter, and award-winning Oatmeal Stout. Good food and great brew, but college-student waiters inspire little hope for the planet's future. Moderate.

**Katy's Smokehouse,** 740 Edwards Street, Trinidad; (707) 677–0151; www.katys smokehouse.com. In town, above the harbor. Daily, 9:00 A.M. to 6:00 P.M. A small seafood market offering whatever is locally fresh and in season, as well as what can be shipped in fresh, including halibut, lingcod, salmon, rockfish, perch, oysters, prawns, shrimp, crab, and lobster. Smoked treats include salmon, salmon jerky, albacore, and halibut. Canned products also available. Gift packs shipped anywhere. Moderate to expensive.

**Los Bagels,** 1061 I Street, Arcata; (707) 822–3150; www.losbagels.com. West of US 101, downtown. Monday, Wednesday, Thursday, and Friday, 7:00 A.M. to 6:00 P.M.; Saturday, 7:00 A.M. to 5:00 P.M.; Sunday, 8:00 A.M. to 3:00 P.M. Fresh bagels, croissants, and muffins. Sandwiches, lox, smoked fish, and freshly brewed coffee. Inexpensive to moderate.

**Seascape Restaurant,** P.O. Box 1007, Trinidad 95570; (707) 677–3762. West of US 101, on Bay Street, at the boat basin. Daily breakfast, lunch, and dinner; weekend brunch. Summers, open until 10:00 P.M.; October through April, open until 8:30 P.M. Traditional breakfast and lunch menu but also a large selection of three-egg seafood omelets, clam chowder, seafood bisque, salads, and seafood Louis. Dinners include steaks and such seafoods as halibut, salmon, scallops, prawns, oysters, calamari, lobster tails, and lobster thermidor. Beer and wine. Moderate.

**Wildflower Cafe & Bakery,** 1604 G Street, Arcata; (707) 822–0360. West of US 101, Sixteenth Street and G Street. Monday through Saturday, breakfast, lunch, and din-ner; Sunday open from 9:00 A.M. to 1:00 P.M. Vegetarian cuisine includes such bakery goodies as raisin-date bars, poppyseed muffins, and apple-bran muffins. Among breakfast offerings are omelets, pancakes, and waffles with fruit and yogurt. Lunch features homemade soups, quiche, steamed-vegetable salad, and Mexican beans and cheese. Dinner includes mushroom stroganoff, chow mein, sweet-and-sour veg-etables, and a daily special. Inexpensive to moderate.

# Museum and Aquarium

**Humboldt State University Marine Lab Aquarium,** P.O. Box 690, Trinidad 95570; (707) 826–3689. Corner of Edwards and Ewing, in town, near the harbor. Monday through Friday 8:00 A.M. to 5:00 P.M., Saturday and Sunday 10:00 A.M. to 5:00 P.M. (weekend hours during school sessions only). Aquarium, touch tank, and tidepool exhibits open to the public.

**Humboldt State University Natural History Museum,** Arcata; (707) 826–4479. West of US 101, G Street at Thirteenth Street. Tuesday through Saturday, 10:00 A.M. to 5:00 P.M. Among the exhibits at this museum, which opened in 1989, are nearly 2,000 fos-sils dating back more than 200 million years, as well as fossils from Europe, Africa, and North America providing information about the planet's oceans as far back as 500 million years. An impressive collection superbly displayed.

# Beaches, Parks, Trails, and Waysides

The Arcata Marsh and Wildlife Sanctuary stands as an example of what people can do to improve the environment when they put their minds to it. South of downtown, via I Street, is an area of some seventy-five acres that until 1979 was what one report euphemistically referred to as "degraded salt marsh." Area residents called it the city dump. Next to it was the sewage-treatment plant. A delightful combination.

Not only did the city clean up the mess, but in the process it also created a beautiful natural area that includes a lake, three marshes, hiking trails, and picnic areas. The lake is stocked with rainbow trout, and salmon are reared in a mixture of bay water and treated wastewater at the treatment plant's oxidation ponds. The lush vegetation also attracts more than 150 species of birds and waterfowl. To make watching and photographing easier, the city has built all-weather blinds along the shores.

If the place sounds unbelievable, see it for yourself. As one resident asked, "How many cities do you know of where people take their sack lunches to the local sewage-treatment plant?"

In the vicinity of Trinidad are a number of beaches offering a variety of activities. Take Scenic Drive south off Main Street for 3 miles to the broad and sandy Moonstone Beach. On the way are several smaller pocket beaches and tidepool areas. North of Main Street, off Trinity Street, is Trinidad State Beach. Agate Beach is at Patrick's Point State Park, 5 miles north of Trinidad.

These are some of the best beaches in California for hiking, beachcombing, and photography. Some stretches are littered with driftwood; others give up agates, jasper, and jade. Offshore rocks, sea stacks, and islets punctuate the seascape and add elements of interest and drama to photographs. They also harbor seabirds by the tens of thousands.

## Water Sports and Activities

Beaches and rocky areas north and south of Trinidad offer excellent opportunities for surfperch fishing and smelt dipping. Sandy beaches and tidal flats are popular, too, for clam digging. Moonstone Beach provides a good surfing area.

The Mad River, just north of Arcata, and Little River, 4 miles south of Trinidad, get seasonal runs of salmon and steelhead. Sea-run cutthroat trout also enter the Little River in late summer. The estuaries of both rivers offer angling for surfperch and other saltwater species.

Trinidad's natural harbor and pier are favored by anglers. Offshore, fishing is good for salmon and bottom fish. Near-shore waters also give up rockfish, lingcod, cabezon, and Dungeness crab.

**Bob's Boat Basin,** Trinidad; (707) 677–3625. At the pier, on the harbor. Bait, tackle, snacks, beverages, and boat rentals (16-foot skiffs). Boats up to 24 feet launched. Charters booked. Source of information on local fishing.

# Travel Information

**Arcata Chamber of Commerce,** 1635 Heindon, Arcata; (707) 822–3619; www.arcata chamber.com

**Greater Trinidad Chamber of Commerce,** P.O. Box 356, Trinidad 95570; (707) 677–0591; www.trinidadcalifchamber.org

## events

| | |
|---|---|
| **March** | Humboldt State University Pow Wow, Arcata, (707) 826–4994 |
| | First Nations Feast, Arcata, (707) 826–4994 |
| **May** | Bebop & Brew, Arcata, (707) 826–2267 |
| | Mother's Day Garden Tour Home & Garden, Trinidad, (707) 677–0467 |
| | World Championship Great Arcata to Ferndale/ Cross-Country Kinetic Sculpture Race, (707) 845–1717 |
| **June** | Trinidad Fish Festival, (707) 677–1610 |
| | Humboldt Folklife Festival, (707) 826–9043 |
| **July** | Fourth of July Jubilee, Arcata, (707) 822–3619 |
| **August** | Humboldt County Fair, Ferndale, (707) 786–9511 |

# Crescent City

**Location:** On U.S. Highway 101, 20 miles south of the California–Oregon state line, 19 miles north of Klamath, and 78 miles north of Eureka.

**Population:** 8,300

During the California gold rush, the towns of Klamath and Crescent City burgeoned simultaneously when mining brought thousands to the nearby mountains and beaches in 1850. The Klamath River bar, however, proved too treacherous for the San Francisco schooners to cross, so Crescent City, with its excellent natural harbor, became the supply depot for the mining camps.

The Crescent City Light Station, generally referred to as the Battery Point Lighthouse, began guiding mariners into Crescent Bay on December 10, 1856. It's located at the west end of the town and harbor, on an islet near Battery Point. Although it ceased operating in 1965, it now functions as a museum that's open during the summer months only. The islet, however, is open to the public all year, though it can be reached only at low tide. Offering a good spot for photography or a picnic on any sunny day, the islet commands an excellent view of the harbor and coastline north and south. It also provides a good vantage for watching whales and winter storms.

Crescent City's first lumber mill was built in 1853, and timber eventually became the area's main industry, followed by commercial fishing, agriculture, and tourism. What draws visitors to this part of northern California today is what attracted the early settlers: the ocean, a safe harbor with no bar to cross, the state's two top rivers for salmon and steelhead fishing, and the magnificent coastal redwood trees.

## Lodging

**Bayview Inn,** 310 Highway 101 South; (707) 465–2050 or (800) 446–0583. South end of town, west side of US 101. Queen and king beds in 67 rooms with cable TV, cable movies, and coffeemakers. Rooms with whirlpool spas available. Laundry facilities on premises. Inexpensive.

**Curly Redwood Lodge,** 701 Highway 101 South; (707) 464–2137; www.curlyred woodlodge.com. South end of town, opposite the waterfront. Queen beds in 36 rooms and family units with cable TV. The lodge was built from a single redwood tree that, when sawed, yielded 57,000 board feet of lumber. Walking distance to waterfront, shops, and restaurants. Inexpensive to moderate.

**Ship Ashore Resort,** 12370 Highway 101 North, P.O. Box 75, Smith River 95567; (707) 487–3141 or (800) 487–3141; www.ship-ashore.com. Located 17 miles north of Crescent City, at the mouth of the Smith River. Cable TV and cable movies in 50 rooms and suites. Kitchen and hot-tub suites available. Riverfront units and ocean-view rooms available. Coffee shop, restaurant, lounge, and gift shop on premises. Boat rentals and guide service. Moderate.

## Campgrounds and RV Parks

**Crescent City Redwoods KOA Kampground,** 4241 Highway 101 North; (707) 464–5744; www.koa.com. Five miles north of town. Has 94 campsites, half with full hookups. Cable TV, showers, laundry, tank dump, snack bar, groceries, ice, beer and wine, souvenirs, redwood and myrtlewood items, propane, firewood, volleyball, bad-minton, horseshoes, tether ball, and nature trails—all on ten wooded acres. Kamping Kabins available. Expensive.

**Del Norte Coast Redwoods State Park,** 1375 Elk Valley Road; (707) 464–6101, extension 5120, or (800) 444–7275; www.redwood.national-park.com. On US 101, 7 miles south of Crescent City. Open year-round, unless closed due to slides or flood-ing. Has 145 campsites with tables and fire pits. Showers, tank dump, inland and coastal hiking and nature trails. More than 6,000 acres. Beach access. Moderate.

**Salmon Harbor RV Resort,** 200 Salmon Harbor Road, Smith River; (707) 487–3341 or (800) 332–6139; www.salmonharborrvresort.com. About 18 miles north of Crescent City, at the mouth of the Smith River. Has 90 full-hookup sites and 10 with water and electricity. Showers and laundry facilities. Beer, wine, ice, and propane available. Recreation room, playground, boat ramp, and dock. Riverfront sites available. Moderate.

**Ship Ashore Resort,** 12370 Highway 101 North, Smith River; (707) 487–3141 or (800) 487–3141; www.ship-ashore.com. About 17 miles north of Crescent City, on the Smith River. Look for the 160-foot yacht parked at roadside. Has 200 full-hookup and 12 tent sites. Cable TV, showers, hot tub, laundry facilities, recreation room, gift shop, general store, and boat dock. Restaurant and cocktail lounge on premises. Boat rentals and guide service available. Tackle shop. Moderate.

**Sunset Harbor RV Park,** 205 King Street; (707) 464–3423. About 1 block east of US 101 at the south end of town. Has 69 full-hookup sites with tables and cable TV. Tent area, showers, laundry facilities, minimart, beer, wine, ice, and supplies. Near the waterfront. Moderate.

**Village Camper Inn,** 1543 Parkway Drive; (707) 464–3544. About ¼ mile east of US 101 via Washington Boulevard exit, north of town. Has 135 full-hookup sites with cable TV and 15 tent sites. Showers, laundry facilities, and tank dump. Wooded setting with playground and horseshoe pits. Moderate.

# Food

**China Hut,** 928 Ninth Street; (707) 464–4921. West of US 101, in town. Lunch and dinner daily. Chinese and American cuisine with specialties in Cantonese and Mandarin dishes. American menu includes steaks, chicken, veal, seafood, and a dozen different sandwiches. Among the appetizers are egg rolls, fried wonton, pot stickers, and barbecued pork. Chop suey, chow mein, sweet-and-sour dishes, egg foo yung, and various combination and family dinners offered. Cantonese specialties include *mar far* chicken, curry shrimp or chicken, scallop *chow yuk,* and chicken with black-bean sauce. Mandarin offerings include Peking spareribs, beef with scallions, and Szechuan shrimp, chicken, or pork. Inexpensive to moderate.

**Harbor View Grotto Restaurant & Lounge,** 150 Starfish Way, Crescent City; (707) 464–3815. West of US 101 at the boat basin. Lunch and dinner daily. Lunch: salads, burgers, oyster stew, clam chowder, fish and shellfish sandwiches and platters. Dinner: large selection of seafood, chicken, steaks, prime rib. Crab, prawns, scallops, oysters, lobster, salmon, halibut, and more—all deep-fried in pure vegetable oil. Cocktails, beer, and wine. Moderate.

# Museums

**Del Norte County Historical Society Main Museum,** 577 H Street; (707) 464–3922; www.delnortehistory.org. West of US 101 at Sixth and H Streets. April through September, 10:00 A.M. to 4:00 P.M. Monday through Saturday. Historical society collections and exhibits of pioneer artifacts in the former jail and hall of records, built in 1926. On display also is the first-order Fresnel lens from the St. George Reef Lighthouse.

**Lighthouse Museum,** P.O. Box 396, 95531; (707) 464–3089; www.delnorte history.org. Battery Point Lighthouse at the foot of A Street, west of US 101. April through September, 10:00 A.M. to 4:00 P.M. Wednesday through Sunday, tides permitting. Lighthouse built in 1856 on a near-shore island, accessible at low tide.

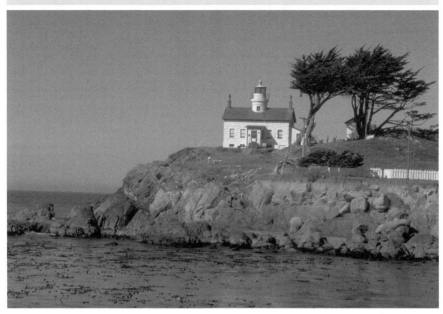

Battery Point Lighthouse *Courtesy of Robert Holmes/CalTour*

# Beaches, Parks, Trails, and Waysides

Nine miles northeast of Crescent City—via Route 199, east off US 101—Jedediah Smith Redwoods State Park lies along the Smith River, amid some of the most spectacular redwood groves in the state. The park offers fishing, boating, picnicking, camping, hiking, sightseeing, and innumerable photographic opportunities.

North of Crescent City and west of US 101, via Morehead Road and Lake Earl Drive to Kellogg Road, Kellogg Beach offers beach recreation and picnicking. The sandy beach spreads before dunes and marshes to the tumbling surf.

The Lake Earl Wildlife Area lies west of US 101 and north of town. From Crescent City, take Lake Earl Drive north to Old Mill Road, turn left, and proceed 1½ miles to the area headquarters. There are few roads and no trails in this 5,000-acre reserve, but there's plenty of room to roam through the stabilized dunes and along the shoreline of Lake Talawa and Lake Earl.

Although fishing is good here, especially in the channel connecting the two lakes, the main attraction for many visitors is the abundant and varied bird life. More than 250 species have been recorded, some extremely rare or endangered. In addition to numerous residents present all year, great flocks of migrants swell the bird population seasonally.

Shorebirds—including black turnstones, dowitchers, godwits, and sandpipers—pour into the reserve in early fall, followed soon by the puddle ducks, such as teal, pintail, mallard, and widgeon. Great flocks of diver ducks follow with the season's first storms, adding bluebill, redhead, canvasback, and others to the colorful gathering.

Rare Aleutian Canada geese arrive in small flocks until they number about 6,000—the world's entire population of this endangered species. Tundra and trumpeter swans, white as wedding dresses, join the gathering flocks.

Among the eighty species of songbirds that have been counted here are chickadees, finches, flycatchers, juncos, larks, robins, sparrows, thrushes, vireos, warblers, and wrens.

With birds, mice, and ground squirrels in such great numbers, raptors are also well represented here. Bald and golden eagles, red-tailed and rough-legged hawks, kestrels, merlins, and black-shouldered kites hunt here by day, while owls take the night shift. Listen, too, for the high-pitched whistle of the osprey as it soars and hunts for fish.

Lake Earl is also a good place to encounter black-tailed deer and smaller mammals, such as rabbits and raccoons. Frequenting the shoreline and marshy areas are river otter, beaver, and muskrat.

Point St. George Public Access is at the end of Radio Road, west of US 101, via Washington Boulevard or Pebble Beach Drive. Here you'll find a trail leading from a large parking area to the beach, where you can explore tidepools, hike, beach-comb, or just enjoy the scenery. The St. George Light, standing about 6 miles offshore, is visible here.

At the west end of town, Pebble Beach Drive parallels Pebble Beach, where you'll find a number of parking areas and easy beach access. This is a wonderfully scenic area, a photographer's delight. The beach is also popular with beachcombers and is a good place to search for agates and other semiprecious gemstones.

Along the northern shore of Crescent Bay lies Beach Front Park, a large, attractive park with play areas, grassy lawn, trees, benches, and picnic tables. There's plenty of parking along the bay and easy bay access. To reach the park, take Front Street west off US 101 to the park entrance. Howe Drive parallels the bayshore for the length of the park.

Crescent Beach and Enderts Beach are west of US 101, via Enderts Beach Road, 2 miles south of town. Both areas offer picnicking, and Enderts Beach has primitive campsites. The rocky beaches are good for examining tidepools.

Four miles south of Crescent City is the 6,000-acre Del Norte Coast Redwoods State Park. Trail systems lead to beaches and into the redwoods. Both sandy beaches and rocky shoreline are here to enjoy.

Del Norte State Park is part of Redwood National Park, established in 1968 and enlarged in 1978 and headquartered at Crescent City. From its northern boundary southward along the coast for 50 miles, Redwood National Park comprises three state parks, virgin old-growth forests, new-growth forests, herds of wild elk, and great stands of the planet's tallest trees: coast redwoods. Within the park boundaries are beaches, overlooks, fishing-access points, a beautiful coastal drive, and miles of hiking and nature trails.

# Water Sports and Activities

The Klamath and Smith Rivers head the list of top-producing streams in California, the former hosting the state's largest salmon and steelhead runs, the latter yielding the biggest salmonids, including steelhead exceeding twenty pounds and chinook salmon weighing more than fifty pounds. Both rivers and their tributaries also offer excellent fishing for sea-run cutthroat trout.

Both coho and chinook salmon move into the Klamath in mid-July, providing angling opportunities in the lower river and at the river mouth until November. Chinook action on the lower and middle Smith occurs from September through December. Steelheading on both rivers runs from August through October. The best angling for sea-run cutthroat takes place in September and October. Native rainbow and cutthroat angling in the upper rivers and their tributaries is good through the summer and into early autumn. Sturgeon are taken from the lower Klamath from midsummer through early autumn.

Angling in the salt chuck focuses on chinook and coho salmon during the summer months. Local bottom fishes include lingcod, cabezon, and various species of rockfish (known locally as snapper), and angling for them is year-round. Seaperch and surfperch are also available all year and at times are abundant.

Saltwater salmon angling is predominantly an offshore sport. The harbor provides excellent launching facilities for those who tow boats and charter services for those who don't.

Bottom-fish angling is also good offshore, but it is available to the shore-bound angler as well. The best bets are rocky coastal areas north and south of town, along the breakwaters, and from the public pier near Battery Point, in town.

Anglers take seaperch and surfperch from the pier and breakwaters on the harbor. Perch fishing is also good near the river mouths and from the beaches. A favorite spot is Kellogg Beach, about 10 miles north of town, near Fort Dick.

Another area that provides excellent angling can't be strictly classified as either fresh or salt water. Lake Earl, commonly referred to as a freshwater lagoon, is fed by Jordan Creek and numerous groundwater sources. During the winter storm season, however, the ocean sometimes breaches the dunes and floods the area, turning the water brackish. Although fifteen species of fish populate the lagoon, the best angling is for large sea-run cutthroat of three to five pounds. Shore access is almost nonexistent, and shallow water and state regulations call for small, shallow-draft boats with outboards not exceeding 10 horsepower; electric motors are ideal here. All motors are prohibited during duck-hunting season. Launch ramps can be found at the ends of Buzzini Road and Lakeview Drive, each off Lake Earl Drive.

**March**        Aleutian Goose Festival, (707) 465–0888

**June**         Bay Blues Festival, (707) 464–1336

**July**         Art Show & Sale, (707) 464–9133

                 Fourth of July Celebration, (707) 464–3174

                 Cele-Bear-Ation—Annual Weekend in Bear Country,
                 (707) 465–3013

**August**       Del Norte County Fair, (707) 464–9556

                 Fuchsia Show & Sale, (707) 464–3827

                 Klamath Salmon Festival, (707) 444–0433

                 Crescent City Triathlon, (707) 464–6636

**September**    Crescent City Kite Festival, (541) 476–7208

                 Jefferson State Bike Tour, (707) 464–8344

**October**      Noll Longboard Classic, (707) 465–4400

                 Sea Cruise Classic Car Show, (707) 464–3174

**November**     Country Christmas in the Redwoods, (707) 482–2551

**December**     Holiday Fair, (707) 464–9556

                 Festival of the Trees, (707) 482–4201

Shellfish, too, are present in the vicinity. Crabbers take tasty Dungeness crab in the harbor area from docks and piers, from December through July. North and south of town, sandy beaches provide good digging for razor, gaper, hard-shell, and littleneck clams. Mussels are found in rocky areas on minus tides.

A mussel quarantine—prohibiting all harvesting—is in effect each year from May 1 through October 31, because mussels can be toxic then. Clams are often affected, too, so the state issues a warning during that same period to clean clams thoroughly and discard any dark parts—this is no time for steamers. Because of dwindling stocks, razor clams are further regulated. Beaches south of Battery Point are open for razor-clam digging during even-numbered years, and north of the point during odd-numbered years.

Sailing, surfing, and sailboarding are also popular in the area, and the rivers attract rafters and kayakers.

# Golf

**Del Norte Golf Club,** 130 Club Drive, Crescent City; (707) 458–3214. Nine miles northeast of Crescent City via North Bank Road (Route 197) at Smith River. A par-seventy-one course amid the redwoods, open to the public. Pro shop, snack bar, and cocktail lounge. Club and cart rentals.

**Kings Valley Golf Course,** 3030 Lesina Road; (707) 464–2886. Five miles north of Crescent City, then east off US 101 via Elk Valley Cross Road to Lesina Road. A nine-hole, par-twenty-eight, executive course with driving range, putting green, pro shop, and snack bar. Club and cart rentals. Cocktail lounge on premises.

# Travel Information

**Crescent City/Del Norte County Chamber of Commerce Visitor Center,** 1001 Front Street, P.O. Box 246, 95531; (707) 464–3174 or (800) 343–8300; www.del norte.org

**U.S. Department of the Interior,** National Park Service, Redwood National Park, 1111 Second Street; (707) 464–6106; www.nps.gov/redw

# Index

# About the Editor

A native Californian, Kathy Strong has lived and traveled extensively throughout the state for more than forty years. Strong is also the author of popular guidebooks *Recommended Bed & Breakfasts California, Southern California Off the Beaten Path, The Seattle Guidebook, Driving the Pacific Coast Oregon and Washington,* and *Recommended Island Inns: The Caribbean.* She and her family reside in the Palm Springs area, where she is the editor of two magazines and writes travel features.